Waterscaping

PLANTS AND IDEAS FOR NATURAL AND CREATED WATER GARDENS

Waterscaping

PLANTS AND IDEAS FOR NATURAL AND CREATED WATER GARDENS

JUDY GLATTSTEIN

FOREWORD BY
C. COLSTON BURRELL

A Garden Way Publishing Book

Storey Communications, Inc.
Schoolhouse Road
Pownal, Vermont 05261

This book is dedicated to all gardeners who have taken a walk on the wild side and brought home ideas for their gardens.

Edited by Gwen W. Steege
Cover and text design by Meredith Maker
Cover photograph © Ken Druse/ Inset and back cover photographs © Jerry Pavia
Text production by Carol J. Jessop
Illustrations by Kathy Bray, line drawing on page 15 by Elayne Sears
Indexed by John Matthews, Wood-Matthews Editorial Services, Inc.

Garden Way Publishing was founded in 1973 as part of the Garden Way Incorporated Group of Companies, dedicated to bringing gardening information and equipment to as many people as possible. Today the name "Garden Way Publishing" is licensed to Storey Communications, Inc., in Pownal, Vermont. For a complete list of Garden Way Publishing titles call 1-800-827-8673. Garden Way Incorporated manufactures products in Troy, New York, under the Troy-Bilt® brand including garden tillers, chipper/shredders, mulching mowers, sicklebar mowers, and tractors. For information on any Garden Way Incorporated product, please call 1-800-345-4454.

Printed in the United States by The Book Press
Color text printed by State Color
First Printing, March 1994
❁Text printed on Recycled Paper

Library of Congress Cataloging-in-Publication Data

Glattstein, Judy, 1942–
    Waterscaping : plants and ideas for natural and created water gardens / Judy Glattstein.
           p.   cm.
    "A Garden Way Publishing book."
    Includes bibliographical references (p.   ) and index.
    ISBN 0-88266-608-8 (HC) — ISBN 0-88266-606-1 (PB)
    1. Water gardens.   2. Damp gardens.   3. Wetland plants.   4. Aquatic plants.   I. Title.
SB423.G58   1994
635.9'674—dc20   93-33378
                CIP

CONTENTS

Acknowledgments

It goes without saying that this book could not have been written without the steadfast support (and computer skills) of my husband, Paul. Grateful thanks are also due to all those who helped, answering my insatiable elephant child's questions: Lisa Beebe, Bill Brumback, C. Colston Burrell, Ken Druse, Sidney Eddison, Sven Hoeger, Nick Klise, Don Knezick, Dick Redfield, Midge Riggs, Joe Scott, Jr., and Mark Hoffman of Glen Gate Company, Morris West, and Bill Young. Mentors and friends, alas now departed, H. Lincoln Foster, John Osborn, and Howard Porter, were influential in my development as a gardener, teaching me to look to the wild for an appreciation and understanding of plants and their communities. And last but far from least, my editor at Storey Communications, Gwen Steege, whose meticulous efforts went to ensure this book was everything that could be wanted.

FOREWORD

Wetland plants, no matter what their individual habitat niches, have one shared characteristic — they require consistent moisture to survive. Knowing this fact alone is not enough to make you a competent water gardener, however. There are differences, both subtle and profound, in the timing, amount, duration, and quality of that water. Knowing which plants require or tolerate what water regimes is essential to success.

When I teach students how to grow plants, I always start with a discussion of their native habitat. Knowing that winterberry *(Ilex verticillata)* comes from the wooded swamps and moist forests of the north tells me that it prefers some shade, requires moist, acidic, humusy soil, and is likely to be intolerant of excessively high temperature and limy soils. While plants often have tolerances beyond their native niches, native habitat is always a good place to start. Winterberry, for example, will grow in full sun, tolerates dry soil for short periods (if the soil is rich), but it is intolerant of lime.

This knowledge of a plant's native range and habitat preference gives us a framework in which to place plants in associations. The cardinal rule — the gardener's axiom — is "match the plant to the site." Our gardens, after all, are plant associations or communities. The most prosperous gardens are those that emphasize plants adapted to the growing conditions of the site and group plants according to their requirements for sun, moisture, and soil type. If we recognize and work within these constraints, we avoid such mishaps as planting wild ginger in the broiling sun or astilbe on a dry sandy bank. Observant gardeners learn these fine points by trial and error. Experience, though often hard-won, is the most poignant teacher. *Waterscaping* is a book based on experience.

Judy Glattstein knows these differences well and her knowledge shows on every page. Judy has produced a book unique among water gardening books available in the U.S. She teaches readers about plants and gardening the way I teach horticulture and design students — from the broad context of the plant's habitat, down to the specific cultural requirements. Beginning with descriptions of each type of wetland habitat, Judy then explains what plants grow in each habitat and how to cultivate them. This ecological approach places plants in context, in relation to natural water cycles, canopy closure, soil types, bloom sequence, and native range.

Armed with this information, gardeners can comprehend and articulate the nature and function of the wetland communities, or remnants thereof, they have on their property. Wetlands are valuable for their ability to improve water quality, recharge aquifers, and mediate floods by holding stormwater runoff. They are important reservoirs for biodiversity as well. They also have intrinsic beauty. This book teaches gardeners to view soggy soil as an asset and tells how to combine plants in a way that does not compromise the ecological quality of the site or degrade the wetland.

For those gardeners who do not have a wet area on their property or who want to increase the water in their gardens, Judy provides step-by-step instructions for installing artificial water gardens, from pools to bogs. She describes the techniques for growing wetland plants in containers and for preparing the plants for winter storage.

Waterscaping is informative and personal, with anecdotes about schlepping through the countryside with open eyes and wet feet. Through the accounts of her adventures, we learn, as Judy did, the intricacies of these beautiful and fragile ecosystems. With the benefit of her experience we can begin to discover for ourselves the secrets of creating splendid water gardens. What more could one book do!

C. Colston Burrell
Minneapolis, Minnesota
1994

Chapter One

NATURAL WATER GARDENING

Water has a magnetic attraction for us, whether we are children or adults. It inspires all of our senses: the sight of a pond on a summer day, sunlight sparkling almost painfully bright on the surface; the sound of a brook purling over rocks; the silken feel of water on our skin; the taste of it when we are thirsty. Water is magical, the only substance that commonly exists as solid, liquid, and vapor within the relatively narrow range of temperatures within which we live, freezing winter cold to summer heat. Even city children know the youthful joy of running through a sprinkler. Those who have the opportunity to chase frogs on the muddy reed-fringed banks of a pond, see dragonflies skim the surface, and watch fish languorously drift through the depths experience true magic. Through the eyes of painters such as Monet we sense anew the enchantment that water held for us as children.

Water, and associated wetlands, are more than beautiful and mysterious, however. They are vital in the scheme of things, not only as habitats for plants and animals adapted to their specific ecosystems but also as agents that perform necessary functions. Swamps and marshes, for instance, serve as reservoirs to contain storm runoff and aid in cleansing pollutants from water.

Most of us automatically associate water gardening with pools and ponds — open water with water lilies floating on the surface. Once thought the province of the wealthy, for the formal garden only, water gardening has undergone a change. Preformed fiberglass shells and flexible liners bring a garden pool within reach of anyone who can dig a hole. The ever-increasing interest in naturalistic design has carried over to water gardening, with the result that small casual ponds with an informal, unaffected appearance replace prim rectangular pools necklaced with stone and plopped into the middle of a lawn. No longer are these water features restricted to large gardens. An urban backyard, a townhouse patio, an apartment terrace all are places where a water garden is possible, adding its unique and peaceful charm.

As delightful as these possibilities are, we can achieve even more if we look beyond obvious, constantly wet situations like ponds and streams where water is present and the land is under water. A wet meadow, an open sunny marsh, a shaded swamp offer both challenges and opportunities for gardeners. Even a small area can be made more attractive, more interesting. If the boundary of your lawn has a swale where the grass grows rank and is difficult to cut because the lawnmower's wheels sink in, consider planting wet meadow flowers that need trimming back once a year rather than once a week. Or, perhaps there is a wet area where your roof gutters and downspouts drain, or a drainage ditch near the road. I think of a beautiful garden that was made from just such an eyesore. The owners took a storm culvert on a relatively steep slope and created a small stream, which terminated in a little pool. Lined with such moisture-loving plants as astilbe, hosta, iris, and rodgersia, the channel became a lovely feature in the landscape rather than an ugly muddy trench. As we arrive at a more coherent understanding of these kinds of wet places, we can develop an appreciation for their unique beauty. We can also learn from the characteristic adaptations developed by the plants that live in and around water, adaptations that enable them to survive where more familiar plants might rot.

A water lily is a true aquatic — it cannot live without standing water. But not all wetland plants are aquatics. Familiar herbaceous garden perennials like astilbe prefer a moist soil. Some native North American plants are found in places such as a marsh or a swamp. Cardinal flower, bee balm, blue flag iris, and ferns such as the stately cinnamon and ostrich ferns are beautiful examples of such native plants. Some of this vegetation may also be found on drier upland sites, but, in general, a variety of different plants live in each of these different wet habitats. They include trees, shrubs, herbaceous plants, and annuals. Add the exotics — non-native plants that originated outside your region, that can also grow in wet sites — and we have a diversity of material to explore.

Understanding and Evaluating Your Site

If you walk in an area of your yard and end up with wet feet, you can have a water garden, for not all water gardens *have* to be pools. If such a place is where you want to plant flowers, choose those that prefer damp to wet conditions: familiar perennials available from any garden center, such as astilbes and hosta. If you are more adventurous, native plants such as swamp milkweed (*Asclepias incarnata*) or Joe-Pye weed (*Eupatorium purpureum*) are good choices. There are shrubs and trees that thrive with extra-moist conditions, too. Years ago, if your property had an area that remained wet, in all likelihood it would have been ditched and drained. In contrast, we now protect watery habitats by federal, state, and local laws. In both large- and small-scale situations they can be made more attractive with the addition of suitable plants.

To select plants that will grow most successfully, you need to know what type of wetland you are dealing with. How much moisture is present? Is it present on a seasonal or a year-round basis? Is the site sunny or shaded? The plants that grow in the standing water of a sunny pond are different from those that are found in a sunny wet meadow; a shaded red maple swamp will have yet another plant community.

Let us begin by understanding how various kinds of wetlands are formed. Unless there is some impoverishing condition — sparse rainfall in a desert or harsh conditions above the treeline in high mountains where winter lasts for nine or ten months — plant populations in nature change. A sunny meadow in the East, for example, becomes a shady climax forest. This is called *natural succession,* a term referring to the aging of a landscape as one type of plant community supplants the previous ones. Succession in wetlands is known as a *hydrosere.* Lakes form where water collects, perhaps draining down from surrounding hillsides. Water entering a lake carries sediments with it, silt and organic debris brought down from the surrounding uplands. Plants adapted to open water grow. They pump moisture into the air; they die and add debris to the bottom of the lake, and build up layers of debris and silt. As the lake edges become shallower, plants that are adapted to the margins can grow further in toward the center. From a lake, the body of water shrinks to a pond; the pond becomes increasingly shallow. In turn, the area that was a pond becomes a marsh and then a wet meadow, and eventually the once-upon-a-time lake becomes forest.

Marsh communities may also arise to fill in the sequestered oxbows cut off from slow-moving, meandering rivers. In the northern plains, marshes exist as prairie potholes, the result of the scooping action of glacial ice that covered the region in past millennia. Numerous enough to have given Minnesota the slogan "Land of 10,000 lakes," each spring these productive marshes fill with rain, an important stopping place for migrant waterfowl, permanent home to a diversity of turtles, frogs, and salamanders.

The many nuances and shades of gray blend in these habitats, it is never just black and white, either wet or dry. Wet meadow conditions can exist along a stream or in a roadside ditch, as well as in low-lying, poorly drained fields. An aging pond may be encircled with shrubs, shrunken to a smaller size than in its prime. A wet forest might have

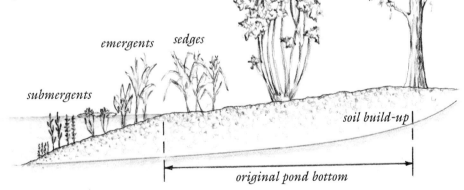

trees

shrubs

emergents   *sedges*

submergents

soil build-up

original pond bottom

A cross section of a pond shore, showing area where soil has filled in and appropriate plants have become established over a period of years.

a small stream flowing through it, passing to an area of shrubs, and opening up to a marshy area as it finally reaches a small pond.

The plant community associated with a pond has a relatively stable water level. Floating leaved plants such as water lilies *(Nymphaea* spp.) and spatterdock *(Nuphar* spp.) grow with their roots in the muck soil at the pond's bottom, with their leaves and flowers at the surface. Along the water's edge grow *emergents,* plants that also have their roots in soil but have more upright leaves, stems, and flowers that rise above the water's surface. Cattail *(Typha* spp.), blue flag *(Iris versicolor)*, yellow flag iris *(Iris pseudacorus)*, and arrowhead *(Sagittaria* spp.) are a few examples.

A sunny marsh, with its shallow water, is home to a variety of soft-stemmed plants. Many grasslike plants, sedges, and rushes as well as cattails, grow here, along with emergents like arrowhead and pickerel rush. In late summer and early autumn, rose mallows *(Hibiscus* spp.) produce enormous hollyhock-like flowers in pink or white. A wet meadow, on the other hand, where the water is usually just below the surface, is the place to grow a number of beautiful native flowers: swamp milkweed *(Asclepias incarnata)*, Joe-Pye weed *(Eupatorium* spp.), asters, ironweed *(Vernonia* spp.), bee balm *(Monarda didyma)*.

In shaded sites with shallow water — the shrub and wooded swamps and riparian woodlands of the Northeast, for instance — woody plants like summer-sweet *(Clethra alnifolia)*, spicebush *(Lindera benzoin)*, swamp azalea *(Rhododendron viscosum)*, red maple *(Acer rubrum)*, and sycamore *(Platanus occidentalis)* thrive. In the cool shade beneath the trees and shrubs grow many kinds of ferns, false hellebore *(Veratrum viride)*, skunk cabbage *(Symplocarpus foetidus)*, and marsh marigold *(Caltha palustris)*. In the Southeast we find bald cypress *(Taxodium distichum)*, sweet bay magnolia *(Magnolia virginiana australis)*, fetterbush *(Lyonia lucida)*, and titi *(Cyrilla racemiflora)*.

Bogs, places with strongly acid conditions, exist either as mats of sphagnum, slowly building up layer after layer in peat bogs, or as the wet sand/peat soils of the coastal plains. These are home to unique and beautiful orchids; bizarre and wonderful carnivorous, insect-eating plants; delightful dwarf shrubs.

Even if your garden does not naturally have these special habitats, it is possible to grow some of the members of these wetland plant communities. Some are adaptable to merely moist conditions; extra attention to watering will suffice. With impermeable liners you can create not only pools but also bog conditions. Containers offer options for small-scale jewel-box gardens. And if you are so fortunate as to have a pond, a swamp, a marsh, or a wet meadow on your property, you have the unique opportunity to discover and grow a wide variety of these fascinating plants.

Chapter Two

Sunny Gardens with Moist Soil: Wet Meadows

Whether your site is relatively small or more extensive, if you have moist soil with sun for six hours or more each day, you are dealing with wet meadow conditions. Here you have the opportunity to venture into the wonderful world of native plants that grow naturally in wet, sunny places, as well as to select familiar herbaceous perennials, such as astilbe and hosta, which are also used under average moisture regimens in the garden. The growth of these cultivated plants is even more luxuriant when they are given the constant moisture they prefer.

Although it is a simple matter to appreciate a wildflower meadow in bloom, the more difficult lesson is to learn from such places in terms of garden design. In the past, tremendous effort was sometimes put into making a wet site "suitable" for growing flowers. Trenching, draining, and ditching, often involving heavy machinery and extensive pipe laying, were considered the most effective means for rectifying what was perceived as an unsuitable situation. Even now, some gar-

deners resort to raised beds as a way of overcoming "problem" conditions. A more natural and creative solution is one I observed at the Shaw Arboretum at Gray Summit, Missouri. Here, a small colony of swamp hibiscus grows in a swale in the one place where it receives extra moisture, since surrounding areas are drier than this plant prefers. Utilizing these micro-habitats permits us to successfully cultivate plants that otherwise fail to grow well. It seems much less effort and more satisfying in the long term to take a lesson like this from nature and use ornamental plants that prefer to grow with wet feet. Many have beautiful flowers; some are good as cut flowers, and others have attractive foliage.

Perhaps your site is relatively small, kitchen table-sized, but located near enough to the house that you want some interest all season long. Consider planting a dozen or more bulbs of Guinea hen flower, to provide their handsome checkered bells in spring. Several plants of monkey musk, together with tufted hair grass, would

In late summer, when surrounding fields often turn brown from lack of rain, these meadows are still green and lush. The dense growth of grasses, flat-topped clusters of white boneset *(Eupatorium perfoliatum)* and lavender-pink Joe-Pye weed *(E. purpureum),* deeper violet flowers of ironweed *(Vernonia noveboracensis),* and elegant yellow spikes of goldenrod *(Solidago uliginosa)* create a pleasing tapestry of color late in the season. Such places may have a shallow film of water in spring but are without standing water during the growing season. The soil is waterlogged to within a few inches of the surface. Usually this high water table is the result of an impervious layer of hardpan, which prevents moisture from seeping any deeper into the ground. Woody plants, both shrubs and trees, are either absent or occasional, scattered in areas where their roots can take hold.

provide summer color. Hardy ageratum adds September flowers. A combination for a slightly larger area might group camassia, a native bulb, with Virginia spiderwort and bee balm. If the wet spot is really spacious, then taller, bolder plants could be selected: magic lily, Joe-Pye weed, and maiden grass. In this chapter, we will consider some plant options and design possibilities for sunny gardens with moist soil.

Grasses and Grasslike Plants

The major component of natural meadows, both wet or drier upland sites, are grasses. They are so prevalent that they lend their name — *grassland* — to describe meadows, prairies, steppes, and savannahs. Insignificant in flower, these plants help support the world: for animals, as forage, and for human consumption, important grains such as wheat, rice, and corn. Turf grasses are mown into the greensward we call lawn, and ornamental grasses have recently become popular as decora-

tive additions to the perennial border. Just as they are fashionable in more traditional settings, grasses are also important in waterscapes. Here are some native and cultivated grasses suitable for wet soils.

NATIVE GRASSES

Rattlesnake grass *(Glyceria canadensis)* and **fowl meadow grass** *(G. striata)* are two common grasses. Rattlesnake grass has slender stems, semi-evergreen leaves, and drooping branches of fat green flower clusters; fowl meadow grass has smaller purple flower clusters. Both blossom in spring or early summer and grow from 1 to 3 feet tall, with a light, airy appearance. **Reed meadow grass** *(G. grandis)* is taller, up to 5 feet high, with an upright, relatively flat flower cluster on long branches. It has a feathery effect in the landscape.

Another plant commonly named **fowl meadow grass,** but of another species, is *Poa palustris.* (This is a good example of common names being descriptive but sometimes confusing.) Both *Glyceria striata* and *Poa palustris* grow in wet places, and because they are similar looking, they may be difficult to tell apart. *P. palustris*

4 to 6 feet tall, it is one of the largest grasses native to the eastern third of the continent. Sheer size relegates it to the background, or the bank of a pond to make a handsome reflection in the water. Even a single specimen can provide a suggestion of tropical luxuriance. The medium to dark green leaves are 1 inch wide and up to 3 feet long. It tolerates light shade but prefers moist fertile soil in full sun. In mild climates with hot summers, if it is planted in light shade, it will have a richer green color.

CULTIVATED GRASSES

Some ornamental grasses are cultivated for their attractive flowers, seed heads, or foliage effect. Generally, these are easier to find at nurseries than are our native grasses. They can be a useful addition to a wet meadow and are helpful in providing a transition from the area that will remain natural and untended to the portion you plan to enhance. Grasses with variegated foliage will not have the same wild, natural look that green leaves provide. They are better used in settings that are more obviously gardenesque. Be

has a delicate airy appearance, with thin branches in clusters. Its flowers are green, bronze, or purple when they first appear, aging to tan.

Eastern gamma grass *(Tripsicum dactyloides)* is a robust, semievergreen grass that grows in dense, large clumps. It grows in pure stands in prairie lowlands, usually not in extensive colonies along roadsides or woods in the East. At cautious with any described as invasive or vigorous. Native plants and wild habitats have enough problems without turning aggressive plants loose in their midst. Just think what damage purple loosestrife (*Lythrum salicaria*) has done (see box, bottom right).

Rattlesnake grass or **perennial quaking grass (*Briza media*)** is a smaller well-behaved clump-forming evergreen grass growing 12 to 18 inches tall. The dense clumps of supple medium green leaves are attractive both for mass plantings and when used as a single specimen. The small florets are an opalescent green when they first appear in spring to early summer. The color becomes golden as they age and shiver and quake on their 2- to 3-foot stems.

∾ DESIGN IDEAS. *Rattlesnake grass would be a good choice for the foreground of a wet meadow, in combination with other, earlier, lower-growing plants.*

Feather reed grass (*Calamagrostis acutiflora* 'Stricta') prefers cooler climates and moist sites. It forms upright arching clumps 3 to 4 feet tall that turn orange-gold in autumn; it remains through the winter. Maintenance consists of trimming back the old foliage in late winter or early spring. The flowers, which are green with reddish bronze tints, appear in May to June and rise 3 to 4 feet above the mound of leaves. They mature to a golden color, age to buff by late fall, and persist into winter. *C. arundinacea* **'Karl Foerster'** will be somewhat more compact and flower 2 to 3 weeks earlier than the preceding cultivar when both are grown in cold climates. This is important in Zone 5 and colder, where the onset of cold weather might have a deleterious effect on flowering. Under milder conditions, they will be nearly indistinguishable.

∾ DESIGN IDEAS. *Feather reed grass is elegant in combination with showier, daisylike flowers.*

Tufted hair grass and **fairy wand grass (*Deschampsia caespitosa*)** is a graceful, semievergreen grass that forms dense tussocks of dark green leaves 1 to 3 feet wide and equally tall. In Zones 4 and 5, the handsome narrow leaves go dormant in winter; in Zones 6 to 7, exposed foliage turns yellowish orange, with some protected foliage in the center of the clump remaining green. Plants that are raised from seed vary in flower color and form. Additionally, since its

WHAT IS A NOXIOUS WEED?

There are federal, as well as state regulations (though not in all states) listing noxious weeds. It is illegal to deliberately cultivate plants so designated. In states where agriculture is vital to the economy these often include thistles.

For example, do not plant the nonnative, naturalized purple loosestrife (*Lythrum salicaria*). Among wetland plants it is the Bête noire. Loosestrife is banned in Minnesota and Illinois, to name but two states that regard it as a pernicious, noxious weed. Attractive as the wands of violet-pink flowers are in July and August, the plant cannot be regarded as anything other than an aggressive weed of pond shores, floodplains, marshes, and wet meadows. It crowds out cattail (*Typha latifolia*), replacing the natural diversity of native plants with a monoculture that provides neither food nor shelter to birds, amphibians, or small mammals that inhabit wet meadows and marshes. Some catalogs advertise "sterile" garden forms, but these produce viable pollen, and are thus able to fertilize nearby populations.

color shifts from green to yellow through shades of bronze and nearly purple as first the panicle flowers and seeds mature, it provides an ever-changing picture in the landscape. Seeming almost afloat, these loose panicles have an airy effect and are so numerous that they hide the leaves. It is one of the earliest grasses to bloom and is thus lovely in the spring garden. There are a number of cultivars: 'Bronzeschleier' and 'Goldenhaenge' are better in warm climates; 'Bronze Veil' is an English introduction; 'Goldschleier' and 'Tardiflora' are late blooming, as is the more compact 'Tautraeger'.

 DESIGN IDEAS. *Since tufted hair grass tolerates moderate shade, it is also valuable for transition situations where the habitat shifts from sunny meadow to shaded woodland.*

Variegated manna grass *(Glyceria maxima)* (color photo, page 27) is a deciduous, 2-foot-tall, vigorously spreading variegated grass that grows well in wet meadows and even shallow water. The new growth in spring is pink, gradually changing to a creamy ivory-white with thin green stripes by summer and aging to a hint of pink again in autumn. It collapses in winter and is uninteresting then. Its invasive habit makes it suitable for checking soil erosion along the banks of ponds where its growth can be controlled — but I would not turn it loose in a wet meadow or marsh. It is tender in Zone 4.

 DESIGN IDEAS. *Manna grass is charming in containers, where it makes an attractive companion to coarser green foliage — perhaps a canna.*

The different species and cultivars of **maiden grass** or **eulalia grass *(Miscanthus)*** are probably the most popular ornamental grasses grown today. Different ones vary in height from a moderate 3 feet tall to stately 15-foot specimens. There are several different variegated forms with either lengthwise stripes of white or yellow or unusual crosswise banding spanning the width of the blade. Deciduous, some exhibit attractive fall colors of orange, yellow, ruddy tones, or even purplish shades before turning to their tawny winter hue. Usually grown for their flowers, they bear silky tassels of silvery white, pinkish tan, or bronze that mature to feathery plumes that persist long into winter. Some flower in early spring; others in autumn, with the latest-blooming forms performing well only in mild climates.

Japanese silver grass *(M. sinensis)* is a sizable clump-forming grass. Where grown en masse,

PREPARING GRASSES AND PODS FOR INDOOR DISPLAY

Grasses are popular for dried arrangements in winter. Be careful to cut the seed heads before they are fully ripe, or they tend to fall apart as they dry. Cut cattails, too, just after they turn brown, and give them a light spray of shellac or hair spray to keep them from dusting your rooms with their fine seeds.

Late in autumn, after the seeds of swamp milkweed have floated away on swan's-down-like parachutes, you can cut their empty pods and enjoy their graceful shape indoors. I also like the seed capsules of iris for winter arrangements. And the woody-textured fertile fronds of ostrich fern *(Matteuccia struthiopteris)* and sensitive fern *(Onoclea sensibilis)* have a wonderful form and texture, too.

it creates an effective screen. It will grow in wet meadows, at the water's edge by a pond, or even in shallow water. Several cultivars worth noting include the following: 'Gracillimus' has a fine texture and showy flowers in late September, especially in warmer climates. 'Morning Light' has a narrow margin of white on the leaves, giving a luminous silvery appearance from a distance; it flowers in October. 'Variegatus' differs in that the white stripes are not confined to the edges but are throughout the leaf. Its habit of growth creates an attractive loose, rather floppy clump 4 to 6 feet tall. 'Cosmopolitan' is an improved, nonfloppy form. 'Purpurascens' begins its color change in September, turning a brilliant orange-red and finally darkening to an autumnal reddish brown. 'Silberfeder', also called 'Silver Feather', is one of the original German introductions. Its rich green leaves grow into an arching vaselike clump 5 to 6 feet tall, with elegant feather plumes of flowers held distinctly above the foliage in August.

Var. *strictus,* frequently (but incorrectly) called zebra grass, has horizontal yellow bands across its stiff, upward-pointing leaves. It is hardy to Zone 4 and grows well in wet soil and on pond banks. 'Zebrinus', or 'Zebra Grass', also has horizontal yellow bands that appear in early summer and a softer, more relaxed arching growth pattern. One of the more recent introductions is 'Yaku Jima' from Japan, which forms a compact, fine-textured clump growing 3 to 4 feet tall. Its flowers frequently fail to rise above the foliage, which is a serious drawback. 'Nippon' is an even newer cultivar with a better display. 'Gracillimus Nana' and 'Kleine Fountaine' are dwarf forms.

For mild climates (Zones 7 to 10), you might want to search for **Formosa maiden grass *(M. transmorrisonensis)*** from Taiwan. It is evergreen, with narrow glossy green leaves that mound into a dense clump 30 to 42 inches high and wide. At the warmer end of its range, it is spring flowering (April); otherwise it produces its silky golden bronze flower spikes in summer. The flowers arch up and out over the clump, producing a wonderfully open, airy display. It prefers moist soil and will brown at the tips if conditions are too dry.

ﾧ GROWING TIPS. *Cut the old culms of Japanese silver grass back in late February or early March before new growth begins. The new foliage is attractive by May, and flowers appear from July to September, depending on the cultivar.*

Purple moor-grass *(Molinia caerulea)* has it all — attractive foliage and flowers, good fall color, and a restrained habit of growth, plus it is easy to grow. The narrow light green leaves grow 6 to 18 inches long and form a fine-textured clump 1 to 2 feet high and wide. The flowers, which appear in midsummer (late June to early July), grow on long, stiff stems held well above the foliage. Foliage and flowers persist through fall, breaking off neatly at the base in late autumn. Purple moor grass grows well in wet meadows, seasonally wet meadows, or open, lightly shaded woodlands. 'Variegata' has attractive yellow-variegated leaves on a more compact plant. It grows best with a little shade, again suiting it for transition areas. Subspecies *arundinacea* has taller flowers, wider foliage, and a strong architectural form, growing 2 to 3 feet tall and wide, with flower spikes a foot or more taller. This creates a marvelous susurrus of sound in response to even a soft breeze. Because it is slow growing, consider beginning with larger plants to create a prompt display; small divisions may take three years before producing a good show of foliage and flowers. 'Karl Foerster' is an older, tall-growing cultivar with flowers on 6 or 7 foot stems. It is named for the noted German plantsman who introduced the concept of naturalistic design; 'Skyracer', 'Windspiel', and 'Bergfreund' are similar.

Gardener's-garters *(Phalaris arundinacea var. picta)* (color photo, page 49) is the variegated form of reed canary grass. It has attractive white-variegated foliage and is a vigorous spreading plant, effective as a ground cover for moist sites with light shade. It grows well along pond banks, even growing in shallow water 2 to 4 inches deep. In full sun, the foliage is apt to brown. 'Feesey's Form' has a pink blush, especially bright on the new growth in spring and fading away by summer. 'Dwarf Garters' is more mannerly in the garden, only slowly spreading and not so invasive. It is charming as an accent near the front of a planting area or in containers. **Golden ribbon grass (*P. arundinacea* 'Luteo-Picta')** has pale golden yellow markings rather than crisp white stripes. It is a rapidly spreading plant and needs light shade to protect the leaves from burning.

❧ GROWING TIPS. *To keep gardener's-garters from being too invasive in a border, confine the roots by growing the plant in a dishpan with drainage holes or a plastic bucket with the bottom removed, sunk in the ground. Cutting the aging foliage away and fertilizing lightly will encourage gardener's-garters into a second flush of growth to finish the summer in a more attractive manner. If nonvariegated shoots appear, they must be removed, or over time they will replace the variegated plants.*
❧ DESIGN IDEAS. *Golden ribbon grass is charming with golden-leaved hosta.*

Native Ornamental Flowering Plants

Many readily available garden perennials, such as peonies and bearded iris, are not tolerant of damp conditions, although some exotics, such as astilbe

and canna, grow in wet places. Native North American plants, however, (sometimes more appreciated abroad than they are at home) are found in shady forests and sunny grasslands, dry fields, and wet meadows. When gardening in wet sites, locally native wetland plants are especially useful, as they are adapted to the growing conditions. Their showy flowers, more colorful than the inconspicuous wind-pollinated flowers of grasses, are an essential part of any garden. In general, those that flower in spring, such as Quaker-ladies *(Hedyotic caerulea),* are rather short, often under 1 foot tall. Summer-flowering species tend to be midsize, 2 to 3 feet tall. Most stately are those that flower in late summer and early autumn; these often grow to 4, 5, even 6 feet tall or more. Peak bloom is in late summer into autumn.

When you are choosing, think beyond the period of bloom. As well as the numerous grasses, there are many plants with grasslike leaves, such as irises, that offer little contrast to the grasses when not in flower. Select plants to provide a variety of foliage. Plan for different blooming periods and consider whether the flowers will be

NATIVE PLANT RESTRICTIONS
Native plants growing on public land in the wild are protected and may not be cut or dug up. Private land belongs to someone, and without permission, the same restriction holds true. Plants on state or federal endangered species listings should not be disturbed. When you grow these wonderful plants in your own wet meadow garden, you are free to enjoy them indoors as well as out.

followed by interesting seed heads. In so doing, you will create an area that is attractive for a longer period and supported by interesting and diverse plants at different seasons. So let's follow the seasons in our examination of native, naturalized, and exotic herbaceous plants that are good prospects for a garden with wet meadowlike conditions.

SPRING

Spring is likely to be the wettest period in any garden — snowmelt in the north and spring rains in general combine to create squishy conditions. Exploring in a wet meadow at this time of year means rubber boots if you want to keep your feet dry. If there is a path or trail through the meadow, the little plants will more likely be observed and enjoyed if planted near its edges. These small, early-blooming plants are best used in groups and masses, rather than sparsely scattered about where they may be overlooked. Taller species can be set back from the edge, especially where they will be permitted to form sizable colonies.

Camassia or **wild hyacinth** *(Camassia cusickii)* is one of the few bulbs that will tolerate wet conditions. It washes the wet meadows of northeastern Oregon in the Pacific Northwest with a haze of blue before going dormant in June. The massive, up to one-half-pound bulbs were used as food by Native Americans. Camassia's 3- to 4-foot spikes of pale blue starlike flowers rise above the grassy foliage. As is common with many bulbs, it goes dormant after flowering. The most cold-tolerant camassia, it will grow in northern New England and even Minnesota. *C. leichtlinii* has blue, bluish purple, or white flowers and is more widespread. *C. esculenta* is smaller, at 2 to 3 feet, with white or violet flowers. Camassia also accepts average soil moisture, pulling its bulbs deep into the soil and forming offsets to make large clumps.

Shooting-star *(Dodecatheon meadia)* (color photo, page 28), a relative of primrose, is a spring ephemeral. Early in the season, a rosette of oblong light green leaves appear. In May and June, a leafless flower stalk appears, surmounted by a cluster of rosy pink, pale pink, or white flowers, looking like a flight of badminton shuttlecocks. After maturing their seeds, the plants go dormant.

Water avens or **purple avens** *(Geum rivale)* is a moisture-loving plant native to wet meadows from Newfoundland and Quebec to Alberta in

"WILD" PLANTS VERSUS "NATIVE" PLANTS

Not all the plants you see growing wild are native. *Native* describes plants that originated in the area where they are found growing. Some people give "native" a very narrow interpretation, and apply it to plants found in a specific state region, such as Southeast, Northeast, or Midwest. Other gardeners apply a very loose interpretation and accept North America as the boundary. *Naturalized plants* are those which, while originating elsewhere, grow and thrive in the wild, reproducing on their own without assistance. Though these immigrants never applied for a green card, they have become a naturalized component of our wild flora. *Exotic* refers to any nonnative plants, naturalized or not, that originate outside the region where they are found growing.

Canada and south to New Jersey, Indiana, and Michigan. The nodding bell-like flowers appear in May and June, several at the top of the stem, each with purple-veined yellow petals cupped in a purple calyx. The plant grows in loose, open colonies from a thick horizontal rhizome just below the soil's surface. Each stem grows about 3 feet high, with mostly basal foliage and smaller leaves ascending the stem.

Quaker-ladies or **bluets** *(Hedyotis caerulea)* is a dainty little plant that grows only 3 to 6 inches tall. Carpeting sunny wet meadows with solitary golden-eyed pale blue flowers above dense tufts of tiny leaves, its fragile appearance is misleading. This is one of our earliest-flowering meadow plants, blooming in April and May. It also has an obstinate character. Should you introduce it and it decides not to grow, it won't, though your neighbor's plants may thrive with seemingly little attention.

Copper iris *(Iris fulva)* is one of the Louisiana irises, with bright green swordlike leaves and reddish brown flowers, two or three to a stem, that bloom in May and June. Native to ditches and swamps from Illinois and Missouri south to Georgia and Louisiana, it is a charming plant for moist sites.

Blue flag iris or **fleur-de-lis** *(Iris versicolor)* is a handsome, easily cultivated species. The narrow swordlike leaves, which grow about 2½ feet tall in a flat, fanlike arrangement, are an attractive glaucous blue-green. The slate-blue flowers repay an observant look, as the lower three petals (called *falls)* are beautifully marked in green with white and yellow veining. They bloom in May and early June, though this will vary somewhat in warmer or colder regions. Unpretentious, the flowers are much smaller and simpler than their highly bred counterpart Japanese iris, making them more suitable for naturalistic

IDENTIFYING BLUE FLAG
Pushing through the shrub tangle that guards a pond in late summer, I slip down the bank into odiferous mucky ooze. The dry weather has shrunk the extent of open water, and I can now reach the iris, whose foliage I want to cut for basketry. Growing with it are cattail, yellow flag iris, and calamus. The deep purple stain at the base of the leaves is a clear indicator of just which species I am harvesting, even after the flowers are gone. Also, blue flag's leaves are straight and tightly folded, while cattail has a jaunty twist at the top of its flat leaves. Both lack the fragrance characteristic of calamus.

landscapes. Native from Newfoundland west to Manitoba and south to Virginia, Ohio, and Minnesota, this iris is found in wet meadows, roadside ditches, and swales, as well as in marshes and the wet soil bordering ponds. Accordingly, it is adaptable enough to use in several sites — those with moist soils and shallow water or the difficult transient situation of vernal pools. It rarely grows by ones and twos and instead is found in sociable colonies of fifty, a hundred, or more.

Cultivated for centuries both as an ornamental and a medicinal plant, **yellow flag iris** *(Iris pseudacorus)* (color photos, pages 30 and 77) is a naturalized European immigrant. This is a vigorous plant, colonizing ditches, swales, pond banks, and the margins of slowly flowing streams. Quite adaptable, it can grow with average soil moisture, in shallow water, or in every situation between the two extremes. The long, wide swordlike leaves form large clumps with yellow flowers in May. Unfortunately the flowers are not held clear of the leaves, weakening the display. *Bastardii* has pale primrose-yellow flowers, and 'Variegata' has creamy yellow markings on the new leaves in spring, becoming progressively greener as the season progresses. Following their flowers, irises have interesting seedpods that look like a three-part brown vase. Held on a stiff stem, they remain an attractive feature in the landscape right through winter.

Blue-eyed grass *(Sisyrinchium angust-ifolium),* with narrow bluish green leaves barely 12 inches tall, has foliage reminiscent of a miniature iris. The rich blue flowers each last but a few hours, but they make up in number what they lack in duration. Inconspicuous when not in flower, where their population is great they can create a low haze of blue over a meadow in May and June. In West Coast gardens, *S. bellum*, with amythest-violet flowers, is more suitable.

Violets *(Viola* spp.) include some that flower in a wet meadow in the spring sunshine and then find welcome shade in summer as other plants grow taller. Most violets are wildly prolific plants, often a nuisance in more cultivated settings. With the dense turf of a meadow, their seeds have a more difficult time coming to earth, and reproduction is not so bountiful. The **American dog violet** *(V. conspersa)* grows less than a foot tall with numerous leafy stems, kidney-shaped basal leaves, and pale blue-violet flowers. It can grow in woodland shade as well as in meadows. **Sweet white violet** *(V. blanda)* is a stemless violet, with roundish heart-shaped leaves and tiny, fragrant white flowers veined with purple. It is adaptable to swamps, meadows, and occasionally even in upland sites. **Lance-leaved violet** *(V. lanceolata)* has halberd-shaped leaves with a slight scalloping to the edges, and small purple-veined white flowers. **Wild white violet (V. pallens)** is similar,

growing perhaps 5 inches tall, with white flowers clustered among the oval to heart-shaped leaves. The lower three petals are finely penciled with brownish purple veins. These flowers appear in May and June, while the cleistogamous flowers appear in late summer. **Common blue violet *(V. papilionacea)*** is a good one here as well.

∾ GROWING TIPS. *Violets can quickly get out of control. One method of dealing with this in a garden, once the plants are established, is to pull many of them out as soon as they are through flowering. The next spring, they will be back in full strength.*

Flower of the west wind, zephyr lily *(Zephyranthes atamasco)* is a southern plant not hardy where the ground freezes. In Virginia to Alabama, Georgia and North Carolina, especially in sites where the meadow grass is mown back, its grassy leaves and shining white lilylike flowers produce a wonderful display in April and May.

Golden alexander *(Zizia aurea)* is charming in full sun where the soil is clayey and wet, or at the meadow's edge, in a site where it gets a little shade (especially in the middle of the day). It has prolific tendencies that suggest caution in smaller sites. The fresh green, sharply toothed leaves are similar to those of parsley. In May and June, the loose, airy umbels of attractive greenish gold flowers appear. In my garden it makes a winter rosette of evergreen foliage, often disguised under fallen leaves at the woodland edge. **Heart leaved alexander *(Z. aptera)*** is very common in wet prairies, moist meadows and open woods from New York south to Arkansas and Florida. It grows 2 feet tall and has small yellow flowers clustered in an umbel from late spring to early summer.

∾ DESIGN IDEAS. *Golden alexander is attractive in combination with Bowles golden sedge (Carex stricta 'Bowle's Golden') and a golden-edged hosta. It looks equally at home in a naturalistic design, where the pinnately compound dark green foliage of golden alexander can associate with the simpler, more architectural leaves of skunk cabbage and false hellebore.*

SUMMER

Wild celery, angelica, or **alexanders** *(Angelica atropurpurea)* (color photos, pages 26– 27) is a coarse, bold plant of wet meadows, marshes, shrub swamps, and forested swamps from Labrador to Wisconsin and southward to Delaware and Indiana. Statuesque, it grows up to 9 feet tall with thick, purple-stained stems that branch near the top. Its long stalked leaves are twice or thrice divided, with five to seven leaflets in each division, giving wild celery a parsleylike appearance. Toward the top of the stem, the

A BUTTERFLY GARDEN

Most butterflies need moisture and can often be found congregating around a damp spot. Wet meadow conditions thus make an ideal location for a butterfly garden. Here are some plants to try.

With its soft rose-pink flowers formed in a flat-topped mass, swamp milkweed *(Asclepias incarnata)* is attractive to butterflies. Those visiting it include fritillaries, monarchs, swallowtails, pale sulphurs, and cabbage whites. If a butterfly garden sounds appealing, you can choose other moisture-loving perennials to attract them as well. Joe-Pye weed *(Eupatorium purpureum),* with its large trusses of soft

A butterfly garden with native wetland plants including New England aster, larger blue flag, beebalm, turtlehead, cardinal flower, and common blue violets.

mauve flowers, white boneset *(E. perfoliatum),* and bright golden-yellow marsh goldenrod *(Solidago uliginosa)* all bloom in summer. Sneezeweed *(Helenium autumnale),* with yellow, orange, or coppery rust-colored flowers; lavender to violet New England aster *(Aster novae-angliae);* and intense red-purple ironweed *(Vernonia noveboracensis)* flower at summer's end. Bee balm *(M. didyma)* with red flowers, attracts not only butterflies but also hummingbirds.

Purple loosestrife *(Lythrum salicaria)* does attract butterflies, but its deleterious traits outweigh this single good point. It is such an obnoxiously invasive plant that I can only urge you not to plant it. (For restrictions on purple loosestrife, see page 8.)

A CUTTING GARDEN

Choose plants with showy long-lasting flowers or attractive foliage. Flowers that grow and close in a single day — daylilies *(Hemerocallis* spp. and cultivars), for example — are difficult to arrange. Those that close at night, like the New York aster *(Aster novi-belgii),* are a poor choice because they are unlikely to remain open under low light conditions indoors. And, to be grown in a wet meadow situation, plants must prefer, or at least tolerate, moist to wet conditions. In summer, hardhack *(Spiraea tomentosa),* has dusty rose-pink spires, good for cutting. Perhaps this could be the starting point for a wet meadow cutting garden.

Some of the plants that attract butterflies, such as swamp milkweed, also make good cut flowers. Similar in color to hardhack but with a very different shape, swamp milkweed is attractive when combined in the garden or in arrangements with hardhack. White boneset, ironweed, Joe-Pye weed, and New England aster also double as excellent cut flowers.

Culver's root *(Veronicastrum virginicum),* with its stiff terminal spikes of white to pinkish white flowers, is an effective contrast in form to the more massive umbels of Joe-Pye weed and the many daisies. Tickseed sunflower *(Bidens coronata),* swamp sunflower *(Helianthus angustifolius),* oxeye *(Heliopsis helianthoides* ssp. *scabra),* cut-leaf coneflower *(Rudbeckia laciniata),* and cup plant *(Silphium perfoliatum)* are different yellow daisies suitable for cutting. Another daisy, sneezeweed, has flowers in the same autumnal color range as chrysanthemums. Liatris is so popular a cut flower that it is used commercially. Lilies can be cut, but only every few years to allow the bulb time to regenerate; for the same reason, leave as much foliage as possible to nourish the bulb for the next season's performance. Violets can be cut for a dainty nosegay in spring. Nonnative plants such as astilbe make excellent cut flowers, and I find the foliage of canna very useful in arrangements.

leaves are less compound. The small greenish white flowers appear in July and August, forming spherical clusters at the tips of long stalks and gathered into a large umbrella-like cluster at the end of the stout stem. It reminds me of a more rounded Queen-Anne's-lace.

❧ EDIBLE PLANTS. *The young stems and leaf stalks of A. Atropurpurea can be gathered, peeled, boiled once, and then covered with fresh water and simmered until tender.* **Be absolutely certain of what you harvest,** *as there is a highly poisonous small-scale version of this plant — water hemlock (Cicuta maculata). It also grows in wet meadows or swampy areas, and resembles an outsized parsley plant with fernlike foliage, purple-flecked green stems, and flat, airy sprays of white flowers. The fleshy white roots are especially poisonous, producing violent convulsions, even death.*

Swamp milkweed (Asclepias incarnata) grows in roadside ditches and swales; in marshes and open swamps; along lakeshores, streams and river boundaries; and in wet meadows. It is a wet-soil version of the familiar orange butterfly weed (*A. tuberosa*), which thrives in dry soils. Color is variable, with individual plants ranging from nearly white to almost raspberry pink. It flowers in July and August with flat-topped clusters of flowers on stems about 2 to 4 feet tall, and is an excellent cut flower. Its natural range is from Nova Scotia west to Manitoba and south to New Mexico, Wyoming, and Florida, so it is a useful species for gardens across much of North America. Its overall appearance and flower color, as well as its blooming period, are similar to those of Joe-Pye weed, so avoid growing them side by side — the result is likely to be too plain to be interesting. Unlike butterfly weed, which has a deep carrotlike root system, swamp milkweed has a more shallow spaghetti-like root system; it therefore transplants more readily.

∾ DESIGN IDEAS. *Good companions for swamp milkweed include white boneset, New England aster, and culver's root.*

∾ EDIBLE PLANTS. *Tender young shoots less than 10 inches tall can be steamed after boiling in one or two changes of water; the unopened flower buds can be steamed until just cooked; and the tiny seedpods, no more than 1½ inches long, can be simmered in a little water seasoned with maple syrup or a tablespoon of honey until tender-crisp and then served hot or cold.*

Queen-of-the-prairie (*Filipendula rubra*) (color photo, page 26) provides a stately display of deep pink to peach-pink flowers in a flat-topped cluster in July and August, as well as attractive foliage and interesting seed heads. This bold plant grows 5 to 6 feet tall or more, with large, fernlike pinnately compound leaves. Despite its size, it remains self-supporting, even under windy conditions. The cultivar 'Venusta' has deep pink to rosy carmine flowers. It can be aggressive. To propagate, or contain, dig alongside the parent plant and remove rhizomes.

Oxeye (*Helianthus helianthoides* ssp. *scabra*) is a wonderful free-flowering, summer-blooming yellow daisy from the prairie grassland. Oxeyes can be in flower for three to four months, from June through September. This is encouraged by deadheading — removing spent flowers. Especially when they have suitably fertile, moist conditions, they are long-lived plants. Oxeye is a popular garden perennial, with a number of cultivars available: 'Jupiter' has enormous heads of single orange-yellow flowers and grows 5½ feet tall; 'Karat' has large heads of single golden yellow flowers on smaller plants growing a little over 4 feet high; 'Summer Sun' has double and semidouble golden yellow flowers on plants 3½ feet tall; 'Gold Greenheart' looks rather like a buttery yellow double zinnia with a greenish center, especially when first open.

∾ DESIGN IDEAS. *An ornamental combination would be the pairing of oxeye with a large colony of blue vervain (Verbena hastata).*

Slender blue flag (*Iris prismatica*), a choice plant for really moist sites, has narrow grasslike leaves and one or two flat, slate-blue flowers on a 2-foot-high stem in June or July. It spreads gradually to form small colonies.

Several of our native lilies (*Lilium*) are native to wet meadows, as well as sunny grassland sites and prairies. They need moist to average soil conditions and will not grow in saturated soil. Growing 4 to 6 feet tall, **Canada lily (*L. canadense)*** is one of our most beautiful wildflowers. It has an impressive candelabra of flowers, like pendulous soft orange bells, spotted purplish brown inside, in early summer. The scaly white bulb differs from that of many other lilies in having a horizontal rhizomelike arrangement with the new shoot forming at the tip. Canada lily is native from Quebec and Maine to Minnesota and south to Indiana and Alabama. **Michigan lily (*L.**

michaganense) is shorter, growing about 2 feet tall. It has black-spotted, red-orange Turk's-cap flowers with strongly reflexed petals, one to three to a stem. It also produces a new horizontal rhizome each year. As it forks, this attractive plant forms a colony, creating a lovely flowering display in late June and July. In part overlapping the range of Canada lily, Michigan lily is native from Ontario to Manitoba and south to Tennessee and Arkansas. **Turk's-cap lily** *(L. superbum)* is an elegant species, well named *superbum*. It, too, has reflexed, maroon-spotted orange-yellow to red flowers, often green in the throat, nodding on long stalks in a pyramid-shaped panicle at the upper portion of each stem; each stem can have three to as many as forty flowers (though twenty is more common). Growing 4 to 8 feet tall, it flowers a little later than Michigan lily, in July and August. Native from Massachusetts and New York west to Minnesota and south to Georgia and Alabama, its rhizomatous roots produce large colonies where conditions are to its liking. Especially the more vigorous taller specimens need adjacent plants for support.

❧ DESIGN IDEAS. *Different species of iris, bergamot, bottle gentian, and culver's root, though not necessarily in bloom at the same time, are possibilities for bracing lilies in a natural manner, and also extend flowering interest over a longer period.*

Mints *(Mentha)* are well-known both as plants that like wet places and as assertively spreading plants. Our native species, **field mint** *(Mentha arvensis),* is no exception. It grows about 2 feet tall, quickly forming large, aromatic, many-branched colonies with small lilac-pink flower clusters in the upper leaf axils in July and August. Native from Labrador to Washington and south to Virginia and California, it will cheerfully inhabit ditches, wet meadows, marshes, and open, lightly shaded shrub swamps.

❧ EDIBLE PLANTS. *Like the leaves of any other species of mint, the aromatic leaves of field mint can be used for flavoring or as a tea.*

Monkey flower *(Mimulus alatus)* has showy lavender flowers, somewhat like snapdragons in appearance, each individually held in the upper leaf axils, that bloom from June to September. The 2- to 3-foot-high stems have thin wings angling outward, and a short petiole holds the leaves away from the stem. *M. ringens* also has the common name of monkey flower and similar flowers, but it blooms in July and August, has square stems, and has leaves that clasp the stem. Preferring a lightly shaded site, it is found in marshes, along the edges of slowly moving streams, and in swamps, sites with really wet soil.

Bee balm or **Oswego-tea** *(Monarda didyma)* is a familiar, troublesome garden perennial. Popular for its red flower heads, which look like a skyrocket going off, this member of the Mint Family has numerous, coarse aromatic leaves that can be used for tea. It has no inhibitions about seeking out fresh territory, even if the area is already occupied by some other plant, and its aggressive tendencies can be a problem in perennial borders. It is held somewhat in check in the more competitive situation of a meadow. 'Cambridge Scarlet' and 'Croftway Pink', with intense red or pink flowers, are but two of the cultivated forms available.

❧ GROWING TIPS. *If you remove spent flowers, you can keep bee balm in bloom for two months. If a dry spell results in disheveled, tatty foliage, cut the stems to the ground and water to produce a second flush of fresh new growth. Mildew can also spoil the appearance of its leaves.*

Meadow phlox or **wild sweet william** *(Phlox maculata)* is like a more refined *P. paniculata,* the species usually seen in gardens. Meadow phlox has a cylindrical cluster of mauve-pink, purple, to white flowers (rather than the broad umbels of garden phlox) on 2- to 3-foot-tall maroon-spotted stems from late May to June; deadheading can extend the flowering period into August. The glossy lanceolate leaves are resistant to mildew, scourge of the common garden phlox. 'Miss Lingard' has pure white flowers; more floriferous 'Omega' has white blossoms with a small pinkish lavender eye; 'Alpha' has rose-pink flowers with a faint darker eye; and 'Rosalinde' has dark pink flowers.

∾ DESIGN IDEAS. *This is a good choice to follow shooting-star or spiderwort. It also looks very good with cut-leaf coneflower.*

The flowers of **obedient plant** or **false dragonhead** *(Physostegia virginiana)* can be pushed into line as though on little hinges, and they'll compliantly remain where you push them. Would that the spreading roots were as obedient! Invasive in perennial borders, it is well-behaved in meadow gardens. Common in gardens, this native from moist, sunny glades and thickets is found in the wild from Vermont west to Minnesota and Illinois and south to South Carolina and Texas. The leafy stems are 3 feet tall, terminating in a spike of rose-pink flowers rather like snapdragons. In the prairies of Missouri and Illinois, I've seen this plant create an attractive contrast to the many daisies that also bloom in August and September. 'Pink Bouquet' is a more vividly colored cultivar, and white forms are also available.

∾ GROWING TIPS. *Obedient plant blooms in late summer, from August until late September, especially if the spent flower spikes are removed. One pleasant way to accomplish this is by cutting the flowers for bouquets.*

Meadowsweet *(Spiraea latifolia)* (actually a shrub) is generally found in moist open sites, such as wet meadows and marshes, from New-

foundland to Michigan and south to North Carolina. It can form large, spreading colonies with a thicket of unbranched or only slightly branched stems in a dense mass. In July and August it bears numerous small white, pinkish white, or pink flowers clustered in a pyramid at the top of the stem. The small dark brown seedpods persist over winter.

Tall meadow rue *(Thalictrum polygamum)* is a stately plant exhibiting an airy grace, proving that large does not always mean coarse. Occasionally 8 feet tall, though usually less, it has handsome foliage reminiscent of columbine or maidenhair fern. The puffy clusters of white flowers that appear in June and July are without petals, formed instead by multiple prominent threadlike stamens.

∾ DESIGN IDEAS. *Tall meadow rue is usually seen as an individual specimen or scattered in small groups. This is also an effective way to plant it.*

Virginia spiderwort *(Tradescantia virginiana)* is a familiar garden perennial that also happens to be a native plant. It has long,

EARLY WARNING

Spiderworts have been planted near atomic power plants; their stamens change color in response to very low levels of radiation and thus provide an early warning system.

narrow grasslike leaves that become shabby after flowering by midsummer. The three-petaled purple, lavender, or white flowers, each lasting for only one day, are clustered at the top of a 1- to 2-foot-high stalk in an umbel. It blooms from June to August. Most of the cultivars are hybrids:

'J.C. Weguelin' has China-blue flowers; 'Zwanenburg Blue' has deep blue flowers; 'Red Cloud' has rosy red flowers; 'Iris Prichard' has white flowers attractively stained with purple; and 'Snowcap' has pure white flowers.

∾ GROWING TIPS. *If cut back, given a light dose of fertilizer, and kept moist, Virginia spiderwort will produce an attractive flush of new growth to finish out the season.*

Culver's root *(Veronicastrum virginicum;* sometimes listed as *Veronica virginica)* has a dense spike of tiny white or pink-tinged flowers from early July though the middle of August. It grows 3 to 4 feet tall and accepts moist to average growing conditions.

∾ DESIGN IDEAS. *Culver's root looks best with companion plants of contrasting form flowering around it — daisies such as New England aster or plants with a more massive, blocky form such as Joe-Pye weed.*

LATE SUMMER/AUTUMN

Asteraceae, that tremendous Aster Family, holds pride of place in the meadows and prairies

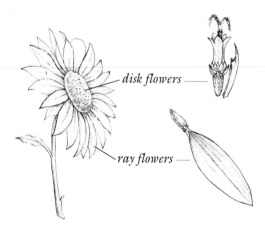

A close-up view of individual disc and ray flowers reveals the clustered community that forms a daisy.

of North America, especially so as late summer falls into autumn. The "daisy" we see is not one but many tiny flowers, clustered together for ease of pollination/efficiency of seed production. It has two types of flowers: *ray flowers* are the petals surrounding the *disk flowers* clustered in the center. Some plants in this family have only one kind of flower: ironweed *(Vernonia noveboracensis)*, for instance, has only discoid flowers.

DAISIES

New England aster *(Aster novae-angliae)* is one of our most beautiful wildflowers, closing out the growing season with a royal purple display. This easy, accommodating plant grows 4 to 6 feet tall. From late August into October, it produces scores of golden-centered violet-purple daisies, with deep rose and clear pink forms occasionally turning up. It is a better choice as a cut flower than **New York aster** *(A. novi-belgii)*, which closes its flowers. You can tell the two apart by their leaves: New England aster has rough, hairy leaves, while New York aster has smooth foliage. Adaptable to average garden soil, this aster usually grows in the wild in wet meadows and moist soil on the shores of ponds or along sunny, slowly flowing streams across the eastern United States. Several cultivars are available: 'Alma Potschke' is a 3- to 4-foot-tall cultivar with vivid cerise-pink flowers; 'Barr's Pink' has semidouble rose-pink flowers on 4-foot-tall plants; 'Harrington's Pink', one of the last to bloom, has salmon-pink flowers on 3- to 5-foot-tall plants; similarly sized 'September Ruby' has rich ruby-red flowers in summer; and 'Treasure' has violet-blue flowers on 4-foot-tall plants. Plants raised from seeds will usually flower the second year. Named forms must be propagated asexually (by division) to remain true.

∾ GROWING TIPS. *New England aster can become*

floppy in cultivation, whereas it is supported by neighboring plants in a meadow situation. One solution is to give it a couple of hard pinches in late spring and early summer to reduce its height and promote branching. Be sure to stop pinching by early July so that flower buds will have an opportunity to mature. Eventually, the enlarging tangle of roots will produce stems only along the circumference of the clump, leaving a bare bald spot in the center. Dig the clump in spring, take divisions from the perimeter and replant them. Discard the worn-out portion.

Swamp aster *(Aster puniceus)* has numerous pale lavender flowers that lack the impact of New England aster's more emphatic coloration. Because of its vigorous nature, this is a good plant for larger sites where its massed flowers can cast a smoky haze and act as a foil to deep purple ironweed.

Tickseed sunflower *(Bidens coronata)* is an annual, but its prolific self-sowing creates a self-perpetuating colony. Plants appear each year, but they are new ones, not reemerging perennials that grew there the previous year. In the wild, the slender plants grow only a few inches apart in dense colonies. This permits the 4- to 6-foot-high stems to support each other as they sway in unison to the orchestration of a passing breeze. In August, they produce a massive display of golden daisies, often to the exclusion of any other plant attempting to grow on their turf. Their other common name — bur-marigold — commemorates their stick-tight seeds, which attach to animals' fur and human clothing as a means of dispersal.

Boltonia *(Boltonia asteroides)*, has clear white flowers that open in late summer. As its Latin name suggests, it has an asterlike appearance. The species grows 5 to 6 feet tall with many 1-inch-wide flowers in large panicles at the end of each stem. Native across the eastern United States, the species is rarely offered in nurseries. Instead you will find 'Snowbank', at 3 to 4 feet a lower-growing, less floppy plant that flowers from mid-August into September.

❧ DESIGN IDEAS. *Boltonia is elegant in combination with the soft mauve coloration of Joe-Pye weed.*

When we think of sunflowers, the huge flowers of the annual 'Russian Mammoth' come to mind. Useful as a source of seeds for feeding birds and pressing for cooking oil, this particular sunflower is of little use in wet areas. Some perennial sunflowers with warm golden flowers do, however, delight in moist sites.

Swamp sunflower (*Helianthus angustifolius)* is native across the eastern United States, from coastal New York and Long Island south to Florida and Texas and along the Mississippi River valley to southern Indiana, in both freshwater wet meadows and salt meadows. In autumn, it produces numerous 2- to 3-inch-wide dark-eyed yellow-orange flowers up and down the 3- to 6-foot-tall stems. Both the narrow grasslike leaves and the maroon stem are rough, almost gritty, when touched. Swamp sunflower produces numerous offspring extending outward from around the base.

Sawtooth sunflower *(H. grosse-serratus)* is variable in height from 5 to 14 feet tall. The leaves are in the same large scale — 15 inches long — and have a fine woolly underside. The numerous bright yellow flowers are striking, yet this sunflower is rarely cultivated. Obviously, it requires ample space to display its towering show.

❧ GROWING TIPS. *If you want to try sawtooth sunflower even though quarters are cramped, try cutting established plants back close to the ground in late May or early June. This will result in shorter, bushier growth. Also, fertilize lightly if at all. It seems to me, however, that it would be easier to select a different species. Although coarse in growth — tall and stately with bold foliage — many sunflowers are gentle giants, noninvasive and unlikely to invade their neighbors' territory. Others, such as Jerusalem artichoke happily spread far and wide. The more you cosset sunflowers with fertilizer, the more vigorous and rank their growth. Such plants often have weak stems and tend to fall over. If you want self-supporting, less aggressive plants, hold the fertilizer.*

Sunchoke or **Jerusalem artichoke** *(H. tuberosus)* may be familiar from the produce counter of your local grocery store. This plant's abundant golden yellow daisies brighten wet meadows and roadside ditches in autumn. In poor soil, it will grow about 5 feet tall, doubling this (or more) in gravelly, rich, alluvial soils. It is aggressive and can take over a garden, so it is better used in naturalistic settings where its spreading tendencies will not be a problem.

❧ EDIBLE PLANTS. *The sunchoke's tubers may be gathered late in autumn, but because they store poorly, harvest only enough for each meal. You can eat them raw like a radish, sliced or diced in a salad, boiled, or roasted. They also make an excellent bread-and-butter-type pickle.*

Cut-leaf coneflower *(Rudbeckia laciniata)* is a superb clear yellow daisy. One September, near Philadelphia, I will never forget seeing a wet meadow hazed with the intense purple-violet flowers of ironweed, in vivid contrast to some cut-leaf coneflower. As the name suggests, the lower leaves especially are divided into three or five lobes, while those ascending the 3- to 5-foot-tall stem are less cut. Green-centered 2- to 3½-inch-wide yellow flowers are produced from late July into September. Cut-leaf coneflower grows in wet thickets and along slowly flowing streams from Canada south to Florida and west to North and South Dakota and Oklahoma. The double

form, 'Golden Glow', is a familiar old-fashioned garden perennial; 'Goldquelle' is a 3-foot-tall double-flowered German introduction.

Cup plant or rosinweed *(Silphium laciniatum)* (color photo, pages 26-27) is yet another stately golden-flowered daisy growing 3 to 6 feet tall. It has attractive stocky leaves that are joined at the stem like those of white boneset *(Eupatorium perfoliatum),* looking as if pierced by the stem. Birds come to drink the small amounts of water held in the cuplike leaves. This is a deep-rooted prairie plant (to 15 feet deep!) and must be moved into its permanent location when quite young. Another species, **prairie dock** *(S. terebinthinaceum),* is similar in size and time of bloom but it has large, coarse basal leaves.

❧ DESIGN IDEAS. *Silphiums are attractive in combination with other tall stately plants, such as angelica, Joe-Pye weed, culver's root, or meadow phlox. Avoid planting cup plant and prairie dock jointly, or with other yellow daisies, to avoid having several similar flowers growing together.*

Marsh or **bog goldenrod** *(Solidago uliginosa)* grows as solitary individuals or in small colonies. The branching rhizome is close to the soil's surface and produces stems up to 5 feet tall. Appearing in August and September, the inflorescence may be 12 inches long, with numerous small heads of tiny yellow flowers in short-stemmed clusters ascending the main stem. It is found in wet meadows and bogs from Nova Scotia west to Ontario and Michigan and south to Maryland and Ohio. Individuals afflicted with hay fever need not avoid goldenrod. Like any other plant with showy flowers, it has sticky pollen, designed to wait for some pollinating insect to transport it from flower to flower. The sneezing, runny nose, irritated eyes, and associated hay fever symptoms are caused by inconspicuous flowering plants such as grasses and ragweed *(Ambrosia* spp.), which use the wind to move their pollen.

DAISIES WITH A DIFFERENCE

Some members of the Aster family are known as "daisies," yet because they lack disk flowers, they may not look like more typical daisies. Some examples include the eupatoriums, liatris, and vernonia.

Blue boneset or **mist flower** *(Eupatorium coelestinum)* is also called hardy ageratum for its resemblance to the familiar summer annual. Smaller than other Joe-Pye weeds, it is one of the few low-growing, late-blooming native meadow plants. In moist sites it produces stems 2 to 3 feet tall and is somewhat late in making its appearance each spring. It has rapidly spreading subsurface rhizomes. Let it romp through a wild site. I remember this along September roadsides in Missouri, where the wetter ditches provided comfortable growing conditions and its flowers tangled attractively with tawny grasses. In cultivation, it will need to be headed back as it stretches for new territory. There is also a white form.

The other Eupatoriums, sometimes called Joe-Pye weeds, are all minor variations on a motif of moisture-loving plants growing 6 feet tall with mauve, lavender, rosy pink, or white flowers in late summer. All of these are good butterfly plants, excellent for attracting monarch butterflies as they gather strength for their migration down the West Coast to California and along the East Coast to Mexico. They are also good cut flowers.

Joe-Pye weed *(Eupatorium maculatum)* grows up to 6 feet tall with sturdy purple-spotted stems topped with dense flat-topped clusters of reddish purple flowers in August and September. It spreads into moderate to large colonies (but not so aggressively as goldenrod), thriving in wet meadows, marshes, and the moist soil around

COLOR TRICKS
Called the "ageratum effect," the soft lavender-blue flowers of blue boneset photograph distinctly pink, as the flowers reflect red light invisible to the human eye but obviously apparent to film emulsion.

ponds or slowly moving streams. Also known as Joe-Pye weed, *E. purpureum* has 12- to 18-inch-diameter heads of rosy mauve flowers massed at the top of hollow green stems 4 to 7 feet high. ∾ DESIGN IDEAS. *Both Eupatorium purpureum and E. maculatum are attractive when combined with tall, moisture-tolerant ornamental grasses and the more intensely colored violet flowers of ironweed or the white daisies of boltonia.*

Boneset *(Eupatorium perfoliatum)* is found in the same habitats as the Joe-Pye weeds, but it is conspicuously different in flower color and leaf form. Its flowers are off-white with a grayish or greenish tint. The bases of the grayish leaves broaden out and the pairs unite, giving the appearance of having been speared by the coarse stems, which grow 5 feet tall. It is native from Nova Scotia and Quebec west to Manitoba and south to Florida and Texas.

Spiked gay-feather *(Liatris spicata)* (color photo, page 25) is familiar in herbaceous borders, where it grows in average soil conditions. In its native home in the prairies of the Midwest, however, it is found growing in quite moist conditions. In summer, it likes wet feet, but moisture in winter can cause it to rot. Less familiar but more spectacular is **prairie blazing-star** or **Kansas gay-feather** *(L. aspera).* From mid-July to early August, it produces bright magenta-pink flowers arranged in buttonlike tufts as they ascend the 2- to 4-foot-high stem. Unlike most other plants with flowers in a spike, all liatris open not from the bottom up but from the top down. Gay-feather makes great cut flowers.

∾ DESIGN IDEAS. *Gay-feather tends to blow over in strong winds. You can provide it support by growing it in community with plants like cut-leaf coneflower, spiderwort, culver's root, stiff goldenrod, Turk's-cap lily, and wet meadow grasses.*

Common ironweed (*Vernonia noveboracensis*) (color photo, page 25) has flowers like a centerless daisy. Its intense violet-purple color adds opulent saturated hue to wet meadows in late summer and early autumn. This color is a rich contrast to the softer shades of Joe-Pye weed and the numerous golden-flowered daisies that inhabit the same sites and bloom at the same time. **Tall ironweed (*V. altissima*)** blooms in moist areas along streams, in low, sparse, open (lightly shaded) woodlands, from July to September. This species frequently gets much taller than 4 feet high. **Great ironweed (*V. crinita*)** grows on sand and gravel bars, so it wants a coarse, open, moist soil. This species is usually about 4 feet tall and forms large dramatic clumps when well established. I've seen swallowtails, monarchs, fritillaries, and other butterflies feeding on ironweeds, practically mobbing the flowers in late summer.

∾ DESIGN IDEAS. *The rose-purple ironweed flowers make a good contrast to grasses, any of the sunflowers, sneezeweed and other yellow daisies, lavender to purple asters, and other end-of-summer flowers.*

OTHER THAN DAISIES

Moving away from the daisies, sunflowers, ironweeds, and their kin, we find a few late flowers with a different appearance.

White turtlehead (*Chelone glabra*), which indeed looks like a dense spike of turtles' heads, is a well-behaved tall plant for moist sites. Growing about 3 feet tall with tidy serrate leaves in pairs marching up the stem, the white or greenish yellow flowers appear in August in dense spikes at the tip of the stem. It inhabits wet meadows, marshes, the banks of slowly moving streams, and lightly shaded shrub swamps from Newfoundland west to Minnesota and south to Georgia and Missouri. **Pink turtlehead (*C. lyonii*)** has deep rose-pink flowers in September and October. I remember once observing with some amusement a corpulent bumblebee that had entered a flower looking for pollen and was having trouble backing out. Her distinctly grumbly buzzing had the whole inflorescence atremble.

Closed gentian, blind gentian, or **bottle gentian (*Gentiana andrewsii*)** is a relatively easy-to-grow long-lived member of this genus, happy in moist soils in sun or light shade, often at the edge of a shrub swamp. It grows about 15 to 24 inches tall, with deep brilliant blue to blue-violet flowers clustered in the leaf axils on the upper portion of the wandlike stems in early September to October. They remain closed at the mouth, hence the common name. One September, I saw this at Schaefer Prairie in Minnesota, where its arching stems displayed its flowers against the tawny grasses. It is native from Quebec west to Manitoba and south to New England, New Jersey, Kentucky, Missouri, and Nebraska, as well as at higher elevations in North Carolina.

Biennial **fringed gentian (*Gentianopsis crinata*)** is the truly difficult one. It is not easy to introduce, as a colony can be established only after seed has been sown two years running. It cannot compete with other, more vigorous plants, and mowing must be carefully timed to allow the seeds to ripen and disperse. Unless conditions are just right, this is an impermanent addition to the garden, but one well worth attempting. The erect stems are 1 to 2 feet tall, with many short side branches, each holding erect a single, deeply

*Prairie blazing-star
or Kansas gay-feather
(Liatris aspera, p. 23)
blooms from mid-July
to early August.*

© LARRY MELLICHAMP

© C. COLSTON BURRELL

*Tall ironweed (Vernonia altissima, p. 24)
flourishes in moist areas along streams in
lightly shaded spots from July to September.*

fringed gentian blue vaselike flower in September and October. It is so beautiful that it repays the careful two-year seed sowing necessary to develop a self-perpetuating colony.

Grass-of-Parnassus *(Parnassia glauca)* flowers in August and September, but you must look closely to find its creamy white green-veined flowers, as they appear one to each 6- to 12-inch-tall stem. It is a dainty, delicate thing, especially in contrast to the huge Joe-Pye weed at whose ankles I have found it flowering. This is more a specialist's flower, interesting with close-up examination but without much impact in the landscape. It is charming in a container, where it is easier to appreciate.

Meadow-beauty *(Rhexia virginica)* grows in wet meadows and seeps from Nova Scotia west to Wisconsin and south to Florida, Louisiana, and Texas. The showy flowers, nearly an inch across, appear in small clusters at the top of the 2-foot-tall stems. The bright yellow stamens cluster in the center of the flower, conspicuous in contrast to the purple petals. Growing from a tuberous root, it is an easy plant to relocate.

Canadian burnet or **American burnet** (depending on which side of the border you are gardening, I suppose) *(Sanguisorba canadensis)* is an interesting, late-blooming perennial with erect white bottlebrush flowers in September to October. The 12-inch-long feathery pinnate compound leaves are clustered at the base of the plant, with the flowering stems reaching 3 to 5 feet tall. Cold hardy but intolerant of heat, it is found from Newfoundland west to Manitoba, south to New Jersey, Pennsylvania, and Indiana, and in the mountains to South Carolina.

Blue vervain *(Verbena hastata)* is disappointing if you grow only one. To be effective, it needs to be grown en masse since each plant has only a few flowers open at any given time. An

With its attractive blossoms and foliage and its upright habit, queen-of-the-prairie (Filipendula rubra, p. 17) is an excellent plant for moist soils.

© C. COLSTON BURRELL

Tall yellow cup plant or rosinweed (Silphium perfoliatum, p. 22) is impressive in a late border with a deep burgundy angelica, a tall ornamental grass, a mound of cheery rudbeckia, and pink cleome.

© JUDY GLATTSTEIN

© JUDY GLATTSTEIN

A Joe-Pye weed (Eupatorium spp., p. 23), combines dramatically with a canna (p. 31) and a grass (Glyceria maxima 'Variegata', p. 9).

upright plant growing 5 to 7 feet tall, it has leafy stems and many terminal spikes of small flowers from July to September.

∾ DESIGN IDEAS. *When grown in profusion, the colony casts a soft haze over the landscape. Slight on its own, it creates a useful background to showier flowers blooming at the same time, such as deep violet New York ironweed (Vernonia novaboracensis), soft mauve Joe-Pye weed (Eupatorium purpureum), white boneset (E. perfoliatum), and yellow daisies.*

Naturalized Flowering Plants

Lady's-smock or **cuckoo-flower** *(Cardamine pratensis)* has settled in and made itself at home as readily in an American setting as in its original European habitats. The slender stems arise from a tuft of pinnate leaflets, bearing four-petaled white or pale blush-pink flowers in May

Dodecatheon sp. (p. 12) is a spring wetland plant.

and June. As is common with many other plants in the Mustard Family, it self-sows freely. **Bitter cress** *(C. pensylvanica)* is a native species with white flowers.

Elecampane *(Inula helenium)* is naturalized, not actually native — another plant from abroad that just made itself at home. These are coarse, bold plants with ragged, tousled 2-inch-wide mustard-golden daisy flowers. Growing 4 to 6 feet high, the plants need room to spread out 16-inch-long basal leaves, which extend even farther out from the stem on 12-inch petioles. As they ascend the stout stem, the leaves become progressively smaller and sessile. If moisture is lacking, the plants quickly go into a decline by

This nonnative white Filipendula (F. palmata, p. 33), known as Siberian meadowsweet, needs very moist soil.

This lush combination of hosta, perennial grass (Hakonechloa), iris (p. 33), ligularia (pp. 33-34), fern, and lady's-mantle disguise a drainage culvert.

mid- to late summer, indicating their distress by becoming brown and shabby. Given full sun and moist, even boggy conditions, they will thrive. **Swordleaf inula** *(I. ensifolia)* is a smaller version, growing only 1 to 2 feet tall and 2 feet wide, with numerous 1- to 2-inch-wide long-petaled orange to bright yellow daisies over a six-week period. The sessile linear leaves are completely different from those of elecampane.

Self-heal or **heal-all** *(Prunella vulgaris)* will tolerate a certain amount of foot traffic, making it useful if you need a ground cover that can occasionally be walked on. It is, in fact, a common invader of the cultivated lawn and often arrives in gardens on its own. This plant has tightly matted, multibranched stems and leaves in a basal rosette. The flower heads remind me of miniature green bee skeps, with lavender flowers darting out here and there. They appear from May to September.

Buttercups tend to be too aggressive for cultivated gardens, but they are often suitable for a natural setting. There they can spread, with only competition from their neighbors to hold them in check, rather than stoop labor to weed them out. In modern cholesterol-conscious times, do children still pick buttercups to hold under a playmate's chin to "see if they like butter"? When I was a child, we did, and the glossy yellow flowers reflected a pale wash of yellow onto the skin. *Ranunculus bulbosus* is a European native with butter-yellow flowers from May to July. It has a bulbous root that can be used for propagation, although once introduced, it reproduces quite freely on its own. **Aconite buttercup** *(R. aconitifolius)* has glossy three- to five-part leaves reminiscent of an aconite's. It bears 1-inch-wide white flowers on plants 2 to 3 feet tall. Native to France, it is adaptable and well equipped to make itself at home.

Yellow flag iris (Iris pseudacorus, p. 13), and Japanese primrose (Primula japonica, p. 76) in the foreground, and rodgersia (p. 34) at the rear grow next to a pool. Note the boardwalk on the right, helpful for tending and walking through the garden.

Nonnative Ornamental Flowering Plants

Gardening books often describe an ideal but hypothetical situation with rich loam, moist but well drained — meaning that the moisture in the soil should be moving not stagnant. Reading on, you will learn that certain perennials grow best with ample moisture. Signs of inadequate moisture can be as simple as wilted foliage, skimpy flowering, or leaves that brown at the edges if the soil dries out. These are the perennials that enjoy wet meadow, marsh, or pond bank situations. Their leaves and flowers are in the sun, and their roots are constantly moist — but not wet with standing water.

Astilbe (usually available as ***Astilbe*** x ***arendsii*** hybrids) (color photos, pages 78–79) is no doubt the most familiar of these plants. Generally, astilbes are 2 to 3 feet tall, occasionally taller. They have glossy medium to dark green, fernlike compound leaves. Cultivars with deep pink or red flowers often have coppery or bronze new growth in spring. The flowers, excellent for cutting, appear in June through July as plumelike panicles that vary in color from white through pale to deep pink or a striking rich red or magenta. The seed heads may be left on the plants for winter interest, but should be cut away in spring before growth begins. Astilbe appreciates good rich soil and flowers better if fertilized.

Canna (***Canna*** x ***generalis; C.*** x ***hybrida***) (color photo, page 27) is often denigrated, suggested for Victorian bedding-out schemes suitable for those without refined gardening sensibilities. I happen to adore canna, but as a foliage rather than a flowering plant. In my opinion, it should be not so much deadheaded

The leaves of cannas like this 'Pretoria' are as much of an asset as the flowers.

as disbudded before it blossoms. Canna's bold leaves add a tropical luxuriance to the summer garden, especially effective in contrast to thin grasslike leaves on iris, and ferny astilbe or meadowsweet foliage. There are cultivars with green leaves, others with copper to purple leaves, and a couple with leaves elegantly striped creamy yellow against green. ∾ GROWING TIPS. *It is commonly accepted that in gardens located in areas colder than Zone 8, cannas should be lifted and stored over the winter. I think they could remain in the ground in Zone 7, especially in a protected site. In Zone 6 or colder, store the rhizomes over the winter in barely damp peat moss at about 45° to 50°F.*

A serene natural-looking garden, including astilbe, Japanese iris, and ferns, bordering a small pool.

❧ DESIGN IDEAS. *Selections with green leaves work well with ferny foliage, while in the garden, showier variegated ones such as 'Nirvana' can be used in containers. The purple-leaved forms such as 'Wyoming' look especially effective with the mauve flowers of Joe-Pye weed (Eupatorium purpureum).*

Siberian meadowsweet (Filipendula palmata) (color photo, page 28) grows 3 to 4 feet tall. Since it has compound leaves, the effect, though bold, is not overly massive and imposing. The numerous 6-inch-wide fattened panicles of pale pink flowers that appear in early June provide a good display, fading to white as they age. Unless the soil stays moist, the leaves brown at the edge, ultimately shriveling and falling off if the situation is not promptly remedied. **Dropwort (F. hexapetala; F. vulgaris)** is a daintier plant growing 2 to 3½ feet tall. Its glossy medium green leaves are pinnately divided, which gives them a daintier, more fernlike appearance. The flowers are creamy white, often with a hint of pink. This species is better able to accept dry soils but prefers situations where it is constantly moist.

Irises. Iris was a Greek goddess who traveled between heaven and earth on a rainbow bridge, and her namesake flowers display a rainbow of colors. As well as our native and naturalized water iris, there are some species that are low maintenance, while others are worth the care they need. Easiest is the **Siberian iris (Iris sibirica).** This is not surprising, as it is found in wet meadows in its native haunts. Its grasslike leaves add an appealing susurrus in response to even light breezes. Sturdy upright stems bear about five blue, lavender, or white flowers well above the 2- to 3-foot-tall foliage in mid- to late May. **Japanese iris (I. ensata**; formerly **I. kaempferi)** is more difficult to grow well. It needs an acid soil high in organic matter with constant moisture, as well as full sun or light dappled shade. Over centuries of breed-ing, the Japanese have developed saucerlike flat flowers as big as 10 inches in diameter — not only singles but doubles with six petals and twelve-petaled peony-style flowers. There are white, pale blue, deep blue, pink, lavender, and purple flowers, some with a yellow streak to the petals, a picotee edging in a contrasting color, distinct veining, or ruffled edges. Such obviously culti-vated forms are not suitable for naturalistic land-scapes and are best used in more formal settings. **Rabbit ear iris (I. laevigata)** is a closely related species that is more suitable for naturalistic de-signs. The 2- to 3-inch-diameter flowers are lavender-blue or pure white, in the selection 'Alba'. Although rabbit ear iris tolerates a less acid soil than does Japanese iris, this species still demands a soil high in organic matter and con-stant moisture at the roots. Wet meadows and damp soil along pond banks and near streams are the most suitable locations.

❧ GROWING TIPS. *Eventually, Siberian iris plants expand to form clumps, which, as they continue to age, develop a bare center. Either in early spring or after flowering, dig the clump, discard the dead center, and separate the outer "fairy ring" into nice-size divisions. Replant promptly, and do not allow the divisions to dry out.*

Ligularias are not the most attractive peren-nial border plants, because their leaves wilt like a broken umbrella on sunny summer days. When they are given a more suitable site, one with constantly moist soil, it's a different story. In a wet meadow, alongside a stream, or around a pond, especially if there is some midday shade, the handsome foliage adds a bold, attractive texture. I find the flowers of some ligularia, just like cannas, not especially attractive — merely an-other ragged orange daisy.

Big-leaf ligularia (Ligularia dentata) has coarsely toothed kidney-shaped leaves up to 20 inches across. There are several cultivars to choose from. 'Desdemona' emerges in spring with beet-red leaves that remain purple on the underside even when they mature; it is a selection with somewhat more compact form than the species but still bold in scale and texture. 'Othello' is quite similar, perhaps not as compact and tidy.

Narrow-spiked ligularia *(L. stenocephala)* is a more attractive species in flower, with a tall wand of 1½-inch-wide starry yellow flowers, which add a pleasing vertical accent. The triangular leaves have a coarsely toothed margin. Even young plants need copious amounts of water. One cultivar is usually available. This is 'The Rocket', which is more compact and has lemon-yellow flowers. Sometimes it is listed (incorrectly) as a cultivar of *L. przewalskii* which has palmately cut, rather than triangular, leaves.

∾ EDIBLE PLANTS. *Ligularia leaves are edible. I had them, prepared as tempura, when I was in Japan.*

Rhubarb *(Rheum* spp.) is often relegated to the kitchen garden. This is a pity, as the plant has impressively massive foliage. The culinary *R. rhabarbarum* has green or red petioles, imposing triangular leaves with a wavy edge, and a billowing froth of white flowers on stems 6 feet tall. If this does not catch your fancy, several other species are commonly grown for ornamental effect. Most renowned of these is *R. palmatum.* Its dark green leaves are 2 to 3 feet wide and deeply palmately lobed. In the form 'Atrosanguineum', the new growth is dark reddish purple as the leaves emerge in spring; the leaves retain the red color on the underside at maturity. The plants demand a constant supply of moisture, copious fertilizer (rhubarb, even in kitchen garden books, is referred to as a "gross feeder"), some midday shade, and substantial room to grow. Compared to this, canna could almost be called dainty.

Rodgersia, (color photo, page 30) like the two preceding genera, comes from China. These plants can survive in average soil conditions, but only with constant adequate moisture do they truly display their architectural foliage. Use them along a stream, near a pond, or at the edge of a wet meadow. They perform best with partial shade in hot summer regions. In such sites, each plant can spread to 5 feet across. **Shieldleaf rodgersia (*R. tabularis*)** differs from the other species most noticeably in the shape of its leaves, which are large, salverlike, and somewhat scalloped, with a small depression or dimple in the center, where the leaf is attached to the 2- to 3-foot petiole beneath. A sturdy petiole supports stout clusters of drooping white flowers. As the name suggests, *R. aesculifolia* does indeed have leaves like those of a horse chestnut (*aesculifolia* means "leaves like an *Aesculus*," the genus name of horse chestnut). It has seven palmately arranged, coarsely toothed leaflets narrower at the base than at the tip. Each leaflet is 4 to 10 inches long. There are shaggy brown hairs on the petiole, flower stalk, and even the main leaf veins. *R. pinnata* has pinnately compound leaves, with five to nine leaflets each 6 to 8 inches long and widest in the middle. When they emerge in spring, especially while the weather is still cool, the foliage has a bronze cast.

As mentioned earlier, few bulbs accept wet conditions while dormant, but a handful might be used to enhance a wet meadow. Foremost of these is the **guinea-hen flower** *(Fritillaria meleagris).* In April or early May, the slender nodding stems, about 10 inches high, support one or two heavy-looking squared-off bells. Usually they are checkered like a chessboard in purple and white. Some are so heavily suffused with color as to appear solidly purple, while others are white with a faint hint of tessellation in pale green. The sparse narrow leaves are grayish green.

≈ GROWING TIPS. *Plant fritillaria bulbs in fall. Since they are small and lack any tunic or covering, I prefer to plant them as soon as they are available. At a minimum, plant ten in a group, more depending on the scale of the garden and the scope of your budget, though they are usually rather inexpensive.*

Daffodils *(Narcissus* **spp.).** Many daffodils tolerate wet conditions, even flooding, while they are growing. In general, however, they need enough drainage to keep them from rotting over the winter. Given the combination of short grass and percolating, not stagnant water, the little **hoop petticoat daffodil** *(N. bulbocodium)* will make itself at home. The most renowned example of this is in the alpine meadow at Wisley, garden of the Royal Horticultural Society. At first its flowers do not even look like a daffodil — not if you expect a miniature of the familiar trumpet-flowered sort. Instead, the flower looks like a yellow funnel, with six small spurs neatly arranged around it halfway between the opening of the funnel and its attachment to the stem. The plants grow about 6 inches tall, often less, and are early into bloom and quick into dormancy. I suggest planting ten each autumn for three years. Compare each group to the others, and see how they maintain their vigor. If they thrive, and perhaps even multiply, you can splurge and plant hundreds.

Magic lily, rain lily, and **resurrection flower** are common names that allude to the habit of *Lycoris squamigera* to produce flowers, unaccompanied by any leaves, in response to late summer rains. Seemingly by magic, the smooth stem with a whitish coating or farina emerges quite briskly, reaching 2 feet tall, and then produces four to seven fragrant rose-pink flowers, each of which looks like a small amaryllis. This is the hardiest species and grows and flowers in my Connecticut garden. In large part this is because leaves do not appear until spring. Looking as if they belong to some huge daffodil, the broad (1-inch-wide), 9- to 12-inch-long grayish green leaves emerge in spring and begin collapsing in June. A moist soil and some shade in late summer when the flowers appear will produce the best results. In southern and southeastern gardens, this flower grows so well and multiplies so freely as to be a "back fence" plant, one passed on from neighbor to neighbor rather than purchased.

A Final Word on Selecting Plants

It is as easy to distinguish the differences between a pond and a wet meadow as it is to recognize a water lily and a water iris. The iris, along with many other plants, can accept the conditions on a pond bank with equanimity; it is only true aquatics, like water lilies, that demand the constant presence of open water. If the idea of gardening in wet meadow conditions is unfamiliar to you, perhaps you might begin with familiar garden perennials. Select rhubarb *(Rheum rhabarbarum)* as a bold accent, and embellish it with three plants of a white-flowered Siberian iris and five to seven plants of a white-flowered astilbe. Should you decide that this would be an appropriate place to grow native plants, then blue flag *(Iris versicolor)*, sensitive fern *(Onoclea sensibilis)*, and swamp milkweed *(Asclepias incarnata)* would be a suitable trio. Or, you could mix and match natives and exotics. Boundaries are often less than clear-cut. In your own situation, you will find that if plants accept one type of sunny wet soil site, they may be adaptable to another. Discovery and exploration are among the pleasures of gardening.

Chapter Three

SUNNY GARDENS WITH SHALLOW WATER: MARSHES

Suppose you have a small pond in your garden, either one you've installed yourself or a naturally occurring one (lucky you!). If you want to blend it into the landscape in a natural manner, then marsh plants such as cattails and rushes, ferns and water iris will create the effect you want. Or perhaps your property abuts a real swamp, and the marshy boundary is too wet for the ordinary garden perennials you've tried to grow there. If it is sunny, at least six hours a day, then marsh plants should be just the thing to add color and interest.

Keep the situation in scale — a mass of cattails would overwhelm a small pool, where a dwarf Japanese cattail *(Typha minima)* would be a more suitable, daintier choice. Add smaller species of ferns, perhaps sensitive fern *(Onoclea sensibilis)* and other small-scale plants: marsh marigold *(Caltha palustris)*, forget-me-nots *(Myosotis palustris)*, lower-growing astilbes, monkey flower *(Mimulus guttatus)*, and sedges and rushes. Plantings such as these are reminiscent of a marsh

in conjunction with even a bird-bath-size pool.

Where the pool is larger, from 3 or 4 feet to perhaps as much as 8 or 10 feet across, and a couple of feet deep, the adjacent marsh plants should increase in stature in order to provide visual balance. This scale would allow the use of various iris such as yellow flag *(Iris pseudacorus)* and blue flag *(I. versicolor)*, as well as taller ferns like cinnamon fern *(Osmunda cinnamommea)*, tall astilbes, rodgersias *(Rodgersia aesculifolia* or *R. pinnata)*, narrow-leaved cattail *(Typha angustifolia)*, and other stately plants. This back-yard pond should be within reach of a garden hose so it can be topped up and the adjacent marsh planting watered during dry spells (see suggestions on the use of water-retentive crystals in chapter 9, pages 165–166). This type of pond/marsh would attract amphibians — frogs, toads, and salamanders. Mated pairs of mallard ducks have been known to accept the "welcome mat" such a planting provides in urban settings where more spacious quarters are limited.

As well as the small-scale marsh-type habitat to be installed adjacent to a pool, there are natural marshlands on a grander scale. Perhaps a degraded, drained marsh basin where once there was wetland may have been altered to farmland. Often there exist state or federal services — water bank subsidies, soil conservation services, department of natural resources, and others — to provide technical assistance and even subsidies to qualified agricultural landowners for the restoration and/or preservation of wetlands. Usually this help applies to large-scale, multi-acre situations.

Some Design Ideas for Marshes or Marshlike Settings

Many plants that grow naturally in marshes are eminently suitable for a pond bank. For quiet simplicity itself, pair the graceful linear foliage of cattail at water's edge with the round leaves of water lilies floating nearby. Flowering rush *(Butomus umbellatus)* adds umbels of pink flowers in summer, its narrow rushlike leaves blending

MARSHES

Similar to a wet meadow in that woody plants are sparse or absent, a freshwater marsh has waterlogged soil that is frequently covered with water. The water is not stagnant; there is some flow through the site. Temporary pools and ponds appear seasonally.

The major plants that help identify these sites are *hydrophytes,* water-loving plants such as grasses and sedges — burreed in shallow marshes, cattails in wetter areas where the open water is semipermanent. These hydrophytes are *emergents,* plants that grow with their roots in wet soil or under water for part or all of their life, but with the bulk of their foliage out of the water. Grasses (such as *Panicum* spp.), cattails *(Typha* spp.), rushes, and sedges (species of *Scirpus* and *Carex)* tend to be the dominant plants. Others frequently found are pickerel rush *(Pontederia cordata),* arrowhead *(Sagittaria latifolia),* and ferns such as sensitive fern *(Onoclea sensibilis)* and royal fern *(Osmunda regalis).* Typically the ferns are growing on sedge tussocks so that their roots reach down into the water but their crowns are above the usual water level.

Marshes may become drier on a seasonal basis, but the plants that grow there are wetland species. Inland marshes fill and deplete, fluctuating as rainfall and evaporation affect them. Water supplies are influenced by rainfall, but usually there is drainage into the marsh from an adjacent watershed, either from a stream or as groundwater below the soil's surface. Usually the soil at the edges of a marsh is wetter than the surrounding area, as seepage from the marsh infiltrates the soil. Thus, there can be a wet meadow fringe surrounding the marsh itself. Often a marsh is found as a lakeshore wetland, where shelving ground rises from the standing water. These emergent aquatics are useful for the transition zone between pond and shoreline, softening the passage from water to land.

inconspicuously with those of the cattail. Arrowhead *(Sagittaria latifolia)* provides ornamental, contrasting foliage.

You can choose among several meadow plants to supply flowering interest. Creeping swamp buttercup *(Ranunculus septentrionalis)* has deep yellow flowers 1 inch across; the stems become stoloniferous after the plant blossoms in March through June. Its bloom time overlaps with yellow flag iris *(Iris pseudacorus)*, which begins to flower in June. Other irises would add different colors, but similar shapes and foliage — too repetitive in a site that already has cattails and flowering rush. Hybrid globeflower *(Trollius x cultorum)* has large double golden yellow flowers so crowded with petals as to be almost spherical. Although most of the cultivars bloom in May, 'Lemon Queen' and 'Golden Queen' flower in June. If cut back hard, they may repeat their flowering again in autumn. Some contrast is needed to accent the yellow theme. Summer snowflake *(Leucojum aestivum)* has daffodil-like foliage and a 15-inch-high stem with several green-tipped white flowers, like well-starched petticoats or small bells. Foot-tall, free-flowering water forget-me-not *(Myosotis palustris)* provides a charming accent of soft blue. Cut back after flowering, they flower well a second time, often remaining in flower from May right through summer. Monkey flower *(Mimulus ringens)*, with violet-blue flowers, adds a stronger emphasis. A taller plant, it will reach 2 feet high.

Foliage is an important consideration, and the sun-tolerant qualities of marsh fern *(Thelypteris palustris)* make it a good choice for this planting. Its lacy fronds add texture and contrast to the predominantly linear or low-growing leaves of the other plants.

By its very character, a marshlike setting must have a naturalistic design. The vigorous nature and rapid spread of most marsh plants make them unsuitable for a formal, intensely structured landscape. Where they are used by a small, shallow pond, care must be taken to see that they do not completely fill in the area.

Sedges, Rushes, and Other Grasslike Plants

Many grasslike plants, especially sedges and rushes, are found in this wetter habitat. It is easy to tell them apart: Grasses have nodes, a thickened portion where the leaf joins the stem; sedges and rushes do not. Grasses usually have hollow stems and leaves coming off in two directions; sedges have solid triangular stems and leaves in a triangular arrangement; rushes have cylindrical stems. Sedges and rushes are found in many different kinds of wet places — marshes, swamps, and bogs, as well as along canals and slow-moving streams. Almost any sunny or lightly shaded place with damp, muddy soil or shallow water is likely to have sedges.

SEDGES

Sedges *(Carex spp.)* have a worldwide distribution. Some form clumps; others ramble about, sometimes invasively. They can have showy flowers, interesting seed heads, and pleasant foliage. **Palm sedge** *(C. muskingumensis)*, with bright green leaves radiating from the arching stems, is native around the Great Lakes. Growth is lax and drooping, more procumbent than upright. It is thus useful as an interesting, slowly spreading ground cover.

Tussock sedge *(C. stipata)* looks rather like miniature brown haystacks in winter. In spring, it sends up fresh green shoots, which are quickly followed by long-lasting attractive brown seed heads. This is the sedge that creates a neat edging around ponds and regular mounds in swamps. Its hillocks form the microhabitat for cinnamon fern *(Osmunda cinnamonea)* and royal fern *(O. regalis)*, providing these ferns with a place to keep their crowns above water while sending their roots down into it.

Drooping sedge is a prosaic, rather unattractive common name for *C. pendula.* Growing in clumps, this vigorous evergreen perennial is one of the most graceful sedges. The tufts reach 4 feet high, with long pendulous flower stalks rising an additional 1 to 2 feet above the foliage. This is an excellent choice for a single specimen, when grown en masse, or displayed in a container. It seeds to some extent.

Variegated river sedge (*C. riparia* 'Variegata') may be fairly described as attractive but aggressive. Growing about 15 inches tall, it has leaves that are dramatically streaked with white, some without any trace of green. It is hardy to Zone 5, but in hot climates, the foliage can burn; in such locations, it needs midday shade. Probably this is safest to use as a container plant,

unless you intend to let it take over everything. Clumps form along the spreading root system, rapidly grabbing new territory. Remember, unlike yellow variegation, white portions of a leaf lack any means of photosynthesis. If the variegated form is this contentious a spreader, imagine what the plain green one is like!

Bowles golden sedge (*C. stricta* 'Bowles Golden') is a better-behaved species, also with attractive, showy foliage. The new leaves in spring display the best color — a clear bright yellow softening to chartreuse by summer. The 2-foot-long leaves have a thin green edge. Found by the same plantsman who discovered Bowles golden grass, the golden sedge is hardy from Zone 5 to Zone 9, with midday shade needed in hot climates.

Cyperus sedge (*C. pseudocyperus*) (color photo, page 40) has nodding golden green flowers 1 to 2 feet tall on sturdy 2- to 3-foot-high stems in spring. The flowers turn brown as they mature, creating an interesting contrast to the yellow-green leaves. Widely disseminated, it appears in boggy areas in North America, Europe,

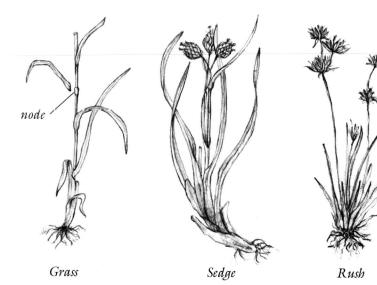

node

Grass　　　*Sedge*　　　*Rush*

The differences between grasses, rushes, and sedges become clear when they are examined side by side: grasses have nodes, and leaves coming off in two directions; the leaves of sedges emerge in a triangular arrangement; rushes have cylindrical stems.

and eastern Asia. The persistent, attractive flowers make it an interesting choice for swamps, pond shores, or containers. Its common name reflects a resemblance to the **umbrella sedges** *(Cyperus* **spp.),** which are primarily tropical and subtropical in distribution, with relatively fewer temperate zone plants.

Carex vegetus is hardy in Zones 4 to 7 and is occasionally grown as a houseplant. It is a vigorous plant, forming loose clumps with medium green evergreen leaves on stems 2 to 4 feet tall and dense, tightly clustered greenish white flower spikes. It reseeds abundantly and is best in a large naturalistic setting where its spreading tendencies are not cause for alarm.

One sedge that can be a problem is **nut sedge** *(C. esculentus).* Its small, hard tubers allow it to spread quickly, and it is difficult to eradicate. The tender species make excellent container plants.

Papyrus *(C. papyrus)* is probably the best-known member of the genus. It can only be grown outdoors year-round in Zones 9 and 10.

Cotton grass, also called **bog cotton** *(Eriophorum virginicum)* (color photo, page 53) is neither a grass nor related to cotton. The common name of this native North American sedge refers to the fluffy, silky bristles crowded into dense, compact clusters that form brownish or whitish cottonlike bundles. For best effect, it should be grown in large colonies, which bend and sway in the late summer breeze, creating a charming picture that one or two plants do not provide. Forming loose colonies, this is a moderate-size plant (2 to 4 feet) with fine-textured medium green foliage. It is a good choice for muddy sites in full sun in Zones 4 to 9. *E. latifolium* is smaller, growing 12 to 18 inches tall with silky white cotton heads in spring (April and May). It grows in clumps and is useful in smaller gardens where the spreading tendencies

of other species might be a problem. Hot weather is not good for it; it grows best in Zones 4 to 7.

Bulrush is the confusing common name for *Scirpus* **spp.** In spite of its name, this plant is a sedge, not a rush. Bulrushes are very widespread and a major component of sunny wetlands. Several species might be able to act as biological filters, removing contaminants such as mercury, lead, cadmium, and phenol from the aqueous environment. My friend Cole Burrell, a landscape designer and principal of Native Landscapes Design and Restoration Ltd. in Minneapolis, pointed out that when biofilters are used on a commercial/industrial scale, disposal becomes an issue because of this. The different species vary from less than 1 foot to more than 7 feet tall. They have thick underground rhizomes by which they spread and which also ensure winter survival. Together with cattail, they grow in dense stands in the muddy soil or shallow water of marshes, pond banks, and river bottoms. They provide nesting cover for waterfowl and some songbirds and habitat for muskrats and otters. Either plants or roots can be set out about 3 feet apart in shallow water or moist soil from the beginning of April to the end of July. Generally, the variegated forms are most widely available.

Porcupine plant *(S. tabernaemontana* **'Zebrinus')** has greenish white or greenish yellow horizontal bands on both leaves and stems (rather like *Miscanthus sinensis* 'Zebrinus'). It grows 2 to 4 feet tall. If it reverts to solid green, those stems should be removed. It is outstanding along a slowly flowing stream and elegant near a pond, as well as in marshes, in Zones 7 to 9. A mass of this plant is stunning, especially when backlit by early morning or late day sun.

White-stemmed club rush *(S. lacustris albescens)*, unusual because of its coloration, forms narrowly upright clumps of white stems thinly penciled with an occasional green stripe — greener at the tips. It rarely produces any leaves, and when it does, they are also white.

∾ EDIBLE PLANTS. *In many of the same ways they used cattail, American Indians used the roots of bulrush, raw or cooked, or dried and pounded into flour. Ground seeds were cooked as a cereal, and the pollen was formed into cakes and baked. Young shoots in late winter and early spring can be eaten raw or cooked, as can the tender core at the base of older shoots.*

RUSHES

The true rushes (different species of *Juncus*) occur in wet meadows and marshes; they need full sun and wet feet. When you roll them between your fingers, they feel rounded; you don't feel the edges of a sedge or the bumpy nodes of true grasses. Useful in naturalistic plantings, rushes create habitats for wetland wildlife and stabilize the banks of ponds and slow-moving streams. **Soft rush (*Juncus effusus*)** is evergreen (at least in mild climates), forming dense vertical clumps, knee to chest high (18 to 40 inches tall), with from only a few to several hundred glossy, soft, round medium green stems. These have long been used for mats and chair seats. Hardy in Zones 4 to 9, soft rush does better if given some midday shade in hotter climates. Preferring a site where it will be inundated for prolonged periods

MEDIEVAL LIGHT

"Rushlights" were used for illumination in medieval times. Twelve-inch lengths of peeled soft rush were briefly soaked in tallow or other grease and lit at one end.

A USEFUL PLANT

Horsetails' rough coating of silica crystals makes them useful as pot scrubbers on a camping trip. They have been used to polish pewter and for fine sanding. Their ability to grow in polluted environments and absorb heavy metals such as lead, cadmium, and zinc suggests their possible use around strip mines. They even assimilate minute traces of gold, and during the California Gold Rush, it was suggested that the stems be dried and burned to reclaim the precious metal from the ashes.

by a few inches of water, it is found in wet meadows, marshes, and roadside ditches, as well as along pond banks and the edges of streams. The tiny green flowers appear in clusters, from May to September, most frequently in early summer, and are an attractive addition to the linear texture of the plants. They turn brownish or rusty red in autumn and persist through the winter. Because soft rush has a creeping rhizome and invasive tendencies, either grow it in a container or plan to thin it on a regular basis. There is a variegated form, 'Aureus Striatus', with strong yellow-green stripes, as well as two white ones, 'Vittatus', which has narrow white stripes, and 'Zebrinus', which has broad greenish white stripes. The variegated forms, usually about 2 feet tall, do better with some midday shade.

Bizarre rather than beautiful best describes a horticultural selection called **corkscrew rush (*J. effusus* 'Spiralis'),** whose stems grow in a curling, spiraling corkscrew fashion, often nearly prostrate. The stems are interesting when seen close-up and are valuable in arrangements both fresh and dried.

Flowering rush *(Butomus umbellatus)* is unique, the only species in this genus. Flowering rush is native to Europe and Asia. It has naturalized, and is found growing from the St. Lawrence River Valley and the Great Lakes west to Michigan and Ohio. The numerous showy rose-pink flowers, each up to an inch across, are borne in a terminal umbel from June through August on stems 2 to 4 feet tall. Although this plant is not a true rush, its coarse-textured medium green leaves have a rushlike appearance, and it grows in similar wet places — in mud at the margins of ponds and right in shallow water. It spreads quickly from tubers that form in autumn and can be used for propagation. I have seen this on the banks and along the edges of smaller canals in Holland.

Scouring rush or **horsetail rush** *(Equisetum* spp.), too, is not a true rush, although it has a rushlike appearance and an aggressively spreading mat of rhizomes. It is a descendant of giant species that grew 65 million years ago during the Jurassic period, in the time of dinosaurs. Horsetails are little changed from their ancient ancestors except in size. The linear stems are made up of a series of dark green segmented tubes that separate easily. Just like ferns, these primitive plants reproduce by spores, which, in the case of horsetails, is produced in a conelike structure called a *strobilus.* Horsetails also multiply by means of their extensive, persistent network of underground roots and tubers. They colonize bare disturbed ground, even railroad embankments, as well as wet meadows, roadsides, and stream banks. The fine linear texture makes a good contrast to other plants, but their spreading tendencies and persistent character suggest caution. Before turning the common evergreen species *E. hyemale* loose in the marsh, consider growing it restrained in a container instead. This

is also the safest course of action with other species.

Dwarf scouring rush *(E. scirpoides)* is a dainty little thing, growing only 4 to 8 inches tall. Found in the north Arctic as well as in temperate regions, its evergreen stems form vigorous, dense mats. 'Curly' is a cultivar with somewhat prostrate, contorted stems. **Giant horsetail rush** *(E. telmateia; E. maximum)* can reach a stately 6½ feet tall, usually less, and is best grown in lightly shaded, moist sites where it combines well with equally majestic ferns. **Variegated rush** *(E. variegatum)* grows 6 to 12 inches tall, and the evergreen stems are streaked green and white.

❧ EDIBLE PLANTS. *When I was in Japan one May, I was taken out to dinner at a restaurant specializing in "healthy wild gathered mountain vegetables." One recognizable plant was tsukushi (horsetail). The young shoots were stripped of their tops and outer sheath, boiled, and served with a dipping sauce of broth, soy sauce, and vinegar.*

GRASSES

Some of the grasses described in chapter 2 are able to grow equally well in the shallow water of a marsh. These include variegated manna grass *(Glyceria maxima)*, maiden grass or eulalia grass *(Miscanthus* spp. and cultivars), gardener's-garters *(Phalaris arundinacea* var. *picta)*, and prairie cord grass *(Spartina pectinata)*.

CATTAILS AND THEIR LOOK-ALIKES

Cattail or **reed-mace** *(Typha* species) is a familiar component of freshwater marshes and pond banks, growing in low swales, inner-city ditches, and other wet situations. Adaptable, they thrive in conditions ranging from moist soil to standing water 2 feet deep. Their vigorous creeping rhizomes can help stabilize pond banks, unless muskrats move in and devour the succulent rhizomes.

Extremely invasive, **narrow-leaved cattail (T. angustifolia)** has slender, flexible irislike leaves that are yellowish green to dark green, less than 1 inch wide, and 3 to 5 feet long on plants growing 4 to 8 feet tall. The male flowers are on the upper portion of the stalk, with a slight separation from the female flowers below. In July or August the 4- to 12-inch-long cattail appears, looking like a fat brown cigar before shattering to tens of thousands of seeds and forming a cottonlike fluff in late fall. (For advice on how to prepare cattails for indoor arrangements, see page 9.) This is an invasive plant best suited to large-scale naturalistic plantings, as it is difficult to contain. Cattail marshes and swamps are highly productive wildlife habitats: red-winged blackbirds build their nests attached to the swaying stalks, waterfowl use the fluff to line their nests, muskrats eat the roots, and the plants themselves remove pollutants such as excess fertilizer — nutrients that lead to eutrophication.

Common cattail (T. latifolia) is an even more strongly competitive plant. It is larger than narrow-leaved cattail, with leaves 6 feet or more long. It is found in freshwater marshes, in shallow water bordering ponds, and along slowly moving rivers throughout most of the United States, Europe, and even Africa. The male and female flowers are adjacent on the stem, with only a slight constriction to delineate the sexes. Better suited to gardens is the more refined and slender **dwarf Japanese cattail (T. minima),** with ½-inch-wide leaves 1 to 2 feet long on plants reaching 2½ feet high. This graceful plant spreads more slowly than the other species, but still in a determined manner. Hardy in Zones 4 to 8, this species is useful in many moist sites.

❧ EDIBLE PLANTS. *Cattail was an important forage plant for American Indians. In late May or early June, the nutritious pollen was gathered to be used to thicken soups or combined with flour in batter for pancakes, biscuits, or breads. The roots can be peeled and eaten raw or cooked. In spring, the tender new shoots can be steamed or boiled.*

CATTAIL OR IRIS?
You can distinguish cattail from iris when the plants are not yet in flower by observing that the bottom portion of cattail leaves clasp the stem, whereas iris leaves are in a flat plane.

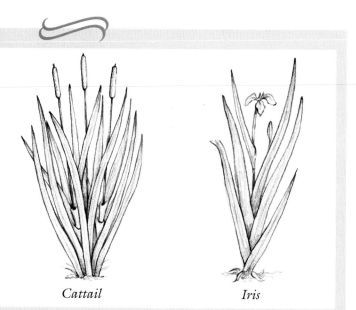

Cattail   *Iris*

Sweet flag was used as a strewing herb in medieval Europe and colonial North America. (Strewing herbs were scattered on clay or dirt floors to provide a pleasant scent when trod upon.) American Indians used the dried roots medicinally: they chewed them as a remedy for toothaches, coughs, and sore throats and used them in a decoction for upset stomachs, colic, and indigestion. Fresh, sweet flag was also boiled in sugar syrup and eaten as a confiture, much like candied ginger.

Cattail has been used medicinally to treat stomach upsets and diarrhea. The leaves can be plaited for mats or twined or coiled into baskets, and the fluffy down was used to pad cradleboards and as diapers.

Sweet flag *(Acorus calamus)* has long, narrow leaves that are a fresh bright green and grow 2 to 4 feet long. It looks a lot like cattail: The whole plant is aromatic, possessing a sweet, spicy scent; a crushed leaf can be identified by its citruslike, spicy odor. The flowers are small and yellowish brown, clustered into a small spike not quite 4 inches long. They appear from the side of the leaflike stalk, partway down from the tip. This structure, called a *spadix,* reveals the plant's kinship with jack-in-the-pulpit *(Arisaema triphyllum),* golden-club *(Orontium aquaticum),* wild calla *(Calla palustris),* and arrow arum *(Peltandra virginica).* All these plants belong to the Arum Family. Sweet flag is native from Nova Scotia and Quebec west to Alberta and Oregon and south to Florida and Texas, where it is found in marshes and shallow water along ponds and sluggish streams. The

variegated form is *A. calamus* 'Variegatus'; a dainty, smaller species from Japan is *A. gramineus.* ❧ DESIGN IDEAS. *Although sweet flag is an excellent companion for bold foliage plants such as arrow arum and the lacier texture of ferns, do not place it adjacent to its look-alikes cattail and iris, for the effect will be monotonous.*

Native Ornamental Flowering Plants

Marsh marigold *(Caltha palustris)* (color photo, page 77) is one of the first plants to awaken in the spring marshes. In April, spread above the roundish, kidney-shaped, glossy dark green leaves, its cheerful golden flowers stand out like a beacon across a sere landscape of last year's fallen leaves. One of the prettiest displays I've seen was in the Eloise Butler Wildflower Garden and Bird Sanctuary near Minneapolis–St. Paul. A carpet of these flowers was the only color; everywhere else were the tawny, winter-beaten stems of cattail and ferns, backed by pale white birch trunks. Marsh marigold is easy to grow in shallow water or wet soil, but it does not tolerate summer heat.

Our native **swamp lily** *(Crinum americanum)* is useful only in mild-winter regions. This beauty is a stunning plant in bloom. A member of the Lily Family, the large, succulent bulb should be planted in 2 to 6 inches of water. Given these appropriately moist conditions, it produces large straplike leaves with a stalklike structure created by a tubular sheath at their base. Delicately fragrant, the spidery white or pink-flushed flowers cluster at the top of the stem in July. Native to marshes, swamps, and sluggish streams from Georgia to Texas in the coastal plain, this is rarely grown and should be more widely used where it is hardy. Northern gardeners could grow it in a suitably large container and bring it into protected conditions in winter. Other, "exotic" species are often more widely available.

Another tender southern bulb is the **spider lily** *[Hymenocallis (Ismene) occidentalis],* native to sunny wetlands, marshes, and sloughs and sandbars in rivers and streams from North Carolina, Georgia, and Alabama west to southern Indiana, southern Illinois, and southeastern Missouri and south to Texas and Florida. Although it prefers wet places, it will accept average moisture conditions if water is supplied during times of drought. A true bulb, it produces six to twelve glossy green leaves about 2 inches wide and 6 to 18 inches long. The flowering stems are about a foot tall, each with three to nine fragrant white flowers in summer (June to August). *Hymenocallis* means "beautiful membrane," in reference to the cuplike corona uniting the six narrow segments of the perianth.

☙ GROWING TIPS. *Where not hardy, spider lily can be grown in a container and moved indoors for winter when it is dormant. It may also be grown in the ground, then dug up and stored in a dry, cool place (at about 45° F to 50° F) in a corrugated cardboard box or paper bag, with the adhering soil permitted to remain.*

Mallows *(Hibiscus* **spp.)** are slow to begin their growth in spring. They produce large, stately, long-lived clumps that flower over an extended period in mid- to late summer. Several native species make an elegant addition to the marsh. **Rose mallow, marsh mallow,** and **sea hollyhock (H. palustris)** are common names for a large plant with sturdy stems that grows 6 to 7 feet tall and bears blush-pink flowers that remind me of oversize hollyhocks, a relative. (Sometimes this is listed as *H. moscheutos* ssp. *palustris.*) Very showy (6 inches across), the beautiful flowers

enhance any garden. Usually they are a soft shell pink, but they can vary from white to a deep purplish pink, sometimes with a crimson eye. They are carried singly in the upper leaf axils from August to early September. The seed capsules are a dark chocolate brown and persist through the winter on the sturdy stems. The large, up to 8-inch-long leaves are wedge-shaped with a somewhat rounded or heart-shaped base tapering to a point at the tip. They are coarsely toothed along their margins, with velvety indumentum underneath. Native from Ontario and Massachusetts south along the coast to Virginia and inland as far as Michigan and Indiana, rose mallow is useful over a wide area. This obliging plant will grow in sunny, moist sites with fresh or brackish water. It forms scattered open colonies in the wild. Another **rose mallow (H. moscheutos)** is found farther south, to Florida and the Gulf states. It blooms in late August, decorating itself with resplendent large white flowers well displayed above the tall grasses of the marsh, as the plants grow 6 to 8 feet tall. Tolerant of brackish water, it is equally at home in salt and freshwater marshes.

A number of other mallows enjoy growing in wet places. **Woolly mallow (H. lasiocarpus)** is an 8-foot-tall perennial inhabiting pond banks, lakeshores, swamps, wet meadows, sloughs, and ditches. The 6-inch-diameter flowers are either white with a dark eye or rose-pink with a dark wine-purple central spot. Flowers appear from July through October. The large heart-shaped leaves have a dense covering of fine hairs on the upper surface. This helps to distinguish woolly mallow from **halberd-leaved mallow** or **smooth marsh mallow (H. militaris),** whose leaves are smooth on the upper surface and which has pinkish flowers with a dark center.

Wild red mallow (H. coccineus) grows in coastal swamps from Georgia and Alabama to

Florida. When I saw this for the first time, I found it staggering: a 10-foot-tall plant with 6-inch-diameter deep scarlet flowers. A more typical plant is 4 to 7 feet tall, but with flowers just as large. The leaves are much divided, deeply cut palmately.

Swamp or **marsh St.-John's-wort** *(Hypericum virginicum)* has pairs of oblong purplish leaves ascending the 2-foot-tall stems. In July and August, small pinkish or purplish flowers cluster at the tips and in the upper leaf axils; these are followed by deep red seed capsules. Not tremendously showy, this plant has a subtle charm, adding color to wet meadows and marshes from Nova Scotia west to New York and Illinois and south along the coast to Florida and Mississippi. Pick a leaf and hold it to the light to see the numerous translucent dots characteristic of most hypericums.

∾ Design Ideas. *Plants like St.-John's-wort, which provide little interest as individuals, are more effective as a garden design element when grown in a sizable assembly.*

Bog arum or **western skunk cabbage** *(Lysichiton americanus)* (color photo, page 54). I am dangerous in a car, either as driver, swerving to the side in response to a fleeting glimpse of something interesting, or as passenger begging the driver to do the same. One May, on the road to Neah Bay on the Olympic Peninsula, a captivating field of bog arum caused such automotive chaos. Their bright buttery yellow spathes, more than a foot high and about 8 inches wide, seemed to glow against the verdant green marsh. Some of the mature clumps were easily 4 feet across, with paddlelike leaves large enough to propel a canoe. Obviously a plant for gardens on a heroic scale, I thought how lovely they would be reflected in the water of an adjacent pond. The appeal is purely visual, however, as the plants are pollinated by

flies and carrion beetles, which they attract with their fetid rotting-meat odor. Bog arum has an Asiatic cousin, **L. camtschatcensis,** found in swampy places in northern Japan, eastern Siberia, and the Kamchatka Peninsula. This petite (by comparison) species grows 2½ to 3 feet high, and has clean, pure white flowers and a pleasant scent. The two will cross and produce offspring with deliciously creamy old-ivory spathes.

Swamp candles or **yellow loosestrife** *(Lysimachia terrestris)* is a 2- to 3-foot-tall plant with nearly one-third of its height a spike of star-shaped yellow flowers, each set off by a maroon eye, in July and August. It grows in wet meadows, marshes, open shrub swamps, and the brighter edges of wooded swamps from Newfoundland west to Minnesota and south to Georgia, Kentucky, and Iowa. This is a rhizomatous plant, sending roots down at intervals; it can spread aggressively to form large colonies. It is variable in the quantity of bloom produced in different populations: Some form bulbils in the leaf axils and little if any bloom; some are quite floriferous and have no bulbils; and others have both flowers and bulbils. Obviously, in cultivation the more floriferous forms are more desirable. In bloom, the effect is elegant — even in the scruffy habitat of a ditch littered with trash, at the outskirts of the New Jersey Pine Barrens, where I saw it for the first time. Our other native species is **fringed loosestrife** *(L. ciliata),* which has clear light yellow flowers and a less invasive habit than its brassy yellow-flowered Asian cousin, **yellow loosestrife** or **circle flower** *(L. punctata).* The latter is a good choice for creating a wash of color in naturalistic plantings of a larger garden. There it could be used to vivid effect in contrast to mauve and magenta flowers, such as the obnoxious purple loosestrife *(Lythrum salicaria),* the more acceptable Joe-Pye weed *(Eupatorium* *purpureum)*, or a tall astilbe such as *Astilbe taquetii* 'Superba'.

Bogbean *(Menyanthes trifoliata)* has an attractive spike of closely clustered white flowers, each looking somewhat like a shallow funnel with hairy edges. Bogbean grows only 12 to 18 inches tall. Its thick, creeping rhizomes form spreading colonies. Long stems terminate in three oval leaflets, each approximately 3 inches long by 2 inches wide. Cold tolerant, it grows from Labrador to Alaska and south to Virginia, Ohio, and Wyoming in bogs, open marshes, and the muddy banks of ponds, occasionally spreading out into shallow water.

Monkey musk is the curious name given *Mimulus guttatus* by the British (color photo, page 49). Native to marshy places in southern and western North America, it has happily naturalized in Britain in squelching, sopping wet places, such as along streams and pond. From June through summer, it produces a succession of bright yellow flowers spotted with reddish brown freckles on the lower lobes. Often grown as an annual, it self-sows quite freely. When soil conditions are not wet enough to suit, it will retreat into shady places.

Golden-club *(Orontium aquaticum)* (color photo, page 76) has a bright golden yellow spadix that lacks the protective spathe or hood found in jack-in-the-pulpit. When it flowers in early spring, it is surprisingly showy for so simple a thing and contrasts well against the soft green long-stemmed leaves. Another common name is **never wet,** for if the leaves are pushed under water, they are dry as soon as they float to the surface — the moisture immediately rolls off the surface. Golden-club is found in the shallow water of swamps and marshes, along sluggish streams, and by ponds from Massachusetts south to Florida, Mississippi, and Kentucky. It thrives in full sunlight and 6 to 12 inches of water over its strongly rhizomatous roots.

Arrow arum or **tuckahoe** *(Peltandra virginica)* is a relative of golden-club and jack-in-the-pulpit. Native from chilly southern Maine west to Michigan and south to the much milder climate of Florida and Texas, this attractive foliage plant grows in marshes, ditches, and muddy places or shallow water along the banks of sluggish streams and ponds. The arrowhead-shaped leaves are up to 18 inches long, with prominent veins in both lower lobes and down the center of the leaf, as well as just inside the margin outlining the edge. Although it is easily confused with duck potato (another emergent hydrophyte), the two can be readily distinguished, as arrow arum has only three distinct veins in each leaf, and duck potato has more. Overall, the plants grow 3 feet tall. The greenish calla-like flower is small and inconspicuous. It blooms in May and June, wrapping the fleshy spike in a green sheath that is paler inside. In autumn, the stalk turns and grows downward, forcing the seed-bearing green berries into the soft mud. Arrow arum grows in sunny to shady sites with shallow standing water. A southern species, **spoon arum** or **white arum** *(P. sagittaefolia),* is found in the coastal plain from North Carolina to Mississippi. Its greenish spathe has a white edge and the fruits are red rather than green-bronze. Less readily available, it is the more attractive of the two species.

☙ EDIBLE PLANTS. *Like golden-club and jack-in-the-pulpit, acrid roots of arrow arum were gathered by American Indians, who steamed them in a heated pit covered with earth. Over a period of 24 to 48 hours, the poisonous calcium oxalate crystals were broken down. The roots were then dried and ground into a coarse meal.*

Umbrella plant *(Darmera peltata;* formerly *Peltiphyllum peltatum)* is the cold-climate gardener's stand-in for tender gunnera. In marshy ground, the creeping rhizomes travel over the soil's surface, helping bind the soil together and preventing erosion on pond and stream banks. Flowers appear in spring, set in wide clusters at the top of a red-tinged stalk. Though individually small and starry, when grouped, the pink clustered blossoms provide a good display. Large, deeply cupped leaves up to 2 feet wide appear after the flowers on 3-foot-tall hairy stalks. The bold mass of foliage can be 4 feet high and 3 feet across. In autumn, the leaves turn a wonderful rich fiery red-copper. Though native to northern California and Oregon, umbrella plant is much hardier than this would suggest and succeeds quite well in Connecticut and other Zone 6 regions. A dwarf cultivar, 'Nanum', is only 1 to 1½ feet tall.

Pickerel rush *(Pontederia cordata)* (color photo, page 51) has beautiful blue-violet flowers. Crowded into a dense spike, they create a nice display in July and August and on into September. Native from Nova Scotia west to Ontario and Minnesota and south to South Carolina and Texas, this is a familiar denizen of pond banks and sluggish rivers, in shallow water or muddy sites. A

© JERRY PAVIA

© LARRY MELLICHAMP

Variegated gardener's-garters (Phalaris arundinacea, p. 11) echoes the variegated hosta for an interesting play of foliage texture and pattern. The bright yellow flowers are monkey flower (Mimulus guttatus, p. 48) and Trollius 'Golden Queen' (p. 53).

Summer-sweet (Clethra alnifolia) 'Rosea' blossoms in mid- to late summer (p. 66).

single, somewhat arrowhead-shaped leaf emerges from each forking tip of the thick rhizome embedded in the mud. You can separate this rhizome and replant it to propagate more. In addition, the small seeds float on water to create more distant new colonies. It has a gentler outline than the sharply angled lobes of arrow arum, and it is not as prominently veined. The plants grow 2½ feet tall, forming dense colonies.

☙ EDIBLE PLANTS. *American Indians and early settlers ground the nutlike starchy seeds of pickerel rush for use as a cereal or for making bread.*

Arrowhead or **duck potato *(Sagittaria latifolia)*** is a plant of many disguises. When growing under water, the leaves are grasslike and can easily be confused with *Vallisneria* species. Some species lack the sagitate (arrowlike) leaves for which the genus is named, and in other species these leaves appear only at maturity. The leaves, which always grow in a cluster from a single base, exude a milky sap when broken. The three-petaled white flowers grow in whorls of three, with males and females in separate tiers. This plant thrives along the shore or in shallow water and protects the soil against erosion.

☙ EDIBLE PLANTS. *The starchy tubers of arrowhead were a staple food of the Chippewa, Pawnee, Algonquian, and Winnebago Indians. These tribes harvested the tubers in the fall by treading barefoot in the muddy ooze around the plants to loosen them from the soil. They dried the tubers for winter storage, then boiled them for use. Fresh, the tubers can be eaten raw, although the taste is somewhat bitter. The flavor becomes sweeter and more palatable when they are roasted or baked for half an hour or boiled until tender.*

☙ GROWING TIPS. *Arrowhead is easy to transplant. Place tubers or plants 3 feet apart in water up to 1 foot deep between the beginning of March and the end of July.*

Lizard's-tail *(Saururus cernuus)* lacks both petals and sepals. Instead, it has a 4- to 6-inch-long flower spike of thickly clustered white stamens that gives it the appearance of a slender, somewhat arched tail when it blossoms in July and August. The flowers, leaves, and roots have a distinct, orange peel or citrus fragrance. Growing about 3½

Moisture-loving shrubs and perennials are artfully combined to create a natural water garden.

feet tall, the jointed, angled stems branch in a Y pattern. The ovate leaves, up to 6 inches long, are heart-shaped at the base and taper to a point. Native from southern New England and southern Quebec west to Minnesota and south to Florida and Texas, lizard's-tail is found in sunny marshes and lightly shaded open swamps, on muddy pond banks, and in shallow water.

🌿 GROWING TIPS. *Propagate lizard's-tail by pressing small pieces of the rhizome into the mud in very moist areas or under shallow water. This is the method the plant itself uses to form large colonies. In less spacious gardens, it should probably be confined in a container.*

Pickerel rush (Pontederia cordata, p. 49) forms dense colonies along pond banks and sluggish rivers.

Powdery thalia *(Thalia dealbata)* looks more like an escapee from some tropical utopia. Not really cold hardy, it is most common in the coastal plain from Florida to Texas. It is a rare Missouri native, found in marshes, ditches, and pond shores northward into Oklahoma and Mississippi. Reaching 6 feet tall, *Thalia dealbata* has huge cannalike leaves dusted with a fine white meal or farina. The purple flowers are carried well above the foliage on a tall wandlike stem in July and August (earlier in warmer regions).

❧ GROWING TIPS. *If its roots are under 2 feet of water, Thalia dealbata usually survives the winter. Cut plants that are growing in wet ground to soil level in autumn and mulch well. In cold-winter areas, it is safer to grow this species in a pot, which can be placed outdoors in summer and brought inside in winter. In mild regions, propagate by dividing the roots and planting them under 1 to 6 inches of water.*

Tall meadow rue *(Thalictrum polygamum)* waves its masses of soft, feathery pure white to purple-tinged flowers above other wetland plants from June through September. At first the stem is light green; by summer it assumes a magenta cast. Up to 11 feet tall, meadow rue is easily one of the largest herbaceous plants in swamps, wet meadows, and low, wet thickets. As the attractive foliage ascends the stately stem, it is somewhat reminiscent of that of columbine.

Orchids. Scarce and growing ever rarer are the terrestrial orchids of temperate North America. They are difficult to please when transplanted to a garden and generally show their displeasure with a lingering decline and eventual death.

© KEN DRUSE

Overhanging stones disguise the edges of this constructed pool.

In this garden pool, the feathery roots of floating, pale jade-green water lettuce (Pistia stratiotes, p. 144) provides shelter for fish eggs and fry.

Nonnative Ornamental Flowering Plants

Globeflower *(**Trollius** species)* (color photo, page 49) is native to boggy areas of Europe and Asia, delighting in squishy ground. Most plants have yellow to orange buttercup-like flowers. They increase slowly and are best transplanted early in autumn. Most popular is a garden hybrid, **T. × cultorum,** a three-way cross between *T. europaeus, T. asiaticus,* and *T. chinensis.* Their flowers look like big double buttercups. Cultivars include 'Lemon Queen', with lemon-colored flowers, orange 'Etna', and deeper orange 'Orange Princess'. As well as attractive flowers, globeflower has handsome dark green deeply divided and lobed foliage, mostly in a basal clump with a

Cotton grass (Eriophorum sp., p. 43) is a good choice for muddy sites in full sun.

few leaves ascending flower stems. Overall, plants grow 2 to 3 feet high and about a foot across. **T. europaeus,** in cultivation since 1581, is a native of wet areas in Britain; 'Superbus' is a selection with lemon-scented citron-yellow flowers.

Cyperus sedge (Carex pseudocyperus) appears naturally in boggy areas.

© LARRY MELLICHAMP

© KEN DRUSE

Bog arum or western skunk cabbage (Lysichiton americanus) set near the edge of a pond where its reflection is captured in the water.

Chapter Four

SHADY GARDENS WITH MOIST SOIL: SWAMPS

*S*wamps and wet woodlands are necessary and important places with a unique beauty. Their spongy soils and tangled mat of well-rooted vegetation act as a reservoir, serving to moderate storm surges as plants slow the water's flow.

Gradually, we have come to understand and accept the necessity of wetlands for their functional properties and for their unique beauty. Picture a Louisiana bayou with still, dark water, stately cypress draped in Spanish moss, and a luxuriant tangle of vegetation growing on the hummocks, home to egrets and alligators. Imagine a Connecticut swamp in early January, covered with a thin rime of snow. Winterberries with their slender black-barked stems beaded with blood-red berries stand amid sedge tussocks as simple and linear as a Japanese woodblock print. Bead-stick fertile fronds of sensitive fern provide a darker brown accent; already emerging from the frozen earth are the flowers of skunk cabbage, intimation of the season's change. Swamps are beautiful!

It may be difficult to envision something as spacious-sounding as a swamp in terms of your home landscape. Consider this scenario: Perhaps you live in a condominium or have a townhouse in an association. Along the back of the property is an unsightly swale, with running water in the spring and autumn, and a muddy ditch in drier periods of the year. The groundskeeper of the condominium association has tried several plants, but the rhododendrons rot out and annuals die — nothing seems to work. An association meeting is called to decide if it would be worthwhile to apply for a permit to bury a pipe for necessary drainage and fill in the swale. Your lawyer is doubtful, because of the regulations protecting wetlands. How much better it would be to devise a planting plan that would use wetland shrubs adapted to those conditions. Because the area needs to be planted in one go, with commercially available material, it is necessary to choose plants that are readily available. In the Northeast, shadbush *(Amelanchier laevis)* would provide

The spreading roots of buttonbush (Cephalanthus occidentalis) are useful in controlling soil erosion.

© JUDY GLATTSTEIN

© A. BLAKE GARDNER

Many kinds of birds are attracted to water, as well as to the plants such as winterberry (Ilex verticillatea) at the right.

© JUDY GLATTSTEIN

SWAMPS

Dominated by the trees and shrubs that grow there, swamps are more or less shaded situations with standing water throughout most of the growing season. They occur where there is a high water table — for example, bordering the banks of wide, slow-running streams or surrounding shallow lakes. As with meadows and marshes, at any given point in time, the water level fluctuates: wetter with snowmelt in spring or after heavy rains; later in the season, although a swale or low spot is wet, adjacent, somewhat higher sites are merely moist. In general, water levels are lowest in summer, especially for those locations that are more dependent on rainfall. The swamp may appear dry, although there can be subterranean water in the root zone. Occasionally, some sites may have open water into summer and even into the winter dormant period.

spring flowers, late summer fruit, and fall color. Summersweet *(Clethra alnifolia)* has fragrant flowers in summer. Winterberry *(Ilex verticillata)* provides winter color with its vivid red berries. Adding a grass, perhaps one of the *Miscanthus* cultivars, introduces a different texture to contrast with the small tree and shrubs, and it will be attractive in summer and winter. In the Southeast, sweet bay *(Magnolia virginiana)* would be a handsome choice, large fothergilla *(Fothergilla major)* and yaupon *(Ilex vomitoria)* would be attractive, with Virginia chain fern *(Woodwardia virginica)* and white spider lilies *(Hymenocallis* spp.) as herbaceous accents. The idea is to work with what you have, rather than make radical changes. Even simple plantings like these would change an eyesore into an attractive addition to the landscape.

Another common situation: Perhaps you are a bird watcher. Although you have feeders, you want to introduce plants that will attract birds in a natural manner, providing food, shelter, and nesting habitat to increase the carrying capacity of the land. The only place you have left to plant is a soggy low spot you've been ignoring while you landscaped the rest of the property, simply because you didn't know what to do with it.

When we first think of water and birds, it is waterfowl — ducks and geese, as well as wading birds such as herons — that come to mind. But many kinds of birds prefer a habitat near water, either in a forest or shrub swamp, or in open, marsh habitats. The "chink, chink" call of a redwing blackbird announces spring's arrival from the cattail marsh. Even those birds that nest in upland situations may feed over water — just think of swallows performing their aerial maneuvers over a pond in the dusk of a summer's day — or of the many water-loving plants themselves that provide food. We buy sunflower seed of the annual species *(Helianthus annuus)*, so the connection to growing perennial sunflowers in the garden is an easy transition. Just don't deadhead (cut off the spent flowers) — instead, allow seed to form. The seeds of many other perennials attract birds. These include goldenrods *(Solidago* spp.), any species of *Rudbeckia*, and grasses. For suggestions, see box on page 58.

ATTRACTING BIRDS TO YOUR GARDEN

Trees, shrubs, and other plants are good food sources for birds. Downy serviceberry is preferred by ruffed grouse, mockingbird, robin, brown thrasher, woodthrush, scarlet tanager, cardinal, and rose-breasted grosbeak. Box elder and red maple attract evening grosbeak, pine grosbeak, cardinal, and robin. Yellow birch provides winter food for small birds like tufted titmouse, northern junco, American goldfinch, and pine siskin. White oak attracts ruffed grouse, bobwhite, and quail. Elderberry is popular with robins, thrushes (including eastern bluebird), cedar waxwings, cardinals, and purple finches. Cardinal flower, bee balm, jewelweed, and Turk's cap lily attract hummingbirds. Some good plants to use if you wish to attract birds are listed below.

TREES

Shadbush (*Amelanchier* spp.)
   Downy serviceberry (*A. arborea*)
   Shadblow serviceberry (*A. canadensis*)
Box elder (*Acer negundo*)
Red maple (*Acer rubrum*)
Yellow birch (*Betula allegheniensis*)
White ash (*Fraxinus americana*)
Eastern larch (*Larix laricina*)
American sweetgum (*Liquidambar styraciflua*)
Black tupelo (*Nyssa sylvatica*)
Eastern cottonwood (*Populus deltoides*)
Quaking aspen (*Populus tremuloides*)
Swamp white oak (*Quercus bicolor*)
Northern white cedar (*Chamaecyparis thyoides*)

Alders (*Alnus* spp.)
   Speckled alder (*A. rugosa*)
   Smooth alder (*A. serrulata*)
Buttonbush (*Cephalanthus occidentalis*)
Dogwood (*Cornus* spp.)
   Alternate leaf dogwood (*C. alternifolia*)
   Red-osier dogwood (*C. stolonifera*)
   Silky dogwood (*C. amomum*)
Winterberry (*Ilex verticillata*)
Spicebush (*Lindera benzoin*)
Willow (*Salix* spp.)
   Black willow (*S. nigra*)
Menispermum canadense

PERENNIALS

Cardinal flower (*Lobelia cardinalis*)
Red-flower bee balm (*Monard didyma*)
Jewelweed (*Impatiens capenis*)
Turk's cap lily (*Lilium superbum*)

SHRUBS

Elderberry (*Sambucus canadensis*)
Mapleleaf viburnum (*Viburnum acerifolium*)
Hardhack (*Spirea tomentosa*)

Design Suggestions for Swamplike Conditions

Characteristic adapted plants grow in the variable conditions of fluctuating water and seasonal shade. In any forested area, the earliest plants to awaken in spring are those that grow closest to the ground. First, the low herbaceous plants begin their growth and flower, then the shrubs, next understory trees, and last the taller canopy trees. Flowering is concentrated in the spring, before the overhead foliage canopy blocks sunlight and available energy is lessened.

Lower shrubs and the scrub willow community grow literally in the shallow water bordering rivers and ponds. A shrub swamp has soil that is not only waterlogged but is covered by 4 to 6 inches of water.

When you begin to improve wetland sites on your property, your first step is certainly to identify existing plants and work around those desirable trees, shrubs, and native plants already present before choosing new additions to the landscape.

When you select which plants you wish to add for a more pleasing display, first decide what effect you intend. If you enjoy walking through the area in the spring, for instance, additional herbaceous plants with early flowers would be your first choice. Since some of these go dormant after blooming, choose other plants with handsome summer foliage to conceal the bare ground beneath which the ephemerals are resting. Plants with a late spring or early summer period of bloom are valuable if you want extended interest. A massed planting of evergreen shrubs can disguise or conceal an unappealing view. If the winter landscape appeals to you, evergreen trees and shrubs, or those with a handsome bark or branch pattern or with attractive fruit, will enhance the scene. The important thing is to decide what you want the plants to do for your landscape and then make your selection. Remember that the denser cover produced by planting more trees will restrict the growth of shrubs, and denser shade furnished by shrubs will hinder the growth of herbaceous plants. A balance must be reached if an interesting diversity of plants is to grow in a healthy, attractive manner.

Assume that the location is a typical red maple swamp. There are a couple of lovely older trees and some scrawny youngsters. Catbriar and poison ivy form a thorny, itchy "Keep Out" barrier. The first step is to clean out some of the weed plants and take an inventory of what woody and herbaceous plants are present. It is important to take note of desirable species you wish to keep and encourage into more vigorous growth. Judicious pruning, which allows more light into the area, provides more options in the selection of plants to add to the area. An area closer to the house, visible year-round from a kitchen or living room window, may benefit with the addition of shadbush *(Amelanchier laevis)*, whose spring flowers, summer fruits (which attract birds), autumn color, and graceful outline provide four seasons of interest.

Perhaps a grouping of one of the native azaleas with fragrant flowers in spring will provide a scented influence, while summer-sweet *(Clethra alnifolia)* will do the same in summer. For spring interest, native perennials such as marsh marigold *(Caltha palustris)*, with its golden flowers, provide early color. Other plants might be selected for attractive foliage. The bold architectural pleated leaves of false hellebore *(Veratrum viride)*, the

WETLANDS REGULATIONS

Often state statutes define wetlands, in part, in terms of the plants that grow there, so specific is the vegetation to the site. Most of these sites are restricted, so be sure to investigate the laws in your area before you begin any work. Regulations fall into three categories — federal, state, and local. Whichever is the most restrictive is the set of rules you will have to follow. Connecticut Department of Environmental Protection personnel indicated to me in conversation that there is usually little problem with a modest amount of landscape manipulation, especially if one uses native plants. Extensive projects like clear-cutting, dredging, or draining, however, are absolutely verboten without a wetlands application, careful review, and ultimate official approval. (For further information about regulations, see pages 100–101.)

lacy texture of tall cinnamon fern *(Osmunda cinnamomea)*, and the fine linear texture of tussock sedge *(Carex stricta)* will create a pleasing summer combination. At the sunnier edges of the wooded wetlands, winterberry *(Ilex verticillata)* may be planted to display its scarlet berries. Another choice is red-osier dogwood *(Cornus stolonifera)*, with bare withes dressed in polished red bark in winter. The two shrubs create a fine display against the tawny sedge clumps and drifted snow of winter.

Trees for Northern Swamps

A forested swamp wetland, where the woody plants are more than 20 feet tall, usually has water twice as deep as in a shrub swamp. Wooded lowlands that are only periodically flooded are often called *riparian wetlands* or *bottomland hardwood forests* to distinguish them from drier upland forests. Representative trees of forested swamps in the Northeast are red maple *(Acer rubrum)*, silver maple *(A. saccharinum)*, and box elder *(A. negundo)*. This community of trees weaves along water courses, forming the next ribbon, back from the willows at the water's edge. Black gum, also called tupelo or pepperidge *(Nyssa sylvatica)*, and black ash *(Fraxinus nigra)* are common inhabitants of riparian wetlands. These tall trees form the canopy layer beneath which shade-tolerant, moisture-tolerant shrubs grow as a lower woody layer. Typical in New England are species such as spicebush *(Lindera benzoin)*, with small chartreuse flowers before the leaves appear in spring; withe-rod *(Viburnum cassinoides)*, with flat-topped clusters of white flowers; alder *(Alnus rugosa)*, with elongated catkins in winter; summer-sweet *(Clethra*

alnifolia), with fragrant white flowers in summer; and clammy azalea *(Rhododendron viscosum)*, with very fragrant white flowers, also in summer.

Red maple or **swamp maple** *(Acer rubrum)* inhabits wooded swamps from Canada through the Northeast, along the Gulf Coast, and throughout most of peninsular Florida. Early in spring well before the leaves appear, its small blood-red flowers open, adding color to the awakening landscape. Maturing at 60 feet tall, this species is useful as a shade tree that is especially tolerant of wet sites, even those difficult situations that are alternately wet and dry. The leaves, at 2 to 4 inches across, are daintier than those on Norway maple *(A. platanoides)* and less of a problem for herbaceous plants growing in their shade. They turn bright scarlet red, often flecked with yellow, in autumn. The ridged trunks and branches have an attractive silvery gray color, interesting in winter and especially attractive with the spring flowers.

Box elder *(A. negundo)* has an irregular growth habit and compound leaves that don't look at all like those of other maples. The stout trunk divides near the ground, the thick trunklike branches ascend, and the result is a globular, broad-headed tree 35 to 50 feet tall, often wider than it is high. The leaves are pinnately compound (although this is not as obvious when there are only three leaflets as when there are five). The yellowish green summer leaf color changes very little before autumn leaf drop. Box elder is found in the wild in floodplain depressions, in wet ravines, and along lake and river margins — anyplace that is wet and sunny. It is native in the eastern United States and nearby Canada. This tree is extremely cold tolerant and is most valuable for situations where few other trees will grow (useful into Zone 2). Although it is adaptable enough for use south to Zone 8, other, more ornamental trees are of greater interest in warmer regions. In wet areas adjacent to a house, the variegated cultivar 'Variegatum', with its crisp white-margined leaflets, is a good choice.

Silver maple *(A. saccharinum)* is almost as cold tolerant as box elder. It grows in Zones 3 to 9, but it is a good idea to look for material that originated in the region where it will be planted. Fast growing, it is a useful shade tree for wet soils. It will quickly reach 80 to 100 feet tall and is frequently wider than it is high. The rapid growth is a forewarning of weak wood, however, and indeed this species is subject to wind and ice damage. Its extreme tolerance of flooding — inundation for several weeks leaves no apparent damage — suggests its usefulness in bottomlands and along rivers, low lakeshore sites, and swamps. The attractive silver-gray bark on the branches and the bright red twigs add winter interest. Like the box elder, its seeds attract wildlife, especially water birds and waterfowl, small mammals, and browsers such as deer.

Shadbush *(Amelanchier laevis)* got its name from its habit of flowering each spring at the same time as the shad come upstream to spawn. I think this is one of our most beautiful small native trees. Its numerous small white flowers appear as the bronze-copper new leaves begin to unfold. In addition, it has tasty blue berries in summer (if you can pick them before the birds do) and leaves that turn a wonderful orange or golden russet color in autumn. Shadbush has a multitrunked growing habit, generally spreading in a graceful and attractive vaselike shape. The trees grow approximately 25 feet tall. **Serviceberry** *(A. arborea)* is capable of reaching 40 feet tall at maturity. Since both of these naturally hybridize with each other, they can be difficult to identify. Both look especially handsome if you plant them with an evergreen background or ground cover.

River birch *(Betula nigra)* is a species found in moist lowland depressions, in swampy river bottoms, and along the oxbow curves of slow-moving old rivers. It is native in the eastern United States north to Minnesota, as far west as Kansas, and south to Florida. Quick growing, it can reach 30 to 40 feet in twenty years, 50 to 90 feet at maturity. This species is untroubled by bronze birch borer, scourge of the white-barked paper birch. Its most attractive feature is the silvery golden or reddish brown bark, which peels and curls in vertical strips, providing an attractive two-tone effect. 'Heritage' is a recent introduction with whiter bark that exfoliates even more, revealing pink-tan new bark beneath. It grows best with an acid pH, becoming *chlorotic* (yellowing foliage during the growing season) in neutral or alkaline conditions. This is an elegant choice for the winter landscape. More difficult to find are **sweet**, **black,** or **cherry birch** *(B. lenta)* and **yellow birch** *(B. alleghaniensis),* both of which prefer a moist soil. You can chew the young twigs of sweet birch if you like a spicy wintergreen taste. The reddish brown to black cherrylike bark of sweet birch is handsome, and the leaves turn a clear golden yellow in autumn. These small trees do not hinder the growth of any daintier plants that grow under them. Yellow birch has handsome amber to silvery gray exfoliating bark. Autumn leaf color of birches, if not spectacular, is an attractive yellow. Catkins form late in the year and persist through winter to expand in spring.

↬ GROWING TIPS. *In general, birches are best transplanted in early spring as balled-and-burlapped specimens. They tend to bleed when pruned, so any shaping is best done in winter or any time other than spring when the sap is rising.*

Tamarack or **eastern larch** *(Larix laricina)* is one of those exceptions that somehow are supposed to prove a rule: it is a deciduous conifer.

In autumn, its short, clustered needles turn a clear yellow and then drop — all of them. Native from eastern Canada and the adjacent portions of the United States to Alaska, this tree is very tolerant of bitter cold. Northern Minnesota (where winter cold is an entirely different order of magnitude from that of New York, New Jersey, and Connecticut) has large tamarack swamps where this species comfortably survives.

Sweetgum *(Liquidambar styraciflua)* reaches 80 feet tall at maturity. This sizable tree is noted for its starlike leaves, similar to those of Japanese maple *(Acer palmatum)*, which turn from summer's deep glossy green to yellow to bronze or red in autumn. Sometimes all four colors are displayed simultaneously. The round, ball-like spiky fruits are a hazard for barefoot strollers. Since the fruits ripen in autumn and often hang on the tree at least partway through winter, they are more of a springtime than a fall peril. Large specimens are difficult to transplant, and it is hardy only to Zone 5.

Black gum, sour gum, tupelo, or **pepperidge** *(Nyssa sylvatica)*, also 80 feet tall at maturity, has oval, glossy deep green leaves about 4 inches long and 2 inches wide; these turn yellow-orange to flaming scarlet red in autumn. The small bluish black fruits are unobtrusive. Difficult to transplant, it needs little care once it is established. Smaller-size trees, container grown (rather than bare-root or even ball-and-burlap) can be moved more successfully. In autumn, black gum creates an elegant reflection in the still waters of a pond at sunset. It is native to eastern North American. A southeastern native, **water tupelo** *(N. aquatica),* is available only as an accidental substitute. If deliberately chosen, it is hardy only in southern gardens. (See page 85).

Sycamore or **American plane tree** *(Platanus occidentalis)* is sturdy, resistant to storm and wind damage, quick growing (70 feet tall in twenty years is commonly reported), long-lived (many trees live for 350 years), readily transplanted, and tolerant of pruning. It is especially appropriate in waterscapes, as it is native to rich bottomland soils along streams and rivers. I appreciate it for the ghostly figures it creates at dusk; the flaked-off, smooth gray-brown exfoliating

EROSION CONTROL

The one constant along a river is change — the rise, flooding, and fall of the water; eroding banks that collapse; the formation of new sandbars. Shrubs like willows that can grow on disturbed, gravelly sandbars protect them from erosion with their suckering roots and dense thicket of stems. These shrubs readily root when in contact with the soil, preparing the way for the next step in natural succession and the eventual development of a riparian forest. Willows tend to appear with cottonwoods and specific groups of trees typical of various geographic regions, as follows:

MIDWEST PLAINS: green ash, hackberry, box elder
COLORADO ROCKIES: quaking aspen, balsam poplar, *Rubus* spp.
CALIFORNIA CENTRAL VALLEY: California sycamore, California white oak, box elder
OREGON AND WASHINGTON: red alder, big-leaf maple, Sitka spruce, western hemlock

bark contains maplike patterns that reveal the creamy white inner bark beneath. The base and lower portion of the trunk of a mature tree (which can reach 100 feet tall) is somewhat furrowed and a neutral grayish or dark brown color; the upper trunk and sinuous branches most prominently display the markings. In autumn, the large, coarse maplike leaves become stiff and brown before sailing off the tree to float to the ground. After they drop, the ball-like buff-tan seed heads trail on pendulous long stalks from the tips of the twigs, like some odd monotone Christmas decoration. Along a stream bank when the roots become undercut by the flowing water, the tree often leans over the surface, as though seining for the reflection of the moon with tangled, ghostly branches. Sycamore is prone to anthracnose, a serious and disfiguring disease that causes twig dieback in cool, damp weather as the leaves emerge in spring.

Eastern poplar or **cottonwood** *(P. deltoides)* is a wide-ranging stately tree, frequently the tallest species growing in the floodplain, wet lowland, and stream edge sites it prefers. Useful in Zones 3 to 9, cottonwood is native from Quebec south to Florida and west to the Rocky Mountains. This is a large, massive canopy tree, frequently reaching 100 feet tall, especially in the best — that is, moist — sites. Because it often grows in windy locations, and it is brittle as well, it suffers frequent ice damage, but its broken branches are quickly replaced. The tree's shallow, fibrous root system makes it an easy one to transplant. Branch drop, leaf litter, and, especially, the copious amount of seeds it produces in late spring and early summer can create a litter problem. The seeds in particular are a nuisance because when they germinate, the result is a fast-growing weed. It is worth seeking out 'Siouxland' or another male cultivar, as these do not produce

the snowstorm of cottony seeds that cling to other plants and window screens and pile up along curbs, creating such a general nuisance each spring.

Pin oak *(Quercus palustris)* is perhaps the most familiar oak for landscape purposes. Many oaks are difficult to transplant because of their deep taproots, which develop at an early age. The root system of this species spreads more than that of most oaks, making it easier to transplant and therefore the most widely offered and planted oak species. It also has an unusual tolerance for poorly drained bottomland situations; in fact, it even grows in swamps. It reaches 50 to 75 feet tall, with drooping lower branches that add a graceful appearance to the tree. The 4-inch-long leaves are deeply cut with narrow lobes. Although they are a glossy bright green in acid soils, they quickly become chlorotic in neutral or alkaline soils. The autumn leaf color is a medium brownish tan; some leaves remain on the tree throughout the winter. Native from the northeast to the central United States, this species is useful over a wide range. **Swamp white oak** *(Q. bicolor)* is a tall, stately tree with wide-spreading massive branches that create a robust canopy. As with the majority of oaks, it has a taproot and is difficult to transplant. It grows relatively quickly for an oak, adding 1½ to 2 feet in height annually and maturing at 75 to 100 feet tall in 125 years.

Eastern white cedar or **eastern arborvitae** *(Thuja occidentalis)* is a useful conifer for wet sites. Native in northeastern North America from Nova Scotia west to Manitoba and south to North Carolina and Illinois, it is useful as a screen when planted in groups or in solitary splendor as a specimen. With an upright, narrowly pyramidal form, it grows to about 40 feet tall. The scalelike evergreen foliage is usually a lustrous dark green. The columnar trunk is clad in a shredding reddish tan bark. This tree is a good choice for northern gardens; it fares poorly in hot-summer regions. I remember hiking with Cole Burrell near Gooseberry Falls in Minnesota one winter, the two of us bundled under so many clothes we could hardly bend. Looking across the watercourse and down at the opposite bank, I saw a small herd of deer step daintily out of a white cedar grove, their large ears swiveling to catch any sound. Now there was a situation in which I could appreciate Bambi and his brethren — something I am unable to do in my own garden!

Shrubs for Northern Swamps

In the Northeast, a shrub swamp is characterized by deciduous shrubs like buttonbush, with its fuzzy white flowers in summer, or winterberry, with sealing-wax red berries on female plants in winter. Several kinds of willows, such as large pussy-willow *(Salix discolor)* and silky willow *(S. sericea),* are also common.

WILLOWS

Whether it is the slender, trailing pendulous stems reaching down to brush the surface of a pond or the furry silver catkins of a pussy willow, willows are synonymous with wet places. Do not underestimate their water-sucking abilities. Farmers used to plant willows to dry out a wet field. If no better source of water is available, willow roots will enter and clog nearby water and sewer pipes. Most of the familiar tree species such as white willow *(Salix alba),* the more tender Babylon weeping willow *(S. babylonica),* and the catkin-laden goat willow *(S. caprea)* are not native.

Black willow *(S. nigra)* is the species most likely to be found on sandbars, along riverbanks and streams, in swamps, and generally in many wet lowland areas from New Brunswick west to Ontario and south to Florida and northern Mexico. Its dense tangle of stems and roots can withstand surging waters at flood. It can grow as a 10-foot-high shrub or a 60-foot-tall tree. The polished yellow bark on young twigs creates a handsome display in winter. **Sandbar** or **longleaf willow *(S. interior)*** is a shrub or small tree that rarely grows over 20 feet tall. It is one of the pioneer shrubs, first to take root along a sandbar, in silty bottomland, along streams, or edging ponds. It stabilizes the soil until the site can support other species, like silver maple *(Acer saccharinum)* and cottonwood *(Populus deltoides).* All willows have simple linear leaves, but this species carries things to extremes, with 2- to 5-inch-long leaves only ½ to 1½ inches wide. It is another species useful for holding soil on easily eroded sites. Growing wild in the northern half of the United States and adjacent Canada, our native large **pussy willow *(S. discolor)*** has somewhat smaller silky catkins but is otherwise similar in appearance to goat willow *(S. caprea).* Pussy willow is more cold hardy than goat willow and can be grown in Zone 3.

VIBURNUMS

Arrowwood *(Viburnum dentatum),* like several other native woodland viburnums, tolerates moist soils, making it a swamp denizen. Found from New Brunswick west to Minnesota and south to Georgia, arrowwood has dark green coarsely toothed leaves with prominent veins, which in autumn turn a bright red in areas that are only lightly shaded. The flattened clusters of creamy white flowers are followed by blue-black berries which are eaten by a number of birds. While arrowwood can grow 10 to 12 feet tall, it is usually smaller.

∾ GROWING TIPS. *Arrowwood suckers from the base and may need some pruning to thin the many stems and control its form.*

Hobblebush *(V. alnifolium)* has rounded alderlike leaves that are toothed along the edges; these turn red in autumn before dropping. Native from New Brunswick west to northern Michigan and south in the Appalachian Mountains to North Carolina, it is useful in regions with cool summers, especially when planted in somewhat shady, moist sites. Its flat clusters of flowers, edged with showy sterile flowers, create an attractive lace-cap effect in mid- to late spring.

Withe-rod *(V. cassinoides)* is a smaller, even shrubbier counterpart of nannyberry (below). It blooms a bit later, in early summer to midsummer, and also has blue-black fruits. Its autumn leaf color is deep purple to scarlet, especially where shade is not too heavy. Withe-rod also is more useful in regions with cool summers. It is native from Newfoundland west to Manitoba and south along the Appalachian Mountains to North Carolina.

Nannyberry *(V. recognitum)* is a large shrub which can grow to 20 feet or more tall. Its suckering habit produces many stems, making this a difficult shrub to train as a single- or few-stemmed specimen with the character of a small tree. It has numerous 2- to 4-inch clusters of small white flowers in late spring, followed by blue-black berries in early autumn to mid-autumn. It is useful across much of the country, as suggested by its natural range from Hudson Bay south to Mississippi and Georgia.

The **American cranberrybush** *(V. trilobum)* is a popular landscape shrub, as it tolerates average, as well as wet, conditions. Growing 6 to 12 feet tall, it is usually higher than wide. The maple-like leaves turn red to maroon-purple in autumn. Flat-topped clusters of white flowers are followed by glossy, translucent, orange to scarlet-red berries in heavy drooping clusters. The berries persist from autumn through late winter. Particularly popular with cedar waxwings, the berries are eaten by other birds as well. Tart and acid, the fruit is edible and can be used for preserves, although some find the musky flavor objectionable. Some experts include this beautiful, shade-tolerant shrub as a variety of the European cranberrybush *(V. opulus)*.

OTHER NATIVE SHRUBS

Smooth or **hazel alder** *(Alnus rugosa; A. serrulata)* is a small tree at best, more often found as a multistemmed large shrub. Its pendulous catkins (the male and female are distinctly different) are among the earliest flowers to appear, expanding from winter dormancy, where they lend subtle interest to the bare branches. Forming dense thickets, smooth alder can be useful in retaining soil along stream banks.

Buttonbush *(Cephalanthus occidentalis)* (color photo, page 56) has midsummer flowers that look like fuzzy white golf balls, as the stamens protrude from the tightly clustered sphere of blossoms. Its spreading roots are useful in reinforcing pond banks and retaining the soil along shallow, slow-moving streams. The glossy green leaves are attractive in summer, but the tree's winter appearance quickly becomes ungainly in a few years. This shrub demands a moist to wet site; it will not thrive in a dry situation.

Buttonbush can easily be rejuvenated. In spring cut all the stems back hard, close to the ground. This will encourage another cycle of renewed, more shapely growth for the next few years.

Summer-sweet or **sweet pepperbush** (***Clethra alnifolia***) (color photo, page 49) is a familiar resident of northeastern swamps. Valuable for its time of bloom in mid- to late summer (many shade-tolerant plants flower earlier), its small white or pinkish white spikes of flowers add a sweet fragrance to the woods. This deciduous shrub grows 8 to 10 feet tall, with a suckering habit that results in a broad thicketlike mass of stems. **Cinnamon clethra** (***C. acuminata***) is a taller, less hardy southeastern species that, though less showy in flower, has attractive glossy cinnamon-brown bark. Perhaps the most interesting species is **Japanese clethra** (***C. barbinervis***), which has a more attractive, graceful habit, trailing horizontal flower clusters, and shredding cinnamon-colored bark. H. Lincoln Foster, doyen of rock gardeners, grew this at Millstream, his internationally renowned garden in Falls Village, Connecticut, where it created a handsome display each summer. This species lends itself to specimen use, while the native species are better in a naturalized planting. Although in drier sites summer-sweet may be infested with mites, they are unlikely to be a problem in moist sites.

Silky dogwood (***Cornus amomum***) is a pondside swamp species of the eastern and north-central United States and nearby portions of Canada. It tolerates a wide range of light, from sun to shade. It grows 8 to 10 feet tall. Late blooming, the flattened clusters of small ivory-white flowers appear in late June and are quietly attractive rather than flamboyant. They are followed in September by pale blue to blue-black berries that provide food for waterfowl and other birds. It is useful for soil retention, preventing stream bank or lakeshore erosion. It can grow in poor soils (it even appears on old strip mine sites in the Midwest). Although the young twigs have a reddish bark color that is most noticeable in winter, they are not as bright and showy as **Tatarian dogwood** (***C. alba***) from Siberia, North Korea, and northern China. The latter species has two cultivars with variegated leaves: 'Elegantissima' (also called 'Argenteo-marginata') has a crisp white margin; 'Spaethii' has yellow-edged leaves. Both are less vigorous than the type and hence less useful for screening. Again, variegated plants are more "gardenesque" in effect and look out of place in a naturalistic design.

A native species that has good bark color and is tolerant of light shade is **red-osier dogwood** (***C. stolonifera***). With a range extending from Newfoundland west to Manitoba and south to Virginia, Nebraska, and the Pacific Northwest, this adaptable species spreads into large, impenetrable thickets by means of stolons. The dense mass of foliage, which is useful for screening in summer, turns red before dropping in autumn. The bark color on first- and second-year branches reaches a peak in early spring. It is especially vivid against snow. Regular pruning of some older growth close to the ground encourages the production of younger stems with the desirable bright color. 'Flaviramea' is a cultivar lacking the red pigment; both autumn leaves and winter bark are golden rather than red in color. The Massachusetts highway department has planted portions of the Massachusetts Turnpike median swales with alternating groups of the red- and yellow-stem varieties, most attractive in the winter landscape. 'Kelseyi', a densely branched, compact dwarf variety that grows 2 feet tall, could be used as a coarse ground cover, perhaps as a deterrent to geese on the banks of a pond. It does not color as well in winter as do the taller varieties.

Leatherwood *(Dirca palustris)* is a deciduous shrub that is native over much of the eastern United States. It is especially useful because of its adaptability to wet soils in colder regions, but it can also be grown in southern gardens. Small pale yellow flowers appear in early spring before the new leaves; these are more interesting when viewed close-up. The rounded medium to light green leaves are sufficiently dense that these shrubs function as an effective low screen when planted in a group. Trouble free, leatherwood is useful in mass plantings and naturalistic designs, especially in wet sites with cold winters.

Winterberry *(Ilex verticillata)* (color photo, page 56) is characteristic of shrub swamps. In summer appearing as a leafy green tangle, it stands revealed in autumn as a slender bush with persistent shining blood-red berries arrayed close to the upper portion of the dark twigs. The scene is most attractive when winter snow covers the ice and tangles of golden sedge tussocks are clustered beneath. As with other hollies, this species is dioecious, and one nonfruiting male is all that is necessary for several female plants if they are to produce fruit. The leaves turn yellow, then blacken and drop quickly in early autumn — a desirable feature as it reveals the glowing fruits. A number of female fruiting cultivars are available: 'Winter Red' and 'Christmas Cheer' are especially fruitful, 'Aurantiaca' has orange berries, and 'Chrysocarpa' has yellow berries. **Smooth winterberry** *(I. laevigata)* has somewhat larger fruits and can be relied on to produce them even when grown as an isolated specimen. Unfertilized, the fruits form but do not contain any seeds.

Spicebush *(Lindera benzoin)* is another native plant unfairly neglected in favor of exotic imports. The common name probably relates to the clean, spicy scent released when the foliage is crushed or the young twigs are scraped with a fingernail. Early in spring, when the first daffodils begin to flower, this handsome shrub wreathes its branches with small clusters of fragrant chartreuse flowers; when seen from a distance, it appears covered in a haze of vernal color. Its aromatic foliage turns a clear yellow in autumn. Female plants have bright red berries, reminiscent of those on flowering dogwood *(Cornus florida)*. Trouble free, shade tolerant, and requiring at least a moist soil if not a downright soggy one, this shrub is excellent for any shady, wet site. In a swale near my home, several spicebush spread their canopy over skunk cabbage *(Symplocarpus foetidus)*. In spring, peepers shrill away in deafening chorus there.

❧ EDIBLE PLANTS. *The winter twigs of spicebush make a refreshing tea. To keep it from cooling down while it steeps for the fifteen minutes or so necessary to extract its flavor, place it in a thermos bottle until it is the desired strength.*

Sweet azalea *(Rhododendron arborescens)* is aptly named for its heliotrope fragrance. It has white flowers accented by red stamens and pistil in late spring and sometimes sporadically through the summer. Although it can reach 20 feet tall in its native habitat along streams and in wet woodlands, more commonly in gardens this species is half that size. It may be kept lower by pruning, which is especially useful if you wish to produce bushy plants. Unpruned, the shrubs tend to be

RED-OSIER WREATHS

I have twined the flexible young withes of red-osier dogwood into wreaths. Not only are they pliable, but the red color remains for months. They provide a handsome contrast to golden willow shoots.

rather leggy and open. If you pinch and prune young plants for their first two or three years, you will get denser growth. Because flowering is best with at least a few hours of sunlight, this shrub works well in a glade opening or woodland edge position. As evening draws night near, its sweet perfume provides a pleasant end to a spring day. Also tolerant of moist situations, but with a less overwhelming fragrance, is **coast azalea (R. atlanticum)**. Native to wet woodlands and coastal plain from Georgia to Delaware, this species is hardy into Zone 6. Peak bloom is in mid-April as the new leaves unfold, but it flowers through the summer. Stoloniferous, this species can be used as a tall ground cover. Counterpart of sweet azalea, **swamp azalea** or **swamp honeysuckle (R. viscosum)** has sparse foliage that turns a soft orange before dropping in autumn. Intensely fragrant white or pinkish flowers appear in early summer to midsummer. The long tubes are sticky to the touch, hence "viscosum." Swamp azalea is native from Maine to Georgia and Alabama.

\ GROWING TIPS. *When I saw swamp azalea in the New Jersey Pine Barrens, they were up on hummocks. In a garden with swampy conditions, I suggest following the same pattern: plant on mounds or shallowly, with part of the well-mulched root ball out of the soil.*

Rosebay (Rhododendron maximum) is one of our most stately evergreen rhododendrons, reaching 10 to 20 feet tall. It creates a wonderful coarse screen in wet shady areas, where its dense mass of deep forest-green leaves 6 to 10 inches long provides a wall of foliage. Although it does flower late (in early summer to midsummer), with large clusters of up to twenty-five small white, pale pink, or rose-pink flowers with olive-brown freckles in their throats, it does not create a great show, as the new leaves are also expanding at this time. It is native across the northeastern United States and adjacent regions of Canada, extending south at cooler elevations in the Appalachian Mountains to Alabama; some magnificent stands of this native shrub also appear in North Carolina. At its best in Zones 5 and 6, it can be grown in protected sites in Zone 4, as well as at higher elevations in regions with moderate summer temperatures in Zone 7, but here it requires summer shade. This species would be even more useful if it were not for the unfortunate predilection of deer to include it as part of their salad bar diet. Repeated defoliation kills the shrub. When large enough specimens can be obtained, the higher, out-of-reach foliage sustains the plant even if the lower branches are denuded as high as the deer can reach rearing up on their hind legs.

Swamp rose (Rosa palustris) must surely be one of our most beautiful wild shrubs, with exquisite single pink petals surrounding a central boss of golden stamens. Native from Nova Scotia west to Minnesota and south to Florida and Mississippi, it grows in thickets tangled with other shrubs at the edge of open water where increased available sunlight aids in flower production. The plants grow on mounds or tussocks, their stems clear of the water but their roots constantly wet.

Swamp dewberry or **running blackberry (Rubus hispidus)** is a useful, almost evergreen ground cover for wet places. Native from Nova Scotia west to Minnesota and south to Georgia, it has prickly trailing stems and glossy foliage.

\ EDIBLE PLANTS. *The fruits of swamp dewberry are black when ripe. Quite sour, they are better used for preserves than eaten out of hand.*

American elderberry (Sambucus canadensis) is a hollow-stemmed, weak-wooded shrub that seems to inhabit almost any sunny, wet site from Nova Scotia west to Manitoba and south to Florida and Texas. Perhaps its popularity with a variety of birds helps to account for its wide dispersal. The medium green compound leaves drop early in autumn without much color change. Huge flattened clusters, up to 10 inches across, are composed of quite small but numerous ivory-white flowers, followed in late summer by equally massive clusters of small purple-black fruits so heavy as to weigh the branches down. Some cultivars have been selected for improved, even heavier fruiting. These include 'Adams', 'Kent', 'Nova', and 'York'. **American red elderberry (S. pubens)** is found in lightly shaded wet sites from New Brunswick west to Minnesota and south to Georgia and Colorado. The smaller, more pyramidal clusters of yellowish flowers in late spring are followed by red fruits in midsummer. Its greater tolerance of shade makes American red elderberry useful in places where American elderberry is apt to grow poorly.

∾ EDIBLE PLANTS. *American elderberries are seedy. I find them better for jelly than for preserves.*

∾ GROWING TIPS. *American elderberry must receive renewal pruning on a regular basis to remove damaged stems and maintain some semblance of form.*

Bladdernut (Staphylea trifolia) is found along stream banks and in rich woods from Quebec west to Minnesota and south to Georgia and Alabama. Its name comes from its inflated bladderlike fruiting capsules. Greenish white or creamy flowers, each about ¼ inch long, form nodding clusters about 1½ inches long in mid- to late spring. The three-lobed pods, from just over 1 inch to 1½ inches long, ripen from greenish white to buff. The bright green leaves are sparsely arranged on stiff twigs and have little color change before they drop in autumn. Its appeal is provided by its interesting fruits, its low maintenance requirements, its ability to grow in moist sites, and its tolerance of cold climates (it is hardy in Zone 4 and even Zone 3 in sheltered locations). Its mature height is about 15 feet tall.

Yellowroot (Xanthorhiza simplicissima) grows a little over 2 feet tall, with a suckering habit from its bright yellow stoloniferous roots. It can be used as a deciduous ground cover for shaded, wet sites or in smaller quantities as a pleasant foliage plant. Flowering in spring before the leaves come out, the minute rusty red flowers contribute a reddish tone to the simple, mostly unbranched stems. The pinnately compound medium green leaves appear soon after, adding an attractive lacy appearance that contrasts with coarse foliage on plants such as false hellebore (*Veratrum viride*), which grows under similar conditions.

∾ DESIGN IDEAS. *Yellowroot grows naturally in association with shrubs like summer-sweet (Clethra alnifolia), buttonbush (Cephalanthus occidentalis) and swamp azalea (Rhododendron viscosum), as well as trees like river birch (Betula nigra), American plane tree (Platanus occidentalis), and tupelo (Nyssa sylvatica).*

Native Perennials for Northern Swamps

Herbaceous plants adapted to swamp conditions carpet the moist soil or grow on sedge tussocks above the water line. Often they are plants that tolerate change, those that can adapt to spring flooding, which delays their growth, and are capable of withstanding periodic inundation. Perennials such as marsh marigold *(Caltha palustris)* and skunk cabbage *(Symplocarpus foetidus)* are prevalent, along with stately ferns like cinnamon fern *(Osmunda cinnamomea)* and annual jewelweed *(Impatiens capensis),* which forms huge stands.

Skunk cabbage *(Symplocarpus foetidus)* (color photo, page 79) is premier among swamp plants. Familiarity breeds contempt — or perhaps it is its common name, for who is fond of odiferous skunks or the redolent scent of boiling cabbage? The pungent aroma of this plant is most apparent when the foliage is crushed. But after all, most gardeners do try to avoid walking on plants other than their lawn, so one need not avoid this plant because of its odor. The pungent, foxy odor of crown imperial *(Fritillaria imperialis)* does not keep this handsome spring bulb from our gardens. So why not use skunk cabbage? Deservedly renamed "harbinger of spring," it would quickly gain in popularity! While winter's icy grip is still firmly clasped around the countryside, skunk cabbage is in flower, having literally generated heat to melt its way through the frozen soil. Like those of its relative jack-in-the-pulpit, its flowers are small and inconspicuous, crowded onto an erect spikelike spadix that is wrapped in a protective sheath called a *spathe*. The sheath is mottled maroon and apple green to a greater or lesser extent, with some appearing purple and others green. It is too early for bees to fly, so skunk cabbage is pollinated by carrion beetles, attracting them with its rotten meat color and odor. In the cold temperatures, the beetles are apparently able to appreciate scents imperceptible to my nose. The foliage is stately, prominently veined, bright medium green, oval, and up to 2½ feet long. It creates a bold accent in summer, mirrored in the still water of isolated pools to which more frantic torrents have shrunk since spring. The fleshy thonglike roots hold fast against the water's tugging.

Marsh marigold *(Caltha palustris),* native to Europe and Britain, as well as North America, is an adaptable wetland plant that grows in swamps, shrub swamps, wet woods, and wet meadows. The bright golden yellow flowers, up to an inch in diameter, appear in a loose cluster on the top of a stem. It can easily be confused with buttercup. The most apparent difference is in the leaves, for buttercup has divided leaves, and those of marsh marigold are rounded. Planted in wet soil, it will flaunt its glossy deep golden yellow petals. 'Flore Pleno' has fully double ranunculus-like plump flowers. Sometimes offered as 'Multiplex' or 'Monstrosa Plena', it has been in cultivation since the seventeenth century. 'Alba' has less conspicuous white flowers. Marsh marigold is handsome en masse, as I saw it early one spring in Minnesota, brightening a birch woods while the leftover foliage of iris and cattail was still straw colored from winter. A trickling overflow below the millstream at Linc and Timmy Foster's in Falls Village, Connecticut, had just a plant or two in brilliant contrast to groups of a small pink-flowered primrose *(Primula frondosa)*. (This superb naturalistic garden was a mecca for gardeners around the world until Lincoln Foster's death in 1989.) The fibrous white roots help anchor it even in fairly swift water. To give it a more secure start, cover plants with a piece of coarse mesh weighed down at the edges with rocks to hold it until the roots have knit into place.

✎ EDIBLE PLANTS. *Marsh marigolds are edible, but must be eaten only as a cooked vegetable, as the raw leaves are toxic. They are best if gathered before the flowers open. Bring them to a boil in two changes of water, and then simmer until done. Serve as any other greens. The flower buds can be pickled like capers.*

✎ DESIGN IDEAS. *At the Chicago Botanical Garden, the double-flowered form of marsh marigold paired nicely with the creamy striped young foliage of Iris pseudacorus 'Variegata', both reflecting in the still water of a small pool.*

Swamp pink *(Helonias bullata)* is a rare native plant found inhabiting swamps and bogs in the coastal plain from New York south into Virginia, as well as along the mountains into northern Georgia. This plant grows best with cooler summer temperatures and is most suitable for northern gardens. In the South, it should be tried only at higher elevations. In April and May, an evergreen plantainlike rosette of foliage sends up a 1- to 3-foot tall scape topped with a dense spikelike raceme of deep pink flowers. These, combined with blue stamens, create a glimmering lavender-pink haze when viewed at a distance. Swamp pink grows in the same habitat as swamp azalea and summer-sweet.

Swamp pink will not be found at your neighborhood garden center, and is offered only in a few specialists' catalogs. One way to obtain it is to raise it from seed. Even seed is hard to find. The seed list of the American Rock Garden Society (available only to members) in 1993/94 offered both garden and wild-collected seed of swamp pink, meadow beauty, and fringed gentian among their literally thousands of offerings.

Waterleaf *(Hydrophyllum canadense)* graphically shows its dislike of dry conditions: its leaves turn black. Spreading from a creeping rhizome, the plant has coarsely toothed leaves with five to nine shallow palmate lobes. The leaves are 1 to 2 feet high and splotched with gray, as if stained by water droplets, in early spring. Often the upper leaves are taller than the flowers, partially hiding them. Waterleaf is found in moderate to deep shade in rich, moist woods from Vermont west to Wisconsin and south to Missouri and the mountainous regions of Georgia and Alabama. *H. virginianum* is another species, also with the common name waterleaf. It has stem leaves deeply cut into three to seven pinnate divisions, with the lowest separated from those above. Both species are grown primarily as foliage ground cover plants, but only if sufficient moisture is available.

Cardinal flower *(Lobelia cardinalis)* (color photo, page 73), with its flowers of the most intense, velvety cardinal-red, is a stunning perennial. Growing 3 to 4 feet tall, it flowers in late summer. It is rather fussy, but given a location to its liking, it will persist and self-sow. If dissatisfied, it will die after one season's bloom. In general, it wants a moist to wet place, even flourishing in running water if anchored by rocks. It also thrives around ponds in moist soil. Although it can grow in sunny locations if the soil is wet enough, I usually find it in at least partial shade in shrub swamps and along stream margins in forested swamps.

✎ GROWING TIPS. *A major problem of cardinal flower is its susceptibility to winterkill. Often plants whose evergreen basal rosettes are literally under water have a better survival rate. Alternatively, a light, airy mulch of pine boughs or oak leaves protects plants against desiccating winds and frost heaving. Plants are readily propagated from seed. Another propagation method, especially useful for variant forms with pink or white flowers, is to bend* a stem over and peg it to the ground. When the roots that appear at the nodes are established, each node can be severed from the next to produce several new plants identical to the original.

Great blue lobelia *(L. syphilitica)*, a North American native like the related cardinal flower, was brought into European cultivation in the early 1600s. It has clear light blue flowers. At 2 to 3 feet high, somewhat smaller than cardinal flower, it produces a nice effect when growing with its cousin. This species is less susceptible to winterkill but generally declines and dies out if not rejuvenated every few years by division and resetting in fresh soil in spring. Although it grows best in moist sites, it does not demand as wet a situation as cardinal flower.

∾ DESIGN IDEAS. *One September in Pennsylvania, I saw great blue lobelia flowering in a ditch adjacent to a wet meadow purple with ironweed (Vernonia spp.) and accented with a few plants of cutleaf black-eyed Susan (Rudbeckia taciniata), whose golden daisies provided just the right accent to the blue and purple flowers.*

Woolly sweet cicely or **sweet javril** *(Osmorhiza claytonii)* and **anise root** *(O. longistylis)* are very similar in appearance. Both have twice ternately compound coarsely toothed leaves, which resemble those of an astilbe; they are softly hairy all over, on leaves and stems; and they bear a parsleylike head of very small white or yellow flowers that are taller than the leaves. The plants grow 3 feet tall. Both prefer to grow in moist soil in rich woods or thickets. *Osmorhiza* means "aromatic root" in Greek, and the highly aromatic carrotlike root of both species has an anise or licorice scent. The seeds of the second species are used as a seasoning for their licorice/anise flavor.

Golden ragwort *(Senecio aureus)* would probably be renamed by nurserymen to "golden spring daisy," to avoid the negative connotations of ragwort/ragweed. Although daisies are a common flower type in grasslands, it is unusual to see a yellow one flowering so early. Golden ragwort has small heads of yellow-orange daisies in May and June, on stems growing 1 to 2 feet tall. The leaves on the stem are narrow and variously lobed, while the basal leaves are rounded and sharply toothed along the margins. Although it is common in wet woodlands, I have seen it flowering along the Blue Ridge Parkway with azaleas. This plant adds a bright sunny color to shrub swamps, the margins of forested swamps, and even ditch borders and swales where more water collects.

Violets *(Viola spp.)* have two kinds of blossoms: showy, easily observed flowers, and cleistogamous, hidden flowers that are hard to see. These are self-pollinating and produce the generous number of new plants that are the bane of tidy gardeners. Fortunately, less rank and aggressive in its habit is the **blue bog violet or blue marsh violet** *(V. cucullata)*, found in shaded, wet places such as swamps, along stream banks, and in bogs. These are all situations where the violet is often inundated, although it will tolerate drier, sunnier sites, where it forms larger, sturdier clumps. It has relatively long stems, and the light violet-blue flowers are charming for a small May bouquet. Perhaps its most notable cultivar is 'Freckles', whose flowers are liberally flecked with purple on a gray background; it comes true from seed. Other violets that require wet places are **lance-leaved violet** *(V. lanceolata)* and **wild white violet** *(V. pallens)*

∾ DESIGN IDEAS. *Blue bog violet is charming with a native such as marsh marigold* (Caltha palustris) *or exotics such as Japanese primrose* (Primula japonica) *and globeflower* (Trollius hybrids).

Golden alexander *(Zizia aurea)*. See page 14.

© KEN DRUSE

© DENCY KANE

Cinnamon, sensitive, and Christmas ferns, hosta, and Japanese primrose (Primula japonica) border this narrow, inviting stream.

Cardinal flower (Lobelia cardinalis, p. 71) provides not only a welcome splash of color to shady spots, but serves to attract hummingbirds, as well.

© JERRY PAVIA

Native and nonnative plants are combined in this peaceful setting, enhanced by the sound as well as the sight of water.

The spider lily (Hymenocallis sp.) is an excellent choice for moist, shady gardens in southeastern United States.

Easy-to-grow Japanese primrose (Primula japonica, p. 76) provides a long period of colorful bloom.

NONNATIVE PERENNIALS

Japanese primrose _(Primula japonica)_ (color photos, pages 30 and 75) is one of the candelabra primroses. Its name reflects its country of origin, and it (along with other candelabra-type primroses) has sturdy flower stems that produce as many as six layers of flowers, which open in sequence from the bottom up, providing an extended display. From 1 to 3 feet tall, the plant may have as many as five or six tiered whorls of flowers. It blooms in late spring and early summer, with flowers varying from a vivid intense cerise pink through rose and pink shades to white. Named forms include 'Miller's Crimson' and 'Postford White'. Both of these cultivars do come true from seed. This primrose is an easy-to-grow hardy perennial — easy, that is, as long as it has ample moisture. It will grow in full sun or partial shade, in wet meadows, along pond or stream banks, or in lightly shaded woodland. In spring, the large, somewhat coarse bluish green leaves quickly expand, spreading until each plant claims a foot or more of space. Where it has satisfactory conditions, self-sown seedlings appear. It may also be propagated by division, after flowering. I have seen these thriving in the University of British Columbia Botanic Garden in Vancouver, at Mount Cuba in Delaware, and in friends' gardens in Connecticut and New York.

FERNS FOR NORTHERN SWAMPS

Although xeric species of ferns thrive in dry, rocky sites, the popular conception is that ferns grow only in wet places. Our mental image of a swamp has pools of still, dark water overhung by trees, from which emerge tussocks of fine-textured sedges surmounted by tall ferns.

There is something magical about ferns. Flowerless, they reproduce by dust-fine spores, a process that has stood them in good stead since Jurassic times. Before this was understood, ferns were given all sorts of magical attributes: the power to confer invisibility, open locks, and reveal buried treasure. Visual appeal is the real treasure they provide through their elegant foliage. In the nineteenth century, this foliage so engrossed the Victorians that they planted gardens entirely devoted to ferns, constructed fern grottos, eagerly sought each minute variation and peculiarity — a difference of color of the chaff on the stipes, for example. The best ferns for really wet, swampy places happen to be taller, more stately ones: the different species of _Osmunda,_ ostrich fern _(Matteuccia_ spp.), sensitive fern _(Onoclea sensibilis),_ and marsh fern _(Thelypteris palustris)._ The first group of ferns — cinnamon, interrupted, royal, sensitive, ostrich, and marsh — also grow in the merely moist soil of a wet woodland; they do not demand the sodden conditions of a swamp. The last five — lady, glade, Goldie's wood, marginal shield, broad beech, and narrow beech — accept or require moist conditions but do not tolerate inundation. Most of these ferns grow in southern as well as in northern areas.

Golden-club (Orontium aquaticum, p. 48) is found in shallow water of swamps and marshes and alongside streams and ponds.

Marsh marigold (Caltha palustris, p. 45) makes an effective display at the base of variegated yellow flag iris (Iris pseudacorus 'variegata').

Osmundas are clump-forming ferns that have a dense root mass made up of fine, wiry black roots, used for growing greenhouse species of epiphytic orchids. A well-established specimen can require a mattock or similar tool to dislodge its unyielding attachment from a longtime site. All grow best and reach their greatest stature in a really moist to wet site. Deciduous, in autumn they turn a lovely soft straw-gold. This can be especially charming when spangled with the small, newly fallen, gold-flecked bright red leaves of swamp maple *(Acer rubrum)*.

Cinnamon fern *(Osmunda cinnamomea)* is strongly dimorphic. That means that the sterile, magnificent green pinnate fronds for which we cultivate the plant are very different in appearance from the cinnamon-brown congested stipes that are the fertile, spore-bearing portion of the plant. The latter generally wither away after the spores have been dispersed. The sterile fronds grow 4 feet tall, given a nice wet situation.

❧ EDIBLE PLANTS. *I find the native Osmundas very fuzzy. On the other hand, a Japanese species, zemmai or flowering fern (Osmunda japonica), which is more closely related to royal fern, is gathered early in spring while it is still in the tightly coiled fiddlehead stage, boiled in water with a little baking soda, rinsed, and soaked in cold water before serving. It can be served hot, sautéed in oil and sprinkled with soy sauce, or combined with tofu and mirin (sweetened sake).*

Interrupted fern *(O. claytoniana)* is also dimorphic, but in this species, the brown fertile pinnae are borne in the middle of the green frond. When they wither away, there is indeed a noticeable interruption.

Royal fern *(O. regalis)* differs from the two preceding species. When its croziers unfold in spring, they are tinged with coppery brown to bronze on top, which is where this species has its

© JUDY GLATTSTEIN

© JUDY GLATTSTEIN

© DEREK FELL

Moisture-loving pink astilbes (p. 31) and pink calla (p. 91) along the bank echo the bright pinks of water lilies in the pond. Skunk cabbage (Symplocarpus foetidus, p. 70) above right , is a true harbinger of spring, as it is one of the earliest plants to emerge through frozen soil.

Umbrella plant (Cyperus alternifolius) with ferns shelters a small pool.

A shady woodland pond surrounded by ferns and perennials.

fertile pinnae. Fronds grow to 5 feet tall, bare for half their length. On the upper portion, they have five to seven pairs of pinnately compound pinnae.

Sensitive fern *(Onoclea sensibilis)* is so named not for any tender feelings, but because it is sensitive to lowering temperatures in autumn and turns yellow with the first frost. This is a freely branching running fern with a dense mat of subsurface rhizomes. It makes a bold ground cover, especially near water. Throughout the summer it sends up new fronds with a somewhat coarse tropical-looking texture. Height is 15 inches or more, occasionally up to twice that. Sensitive fern is also strongly dimorphic, with the fertile fronds looking like stiff little beaded sticks 12 to 15 inches tall, adding interest to the winter landscape.

∾Design Ideas. *Sensitive fern is excellent in combination with taller shrubs such as swamp azalea (Rhododendron viscosum), spicebush (Lindera benzoin), and summer-sweet (Clethra alnifolia).*

Ostrich fern *(Matteuccia struthiopteris)* shares the running habit and dimorphic character of sensitive fern. Native to bottomland and wooded swamps, it grows with statuesque vaselike clusters of fronds reaching as high as 5 feet tall, usually a foot less. Underground runners spread out in all directions, erupting periodically to create new shuttlecock clusters of fronds. The fronds taper at both ends and are widest about

one-quarter of the way down from the tip. The fertile fronds appear in late June to early July. They are about half the height of the sterile ones. Looking rather like miniature ostrich plumes, they become dark brown and woody and persist through the winter. Unless this fern is given ample room, its spreading tendencies will be pitted against the gardener's need to restrict its territorial aggressiveness. In addition, without constant, ample moisture, it begins to look shabby, which it often does by late August anyway.

∾Edible Plants. *The sterile fiddleheads of ostrich fern may also be consumed as a spring vegetable gathered from your garden. It is the best species to harvest in North America. Immature, green, but still tightly coiled fronds of cinnamon fern, called fiddleheads, are gathered as a wild food in spring. Sometimes they are commercially available, usually in stores catering to the upscale market. When you harvest, remember that next year's growth is initiated in late summer and autumn and the tightly coiled fronds must wait through the winter for spring. Any fronds you gather in spring will not be replaced until the next year. Avoid eating bracken (Pteridium aquilinum) fiddleheads, as they are high in carcinogenic compounds.*

Marsh fern *(Thelypteris palustris)* also has quickly spreading, wandering roots that rapidly extend the area in which it grows. This species is suitable only for larger sites that remain quite wet. It has a fine, delicate lacy texture, with light green to yellowish green fronds anywhere from 12 to 40 inches tall and about 5 inches wide. The variation in height is often an adjustment to competing vegetation, with taller fronds a response to dense thicketlike growth. Given sufficient moisture, it grows in either sun or shade, in wet meadows or shrub swamps. The sterile fronds appear first, each rising singly but closely spaced in dense masses on the branching rootstock in early spring.

By late June, their color deepens, and the fertile fronds appear. These have a wilted appearance, because the edges of their segments are rolled.

Lady fern *(Athyrium filix-femina)* is one of the easiest ferns to grow, and it has a cosmopolitan distribution, including Great Britain and North America. This species was beloved by the Victorians for its tremendous variation: *capitate,* with the apex of the frond crested; *cristate,* where the apex of each frond and each pinnae on the frond is crested like a fan; *corymbose,* with the apex divided in several planes, producing a bunched tassel-like appearance; *plumose,* with pinnate or bipinnate pinnae, producing an extremely full, feathery appearance; and many more distinctive variations. Two of the most amusing, absurd, or attractive (depending on your point of view) are **tatting fern** *(A. filix-femina* 'Frizelliae'), on which the pinnae are reduced to tiny beadlike balls, resulting in fronds that look like a necklace of green beads, and 'Victoriae', on which each pinna is reduced to a pair of pinnules set at right angles to the opposite pinna to form a cross. The result looks like the first stages of macramé, a very neat and tidy set of X's marching up the stipe. Lady fern tolerates average soil moisture, but with constant moisture, the lacy, feathery fronds remain in good condition until late summer. In spring, the crosiers, heavily covered with dark brown chafflike scales, quickly expand to their mature 18- to 36-inch height, with larger specimens having fronds as much as 12 to 15 inches wide. The color varies from green to a light yellow-green. Additional fronds are produced throughout the summer, especially with ample moisture. This species is found in moist woods and wet meadows and along stream banks from the St. Lawrence Valley in Quebec to central Pennsylvania and Ohio.

∾ GROWING TIPS. *The crowns of old established tatting fern tend to stretch out of the ground. At this stage, replanting, possibly coupled with division, will restore vigor. Mulching with leaf litter also useful.*

Glade fern *(Athyrium pycnocarpon)* is somewhat dimorphic and has long, narrow fertile fronds 2 to 3 feet long and 6 inches wide. These are more erect than the sterile fronds, and they are shorter and broader. When they first appear in spring, the young fronds are a luminous light green; they mature to dark green and then turn russet in autumn before going dormant. New

EXOTIC PERENNIALS FOR NORTHERN SWAMPS

By description alone, butterbur *(Petasites hybridus)* sounds intriguing. It has broad, kidney-shaped or rounded long-petioled leaves that are somewhat woolly beneath, is up to 16 inches across, and bears sweetly scented winter flowers. The other side of the coin is its questing roots, which spread dangerously far from the original planting site. In places like a wild garden at lakeside, where the roots have ample room to roam, they can form an almost impenetrable ground cover. In Japan, China, and Korea where butterbur is native, the young, still-folded leaves are harvested early in spring and served tempura style with a dipping sauce. Giant butterbur *(Petasites giganteus)* has leaves 4 feet across on 6-foot petioles. Both species are hardy to Zone 4 and south to Zone 9.

fronds form throughout the summer if there is adequate moisture. Although this species does spread via creeping rhizomes, it is not invasive. Glade fern is native to shady, moist woodlands from Quebec and Ontario west to Wisconsin and south in higher elevations to Georgia, eastern Kansas, and coastal Louisiana.

∾ GROWING TIPS. *Glade fern needs calcareous to about neutral pH (7.0), deep, moist soil that is high in organic matter and in a shady location. If your soil tests acid (or you deduce it is acid because of the acid-loving plants, like rhododendrons that thrive), you will need to add lime to succeed with these plants. I find dolomitic limestone, readily available at nurseries and garden centers, the most satisfactory.*

Goldie's wood fern or **giant wood fern** (*Dryopteris goldiana*) is one of the most majestic ferns forming large clumps 18 to 24 inches across. In early autumn, you can see next spring's tightly furled crosiers, shaggily covered in white to golden or pale brown chafflike scales, snuggled like eggs in a nest in the center of each clump. Individual fronds are 8 to 14 inches wide and 30 to 48 inches tall — 60 inches under extremely favorable conditions. This deciduous species is native to humus-rich, moist woodlands from New Brunswick west to Ontario and south to Iowa and in higher elevations of Georgia, North Carolina, and Tennessee. Requiring a cool root run, this is not a fern for gardens in the Deep South. Planted singly, it makes an elegant specimen; when massed, it creates an excellent background for lower-growing plants.

Broad beech fern or **southern beech fern** (*Phegopteris hexagonoptera;* formerly *Thelypteris hexagonoptera*) and the **narrow beech fern** or **northern beech fern** (*Phegopteris connectilis;* formerly *Thelypteris phegopteris*) are two deciduous running ferns that I use for a loose, open ground cover. The broadly triangular medium green to yellow-green fronds of broad beech fern are 12 to 24 inches long. The two lowest pinnae point downward toward the rachis. Fronds are individually spaced more or less an inch apart on the running, repeatedly branching rhizomes just below the soil's surface. This spacing allows other herbaceous plants such a jack-in-the-pulpit (*Arisaema triphyllum*) to grow interspersed with the fern. It is native to woodlands with moist, acid, fertile soil from Ontario and Minnesota east to Maine and south to northern Florida and eastern Texas. I find it useful because it continues to make new fronds throughout the season, so it always looks fresh. This is also a valuable trait because it hosts a caterpillar that eats the early pinnae in spring. Because replacement fronds quickly form, this is not a severe problem. Narrow beech fern has narrowly triangular light green fronds that are 12 to 16 inches long and about 5 inches wide at their broadest dimension. The basal pinnae stretch outward and downward in an even more pronounced manner than those of broad beech fern. This is an easy species to grow when it is provided with moist woodland conditions. The closely spaced fronds produce a denser appearance than do the fronds of broad beech fern. It is native to cooler climates: Newfoundland west to Alaska and south at low elevations to southeastern Pennsylvania and in the mountains to North Carolina and Tennessee.

Trees for Southeastern Swamps

Tupelo (*Nyssa sylvatica*) is a common inhabitant of southern forested wetlands, often found growing with bald cypress (*Taxodium distichum*). Another tree, seen in shallow water, is swamp cedar.

Bald cypress *(Taxodium distichum)* elicits the same frantic autumn calls in the Southeast from someone convinced that his or her conifer is dying as a tamarack or metasequoia elicits in the Northeast. This tree is hardy to Zone 5, however, and can thus create the same dismay in Connecticut as in the Carolinas. All three of these conifers have fine needles that turn gold to warm russet red before dropping — a disconcerting trait to those who associate "conifer" with evergreen species such as spruce, fir, or pine. Bald cypress is native to river basins and coastal areas of the southeastern United States and north to Delaware and Indiana. In cultivation, it accepts average moisture conditions, but in its native haunts, it grows in the heavy, mucky soil beneath the open water of shallow lakes or ponds. The seedlings establish during drought years when standing water is absent. With maturity comes the development of swollen, buttressing lower trunks and the characteristic knees, which allow an interchange of carbon dioxide and oxygen. Growing to 100 feet tall with a symmetrical conical form, old specimens have a picturesque appearance. The fibrous red-brown to silvery bark, which peels in long, narrow strips, adds winter interest. This is a long-lived tree, commonly living 400 to 600 years; some have been recorded at the extreme age of 1,200 years.

Sweet bay *(Magnolia virginiana)* flowers in late spring and early summer with smaller, 2- to 3-inch-diameter creamy white, sweetly lemon-scented flowers whose fragrance is less cloying than that of bull bay magnolia. This lovely tree is much hardier, even viable in Zone 5. Native along the coast from Texas and Florida to Massachusetts, it is evergreen in the South and deciduous in northern gardens. Variety *australis,* named 'Henry Hicks', is a selection from the southern coastal plain that is fully evergreen and exceptionally cold hardy. I have seen it thriving in gardens around Boston, Massachusetts. The lustrous leaves, up to 5 inches long, are bright green on their upper surface, silvery white beneath. In the southern portion of its range, sweet bay is found in cypress and tupelo wetland forest communities. In cultivation, it is typically grown with average moisture, but it is naturally a wetland species.

Swamp cedar or **Atlantic white cedar** *(Chamaecyparis thyoides)* is native from coastal Alabama and Mississippi to northern Florida and north to Maine. In crowded conditions in the wild, it forms a slender, sparsely branched tree. Where it is growing in a more open situation, free from competition, it is similar in appearance to the common **old field cedar** *(Juniperus virginiana),* one of the trees in the first stage of succession from upland meadow to forest. It is valuable for its rot-resistant timber, but most of the original forests of the southeastern states have been logged for its wood. In southern regions, Atlantic white cedar reaches 80 feet tall; in northern sites, it reaches only half that height.

Swamp cyrilla *(Cyrilla racemiflora)* is also called leatherwood or black titi. Although it is often a large shrub or small tree, it occasionally grows to 32 feet tall. It will tolerate average moisture, but it grows best in wet soil along streams, ditches, and seepage areas, as well as along swamp edges with full sun. Its natural range is from southeastern Texas along the coast to Florida and Virginia. The flowers look like long, narrow, drooping white bottlebrushes, angling out from the base of new growth in July. The flowers and the size of the raceme can vary greatly from one shrub to another. As it has a loose, informal, rather open habit of growth and irregular and spreading branches, it is perhaps best suited for naturalistic plantings. In Zone 8 or 9, it is practically evergreen. In Zone 6 and 7 and the cooler parts of Zone 8, the leaves turn red or orange before dropping in autumn.

Loblolly bay *(Gordonia lasianthus)* is a 60-foot-tall tree found in coastal plain wetlands from Florida to North Carolina. In summer, the glossy dark green foliage provides a superb backdrop to numerous large, fragrant waxy white flowers that are 2 to 3 inches across. Difficult to transplant and intolerant of fertilizers, it grows best in poor wet soils. The 6-inch-long evergreen leaves make it suitable for screening. Hardy only in Zones 8 and 9, it has been used at Walt Disney World in Florida.

Buckwheat tree *(Cliftonia monophylla)*, native to the Southeast, is a large shrub or small tree that grows to 25 feet tall. It grows well in sunny, moist to wet soil, where it forms luxuriant thickets. The fragrant upright spikes of white or pinkish white flowers appear in early to mid-spring. The seedpods resemble buckwheat and give it its common name. The thick, glossy dark green evergreen leaves are leathery, with a pale chalky bloom on the underside. Use buckwheat tree for naturalizing along streams, on pond banks, or in low, poorly drained areas with constant moisture.

Tupelo *(Nyssa sylvatica)* is one of the best shade trees for wet soils. A variety of this species found in the southern portion of its native range, **swamp gum** *(N. sylvatica biflora)*, prefers shallow water and is occasionally found in shrub swamps. **Water tupelo** *(N. aquatica)* tolerates deeper water. Native to the southeastern United States, it would be the most suitable choice for wet sites in the Deep South if it were more available. *Nyssa* species form abundant forests along coastal plain rivers, their dense foliage producing a heavy, dark shade that inhibits the growth of other vegetation, both shrubs and herbaceous perennials.

Shrubs and Vines for Southeastern Swamps

Waterlogged soils in the shallower swamps of the Southeast are home to many shrubs. Titi, also called swamp cyrilla *(Cyrilla racemiflora)*, is one of the most tolerant of such situations. Evergreen fetterbush *(Lyonia lucida)*, with its bright green lustrous foliage and axillary clusters of small pinkish to white flowers in late spring (resembling those of blueberries), is another typical shrub. Growing up to 6 feet tall, it is useful for naturalizing or mass plantings and creates a handsome screen.

Although the following plants are native to warm regions, many (including *Magnolia virginiana*, sweet shrub, fothergilla, and *Itea virginica)* may be grown in northern areas. Though some of the plants described here are scarce or difficult to obtain, it is important to learn about them. As interest in these plants increases, they are likely to become more available. One hopeful sign is the emergence of nurseries specializing in native plants. Just starting up, many are part-time, small-scale, backyard operations, with no mail order.

Sweet shrub *(Calycanthus floridus)* has long been popular as a garden shrub for its unusual, sweetly scented purple-brown flowers. The fragrance is variable, however, and it might be best to select from plants in bloom if this characteristic is important to you.

Dwarf fothergilla *(Fothergilla gardenii)* needs a moist site if it is to survive. In light shade, it can grow to 4 feet tall, though it is a more compact 3 feet high in sunny locations. This witch hazel relative has flowers like white bottlebrushes in spring just as the leaves are emerging. Autumn color is most intense in sunny places, with purple, orange, and golden yellow splashed onto a single leaf. Some bushes have a sweet honeylike fragrance, while others have a musky odor. **Large fothergilla** *(F. major)* grows to 9 feet tall but can be kept lower with pruning. Both are native to the Southeast, growing wild in northern Alabama and Georgia, southwestern North Carolina, and Virginia, but they are hardy to Zone 5. They prefer a moist site to standing water and where native are often found on higher ground in swamps or adjacent to marshy areas. An evergreen background sets off both their spring flowers and autumn color.

Smooth hydrangea *(Hydrangea arborescens)* is a trouble-free shade-tolerant shrub. Unlike many other species in the genus, it flowers on current growth, which means it can die back to the ground in winter and still come back to flower the same year. Its large (6 inch diameter), flat clusters of white flowers have a lacy appearance, with the smaller, more inconspicuous fertile flowers in the center and the showier sterile flowers around the edge. The coarse foliage is not especially showy but creates an attractive background for the flowers; it turns yellowish brown before dropping in autumn. If pruned back each year in spring, smooth hydragea forms a tidy mound. Native from Georgia to New York, it is useful over a wide area. 'Annabelle' has showier flower clusters than other varieties; they are composed almost entirely of sterile florets in a globular cluster 8 inches across. Subspecies *radiata* has a white undersurface to the leaves — most attractive when a breeze blows and they flash their petticoats, so to speak. A close relative is **wood-vamp** *(Decumaria barbara)* a vining plant native to the Southeast. It climbs 15 to 30 feet high on trees, clutching their trunks with aerial rootlets. Its leaves are smooth and shiny, and it has white flowers in late spring. This needs at least fairly moist soil and partial shade.

Florida anise tree *(Illicium floridanum)* rarely grows more than 10 feet tall. It has deep reddish flowers in mid-spring and large, fragrant 6-inch-long leaves. It is very tender — useful in Zone 9 but requiring a protected site in Zone 8. Somewhat taller is the equally tender *I. parviflorum* from northern Florida. This species has white starlike flowers and dense evergreen foliage. "Exotic" **Japanese anise tree** *(I. anisatum)* is the most readily available species. Reaching a height of 16 feet or more, it is useful for screening when grown in a mass. The 4-inch-long smooth, dense, leathery olive-green leaves are aromatic when bruised or crushed. The fragrant white to yellow flowers appear in late spring.

Yaupon *(Ilex vomitoria)* is an evergreen shrub native to the southern United States. As with other hollies, an individual shrub is either male or female, and in either instance the flowers are not particularly showy. Female plants, however, have small, showy red fruits, one or three to a cluster, that often cover the twigs. They persist until spring and are especially attractive displayed against the background of lustrous green leaves. This species can be grown as a small tree or shrub in Zones 8 to 9, but only as a shrub in the warmer parts of Zone 7. It can be sheared for a hedge in spring, lightly trimming the new growth. The timing is critical, as it fruits on the previous year's growth. If you prune too soon, before growth has begun, you will cut off the older, flowering/fruiting wood.

Virginia sweetspire (*Itea virginica*), a native shrub, is attracting attention in the nursery trade. The 3-inch-long drooping racemes of bell-like white flowers appear after most spring-blooming shrubs have flowered and faded — about mid-June in Baltimore, earlier in more southern gardens. While it will grow in full sun, some midday shade is helpful in regions with hot summers. When it is grown with some direct sunlight for at least part of the day, the fall foliage has an attractive reddish color. This is most pronounced in the cultivar 'Henry's Garnet', whose leaves turn reddish pink in light shade, scarlet and burgundy in sunnier sites. This cultivar also has larger flower spikes, up to 6 inches long. It is semideciduous in all but the mildest locations, with the leaves persisting well into winter. Native from Virginia to New Jersey, this shrub is found along streams, in swamps, and in coastal plain regions of the Southeast. In northern gardens and in sunny locations, it grows about 3½ feet tall, but it can triple that height in southern gardens if planted in wet sites.

∾ GROWING TIPS. *Fertilize Virginia sweetspire lightly, as you do rhododendrons or azaleas. Prune by removing individual shoots to ground level in late winter.*

Flowering jasmine (*Jasminum floridum*) is attractive as a scandent, trailing climber for fences or when allowed to trail over retaining walls. It is hardy only in the warmer parts of Zone 7 and on into Zone 9. Evergreen, its graceful, fine-textured foliage creates an attractive landscape feature, accented by fragrant, ½-inch-diameter bright yellow flowers. Arranged in clusters of five or more, these flowers appear in late spring and intermittently throughout the summer.

∾ GROWING TIPS. *Prune flowering jasmine annually by thinning out some of the old stems on established plants. If the plants have been neglected and are beginning to look shabby, the best course is to prune all the branches back close to the ground early in spring before the new growth begins.*

Corkwood (*Leitneria floridana*), another useful native, is rarely used because of its limited availability. It prefers low, moist, poorly drained sites in full to partial sun. Effective for naturalized plantings in wet areas, it functions as coarse-textured screen. Somewhat more cold tolerant than flowering jasmine (Zones 6 to 9), corkwood is a rare native to Texas along the Louisiana border in brackish or freshwater swamps. It also ranges east to Florida and north to Georgia and Missouri. The wide-spreading suckering roots are effective in erosion control on a pond bank. Tallest in milder regions, it grows to 16 to 20 feet tall as a loose, open, slender-stemmed suckering tree. The bark is smooth and brown when young, becoming fissured and textured with age. The long, narrow, smooth light green leaves have a faint layer of fine silky hairs. In colder regions (Zones 6 and 7), it rarely grows above 10 feet because of winter damage.

∾ GROWING TIPS. *Lanky stems of corkwood can be pruned back periodically to make a more compact screen.*

Moonseed *(Menispermum canadense)* does not deserve its romantic name, for the bluish black clustered grapelike fruits on female plants are toxic. These poisonous fruits might cause you to decide against it if you have small children. Its crescent-shaped seeds gave rise to the common name. Its greatest landscape value is as a picturesque seasonal screen, effective from the time the leaves expand in early June through leaf drop in mid-October. Deciduous, the lustrous, round-lobed dark green leaves reach 4 to 8 inches across. The rapidly growing vines twine on a supporting fence or trellis to heights of 10 to 13 feet before being cut back by winter weather. Native from Quebec west to Manitoba and south to Georgia and Arkansas in swamps and along stream banks, it grows in shady sites in forests and old fields and is very tolerant of flooding. This vine is useful where it is maintained; without attention, it can become overly aggressive.

⌁ Growing Tips. *Maintenance consists of cutting back moonseed when it threatens to spread out of bounds and removing winter-killed growth.*

Swamp red bay *(Persea palustris),* which grows 6 to 18 feet tall, is a shrub with aromatic foliage. Its common name refers to the rusty appearance of the underside of the evergreen leaves. It is also attractive in fruit, with lustrous blue-black berries — often with a powdery bloom — on red pedicels in late summer into early autumn. It is native to low pine woods, coastal woodlands, and bay shore swamp regions from Delaware south to Florida and Texas. Infrequently available, container-grown specimens will establish more readily.

Corkwood *(Stillingia aquatica)* has wood even lighter than that of cork. This 6-foot-tall shrub is native to the coastal plain from South Carolina to Florida, Alabama, and Mississippi, where it grows in ditches and other shallow-water

locations, such as along a pond shore. It has somewhat glaucous reddish or purplish branches. Almost evergreen, some of the finely toothed leaves often winter over. The terminal flower spikes — sometimes yellow, sometimes green or red — are followed by coarse silvery gray seeds.

Native Perennials for Southeastern Swamps

Several of the plants suitable for northern gardens (including the ferns described on pages 76 –83) are adaptable to the warmer climate of the Southeast, especially where higher elevations moderate summer heat. Consider planting various mallows *(Hibiscus* spp.), swamp candles *(Lysimachia terrestris),* swamp buttercup *(Ranunculus septentrionalis),* and lizard's-tail *(Saururus cernuus).* Bulbs such as spider lilies *(Ismene; Hymenocallis* spp.*),* color photo, page 75) and atamasco lily *(Zephyranthes atamasco)* will be right at home. Check the descriptions of plants for wet meadows. Often in a hotter climate, some plants will do better with light to moderate shade, especially at midday. The problem is not heat alone but temperature differential between day and night. If it remains hot at night, some plants cannot survive. If you live where the temperature moderates after dark, both you and the plants will have an easier time of it.

Fly-poison *(Amianthium muscitoxicum)* is found in bogs, savannas, pine lowlands, and wet woodlands from Florida and Mississippi north to Missouri and New York. In the past, its bulbs were mixed with sugar and used to kill flies. The numerous narrow daylily-like leaves are also toxic to cattle and sheep. A dense raceme of showy white flowers, which persist and age to chartreuse or green after pollination, appear in late spring or early summer on stems 1 to 2 feet tall. The May/June flowering period is a time few other forest perennials are in bloom. In cultivation it prefers an acid moist soil, lightly shaded.

Goatsbeard *(Aruncus dioicus)* is a familiar garden perennial with twice or thrice pinnately compound foliage that forms stately, imposing clumps 3 to 5 feet tall. In May and June, the plants have astilbe-like plumes of white flowers. Dioecious male plants have the showier flowers; female plants produce volunteer offspring. It is native in fertile moist woodlands from Pennsylvania and Iowa south to North Carolina, Alabama, and Arkansas. In the Deep South, it is often marginal at lower elevations.

It is easy to confuse this perennial with **false goatsbeard** *(Astilbe biternata)*, another bold, statuesque perennial 3 to 6 feet tall. False goatsbeard, too, has compound foliage and large panicles of white to ivory-yellow flowers in May and June. A close look at the terminal leaflet will distinguish them: on goatsbeard it is unlobed, while on false goatsbeard it is three-lobed. Native to shaded, wet woodlands from Virginia and Kentucky south to Georgia, the latter is a better choice for southern gardens.

Bunchflower *(Melanthium virginicum)* is a coarse, stately plant with 3- to 4-foot-high stems. The narrow grasslike foliage is mainly grouped at the base of the plant. Numerous small greenish white to yellowish flowers in a branched spike appear in June to August, carried high above the leaves. The general range is throughout the Atlantic coastal states from Texas and Florida north to New York in low pinelands. In the garden, provide a site with a moist, peaty, acid soil and light shade to partial sun.

Spotted phacelia *(Phacelia bipinnatifida)* is a biennial that often functions as a perennial through self-sowing. An attractive addition to the moist, shady garden, it is native from Virginia west to Ohio, Illinois, and Missouri and south to Georgia, Alabama, and Arkansas. It is found in ravines and moist woodlands with calcareous soil. It flowers in April and May with masses of attractive bell-shaped lavender-blue flowers about ½ inch across. The twice pinnately compound leaves are 2 to 3 inches long. In suitable locations it replaces itself through generous self-sowing to form permanent colonies, but it is not invasive or obnoxious.

Virginia chain fern *(Woodwardia virginica)* is an elegant addition to larger gardens. Sending up its reddish brown crosiers amid the stubble of the previous year's fronds, it begins growing somewhat later in spring than the cinnamon fern *(Osmunda cinnamomea)*. There is little difference in the appearance of Virginia chain fern's fertile and sterile fronds. As they unfold and mature to their full height of 18 to 24 inches, the pinnae change to dark green. The supporting petiole is dark brown to black where it joins the rhizome, which runs along the surface, quickly forming large, dense, tenacious mats that can be removed only with difficulty. Found along the coastal plain from Florida to Texas and sporadically north to Nova Scotia, Michigan, and Long Island, it grows in swamps, marshes, and roadside ditches. Given adequate, constant moisture, it will grow in full sun.

Small chain fern *(Woodwardia areolata)*, a related species, does exhibit dimorphism. The sterile fronds, which grow about 12 to 20 inches tall, have glossy light green pinnae, and the fertile fronds resemble those of sensitive fern *(Onoclea sensibilis)*. This species also quickly forms large colonies in suitably wet sites. It is found over much the same range as Virginia chain fern, in partial to lightly shaded sites such as wooded swamps and glade openings.

Widespread **maiden fern** *(Thelypteris kunthii)* is suitable only for gardens in the Deep South. It is native to river and stream banks and in wooded swamps along the coastal plain from South Carolina to Texas and south into Central America. This is an elegant species, with fronds 20 to 40 inches tall and 6 to 10 inches wide. The fronds are a beautiful light green and somewhat hairy, resulting in an attractive, soft appearance. As this species is naturally found in calcareous soils, add some ground limestone or a stick of white blackboard chalk to the planting holes if the pH is not somewhat alkaline.

Marsh fern *(T. palustris)* is also suitable for use in the Deep South, as is **downy wood fern** *(T. dentata)*, a pantropic species with 3-foot-long fronds growing from creeping rhizomes, and **Mariana maiden fern** *(T. torresiana)*, a large fern growing over 3 feet high with numerous offshoots from the creeping, branching rhizome. All are closely related to *Dryopteris*. **Southern shield fern** or **Florida wood fern** *(Dryopteris ludoviciana)* is a highly desirable species for southern gardens in the coastal plain from North Carolina to Texas.

Hammock fern *(Blechnum occidentale)* is a suitable terrestrial fern for southern Florida and other hot, humid locations. The new crosiers are thickly covered with long brown scales. As they unfold, the new leaflets are coppery green, slowly changing to copper and green and becoming deep green at maturity. Mature fronds are 12 to 24 inches high and 2 to 3 inches wide. The spreading rhizomes produce an attractive mix of coppery young fronds and older deep green ones. This fern needs a shaded location in a moist, not overly wet site, in loose, open humus-rich soil. It prefers an alkaline situation; crushed oyster shells or dolomitic limestone may be used to adjust the alkalinity. Native to the West Indies

and Central and South America from Mexico to Argentina, it is a rare native of northwestern peninsular Florida in limestone regions. **Swamp fern** or **saw fern** *(B. serrulatum)* is a taller species (over 3 feet tall). It has branching rhizomes with the fronds spaced an inch or more apart. As the common name implies, it needs moist to wet conditions.

Florida tree fern *(Ctenitis sloanei;* also *Dryopteris ampla)* is native to south Florida. The fronds have hairy stalks that grow in a tight spiral to form an arching umbrella-like canopy of lacy fronds 3 feet in diameter. It can produce a short, erect stem, which forms a small trunk 1½ feet high on well-grown mature specimens and gives a treelike appearance.

Nonnative Perennials for Southern Swamps

Elephant's-ear *(Alocasia macrorhiza)* is a handsome plant from tropical Asia with lush arrowhead-like leaves that are 2 feet long and grow on stalks up to 5 feet tall. Specialists in tropical plants offer a number of cultivars with ornamental foliage flushed with copper or purple. Resembling those of jack-in-the-pulpit, the small, inconspicuous flowers are clustered on a spike surrounded by a greenish white spathe. The plants need ample moisture, high levels of organic matter in the soil, and frequent fertilization. Dappled light and protection from wind are also important. Evergreen to 30°F, it will regenerate if the frosts are neither too severe nor too prolonged. The luxuriant tropical appearance of the foliage makes a good background for the lacy fronds of ferns.

Caladium is a popular bedding plant for seasonal use in the North, but it can be used year round in warm-climate gardens. Thriving in hot, humid, moist conditions, the tubers produce showy arrowhead-shaped, long staked translucent leaves that are banded and splotched with red, rose, pink, and white, and sometimes veined or edged in green. It needs a moist but not soggy soil that is high in organic matter. This plant also is a good partner to ferns.

Taro or elephant's-ear *(Colocasia esculenta)* is a tender perennial from tropical Asia and Polynesia. It grows from tuberous roots, which in some species are used for food. The mammoth heart-shaped grayish green leaves quickly grow to 6 feet tall on large stalks. Wind shreds the large leaves, so plant in a protected site with rich, moist soil and filtered shade. Fertilize lightly once a month while the plant is in active growth. Like the other elephant's-ear, tops are damaged at 30°F.

Calla lilies *(Zantedeschia* spp.) are elegantly flowered relatives of jack-in-the-pulpit from South Africa. They need frequent, heavy watering, even when grown in swampy, boggy situations. In hot-summer regions, light dappled shade prevents leaf scorch. Feed calla lilies weekly during the active growing season with a dilute liquid fertilizer. In mild-winter areas, the plants are evergreen. **Common calla** *(Z. aethiopica)* has large clumps of green leaves 18 inches long and 10 inches across at their widest point. The pure white or creamy white spathes appear mostly in spring and early summer. This is a very popular florist's flower.

Spotted calla *(Z. albomaculata)* is smaller. It has white-speckled leaves and white or creamy yellow flower spathes blotched with crimson-purple at the base.

Golden calla *(Z. elli-ottiana)* is the same size as spotted calla — about 18 to 24 inches tall. It also has white-speckled foliage, and greenish yellow spathes that mature to a rich golden yellow. Full sun, even in hot-summer regions, is preferred.

Pink calla *(Z. rehmannii)* (color photo, page 79) is a daintier plant growing 12 to 18 inches high with narrow, lance-shaped plain green leaves about 12 inches long. The flower spathes are pink to rosy pink.

Chapter Five

POOLS AND PONDS

hree different types of water plants are found in natural ponds: aquatic, submerged, and floating. Water lilies are the prime example of aquatic plants. They have their roots in the pond bottom, and their leaves float on the water's surface. Submerged plants, such as *Elodea,* are also firmly rooted, but their leaves and stems are submerged. Floating plants like duckweed and water hyacinth actually float on the surface; their roots are in the water rather than in the pond bottom. All three groups are the least adaptable of wetland plants, for they are *obligate wetland plants* — without standing water, they cannot survive. They also are not adaptable to different wetland habitats. Unlike many marsh plants that may also be found in a wet meadow, pond plants need standing water at all times. Water lilies cannot grow in a vernal pool that dries out in summer. Water lilies and most other pond plants are also sun-lovers that require a minimum of six hours of direct sunlight each day of the growing season; they are not plants for a shaded woodland.

The traditional concept of a water garden has been a pool or pond, often rather formal in design, where water lilies could be grown. Not really gardens to my way of thinking, these rectangular or circular concrete pools, outfitted with a necklace of cut stone for an edging, looked as if they are in quarantine, isolated from the rest of the garden by a sweep of lawn.

The arrival of fiberglass pools and flexible liners on the market suddenly made pool installation a weekend operation, with certain caveats. For instance, although flexible liners can be used to create pools with more bends than a french curve, it takes considerable effort to place a liner smoothly, without any puckers or folds. Too often these pools have a bungled look, with the edge bunched up and visible under the rock necklace — which in this incarnation, tends to be anything found while excavating the hole for the pool. It is true that there are excellent, attractive owner-installed pools, but a hole in the ground filled with water is not automatically beautiful.

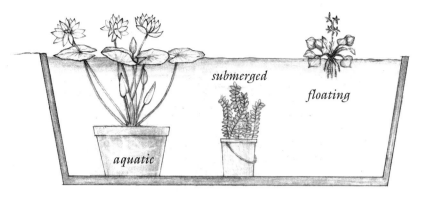

Examples of types of water plants found in natural ponds: from left to right, aquatic (water lilies), submerged, and floating.

Pools should be as large as possible, within the limits dictated by available space and your budget. A depth of 18 to 24 inches, which protects against rapid temperature fluctuations, is necessary in Zone 6 to protect overwintering fish. In fact, for insurance, it's a good idea to build in a small pocket an additional 6 to 12 inches deeper. In warm climates, a shallow pool heats up to temperatures that not only are harmful to fish and plants but also encourage the growth of algae. In addition to the depth itself, the pond must also contain an adequate volume of water, proportional to the surface area. Aim toward an average of 10 gallons of water for each 1 square foot of surface area. For example, a pool 6 feet wide by 7 feet long should be a *minimum* of 15 inches deep, resulting in about 8 gallons of water per square foot of surface. A depth of 24 inches provides a little over 12 gallons of water per square foot of surface, a more desirable amount.

Before you install any pool, it is wise to check local zoning regulations. For example, state code in Connecticut classifies anything 24 inches deep as a swimming pool, thus requiring fencing. One inch less, and it is a lily pool.

PONDS

To my dictionary, a pond is a body of water generally smaller than a lake; a pool is a small, rather deep body of usually fresh water or a small body of standing water. According to one college text, the important, deciding difference between a lake and a pond is that lakes are more than 6 feet deep; ponds are more shallow and contain vegetation — trees, shrubs, and persistent emergent plants growing in the water. Large ponds and lakes are more stable than smaller ones because they provide more room for the growth and expansion of plants before the water area begins to fill up. (If shallow water is completely covered with water lilies, it rather quickly becomes even more shallow, fills in, dries up, and becomes a wet meadow.) If the pond is not to become a marsh, it is necessary that a portion of its surface remain free from the territorial expansion of both marginal and aquatic plants. With human intervention in the form of regular maintenance, shallow ornamental pools can be kept open.

ESTIMATING YOUR POOL'S CAPACITY: A LITTLE MATH LESSON

If you know the length, width, and depth of your pool, it is easy to calculate its surface area and capacity.

- To calculate the square feet of surface area of a rectangular or square pool, multiply the length by the width. To calculate the capacity of the pool, multiply the length by the width by the depth. That number, multiplied by 7.5 (gallons per cubic feet), gives the volume of water the pool will hold, in gallons.

- To figure out the surface area of a circular pool, in square feet, multiply the diameter by the diameter, divide by 2, and multiply by 3.14 *(pi)*. To find its capacity, multiply 3.14 *(pi)* by the radius by the radius by the depth. That number, multiplied by 7.5, gives the volume of water the pool will hold, in gallons.

A CONCRETE POOL

Concrete is a wonderfully plastic material (at least before it sets up) but unless you are skilled in masonry, I think anything in concrete larger than a birdbath saucer is better left to more expert help. Here are a couple of tips to keep in mind if you do decide that you want a concrete pool.

- Any side wall approaching vertical will require the use of forms to retain the concrete until it sets. Reinforcement, in the form of either rebars or special concrete reinforcing wire, helps hold the concrete together, like the armature in a sculpture.

- A compacted mineral subsoil is important so that the concrete shell does not subside and crack. Both freezing temperatures and tree roots can crack concrete. I saw one pool in Massachusetts that had been invaded by bamboo, which had grown right through its side.

- New concrete is harmful for fish and plants because it leaches chemicals into the water.

(Alkalinity leaching from a new home's concrete foundation raises the pH and upsets the iron/calcium metabolism of foundation plantings. Ericaceous shrubs such as rhododendrons and mountain laurel become chlorotic.) Before it is safe to introduce animals and plants to your new pool, fill it with water, let the water stand in it for up to two weeks to allow chemicals to leach, then empty the pool. Refill and flush it several times in the same manner. To speed the process, add 1 gallon of vinegar for every 200 gallons of water. Let the mixture stand for five days, empty, and rinse. Or wash the concrete with potassium permanganate. (Be careful with this chemical: it stains anything it touches purple, including skin and clothing.)

- A somewhat simpler alternative to poured concrete for formal rectangular pools is to dig a hole, build the sides with concrete blocks, and use a flexible waterproof membrane as a liner.

RIGID FIBERGLASS POOLS

Certainly the simplest pool to install is a rigid fiberglass shell. This is what I used for my own garden pool. This material's limitation is that the shape of the pool is dictated by the shape of the shell you purchase. A more creative friend built up her own shell, using several layers of fiberglass

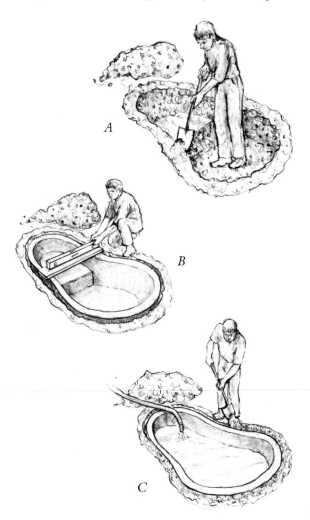

To install a rigid fiberglass pool, (A) dig a hole larger in all dimensions than the pool shell. Line the bottom of the hole with sand, then (B) put pool in place and check to be sure it is level. (C) Back-fill the sides as you fill the pool with water.

fabric and resin hardener that she bought at an automotive supply shop.

I have not had a problem with overheating, but my pool is situated where it is shaded for part of the day. Although I do remove the fish before winter arrives, the water lilies remain in the pool year-round. They have come through unscathed in 3 inches of water below 14 inches of ice in the worst winter.

To install a rigid fiberglass pool, dig a hole larger in all dimensions than the pool shell. Remove any sharp, hard objects from the bottom and place a 1-inch layer of sand as a protective cushion. To prevent distortion, backfill the sides as you fill the pool with water.

Preformed pools are available in a variety of shapes, usually ranging from 14 to 17 inches deep. These hold less water than is ideally recommended (see page 94). For example, an irregular shape 6 feet by 5 feet by 18 inches deep holds 165 gallons or 5½ gallons per square foot of surface; a 9-foot by 8-foot by 16-inch-deep pool holds 450 gallons, or a little more than 6 gallons per surface square foot.

FLEXIBLE LINERS

Flexible liners have the advantage that the name denotes. In addition to creating an informal, irregular shape, you can also make planting shelves for a variety of marginal plants. The drawback of flexible liners is that they are more easily punctured than fiberglass, meaning leaks, and they are difficult to mend.

Flexible liners are usually made of PVC (polyvinyl chloride) or rubber. Liners come single and double ply and in different weights: 20 mil, 32 mil, 45 mil. A single-ply, 20-mil PVC liner has an estimated life expectancy of 10 years, while double-ply, 32-mil liners have a 15- to 20-year-life expectancy. Rubber liners, made from ethylene propylene diene monomer, must be *fish grade* to avoid harmful effects. A 45-mil rubber liner is expected to have a 30-year life expectancy. Relative costs are as might be expected, with the price of 20-mil PVC liners about 60 percent that of rubber liners.

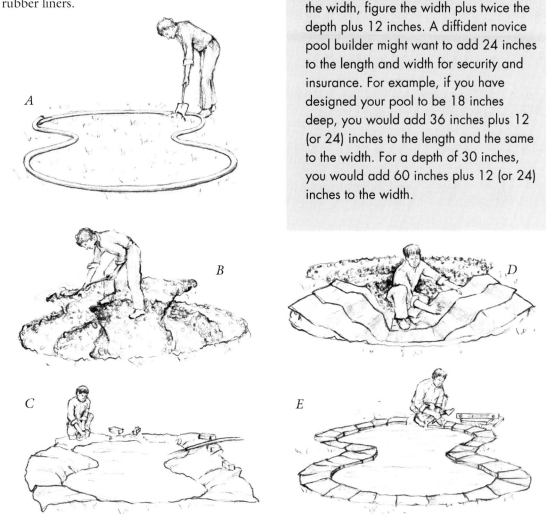

To install a pool with a flexible liner, (A) lay the design out with a hose. (B) Dig the hole, with the sides sloping slightly inward from top to bottom and with ledges for marginal aquatic plants, if desired. (C) Line the bottom with 1 inch of damp sand and geo-textile, rubberized horsehair, or old carpet. (D) Drape liner loosely into the excavation, leaving an overlap all around; hold liner in place temporarily with bricks or smooth stones as you ease it into the hole and begin to fill the pool with water. (E) Lay stones along the perimeter, overhanging the water 1 or 2 inches.

The manufacturers of flexible liners provide simple, clear instructions for installation. Before you begin, decide where to place your pool, approximately how large it should be, and what shape to make it. Lay the design out with a hose to get an idea of how it will look. This is the time to make any adjustments, not after you've begun digging!

It is amazing how much soil comes out of a hole — more, it seems, than was there before it was disturbed. Decide where you are going to put the spoil material before you start digging.

Test the site with a pry bar to determine whether there is any ledge or large boulders where you intend to put the pool. If there is extensive rock outcropping, it might be easier to put the pool some place else. Rocks, protruding roots, or anything else that might pierce the membrane must be removed.

When you shape the hole, remember that the sides should have a slight inward slope from top to bottom. Make the pool 15 to 24 inches deep. Check the depth by laying a 2 x 4 board across the excavation and measuring to the bottom in several places with a yardstick held perpendicular to the board. To make it easier to drain and clean the pool, create one area 18 inches across and 1 inch deeper than the rest of the pool. For marginal aquatic plants that require shallow water, form ledges about 12 inches wide, 9 to 12 inches below the top edge of the excavation.

After the excavation is completed, line the bottom with 1 inch of damp sand. Since sand cannot be used on the sides of the excavation, use an underlay of geo-textile to protect the sides. For extra security, you can also place geo-textile across the pool's bottom, on top of the sand. You can lay down used rubberized horsehair or rubber carpet pads instead of geo-textile if you wish.

Most liners, even small ones, take two people to maneuver into place. Let the liner warm on a paved, sunny area for a few minutes, so it will be as flexible as possible. (Do not lay it on your lawn, as it can quickly heat up enough to kill the grass. My fiberglass pool killed the grass beneath it when we took a lunch break.) To avoid damaging the liner, never drag it across the ground. Unfold the liner and drape it loosely into the excavation, keeping an even overlap all around the perimeter. You can hold it in place temporarily with bricks or smooth stones as you work it into the hole. As the pool fills with water and the liner snugs into place, ease off these weights.

After the pool is filled, wait a day to allow sufficient time for the liner to stretch and fit the contours of the ground, then trim the surplus overlap with a pair of large scissors, leaving a 6- to 12-inch flap.

The liner needs protection from sunlight, as ultraviolet rays will damage it. Trim back any turf about 2 feet from the edge. Hold the liner in place

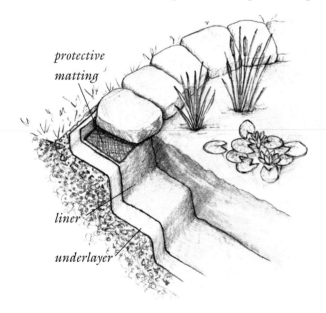

protective matting

liner

underlayer

Edge pool with flat stones placed on a shallow shelf just below water level.

by driving 10-inch spikes directly through it into the ground. Trim it more closely where you want to re-lay sod as a turf edging to the water.

For a stone coping, first place metal lathe along the edge of the liner. Lay 2 to 3 inches of mortar mix over the lathe, then lay the stone in the mortar, checking the edges for evenness as you work. The stones should overhang the water for 1 or 2 inches, protecting the liner where it lips over the edge.

Another attractive stone edging requires planning as you excavate. Create a shallow shelf inside the pool area along a portion of the edge. Lay concrete pavers directly on the soil and bring the underlayment up over them before you put the liner in place. Add a second layer of protective matting on top of the liner. Be sure to trim the matting so it will be beneath the water's surface when the pool is filled, or it can act as a wick, drawing water out of the pool by capillary action and feeding it into the surrounding soil or allowing it to evaporate. Place solid rocks, granite for example, on the shelf you have created. Materials like granite neither crumble nor release minerals into the water as soft limestone might. If the rocks have a flat side to use on the bottom, so much the better, as they are more stable. This technique creates a very natural look with the base of the stone(s) submerged in water. In larger pools, you can make the shelf wider and gently sloping. Cobbles and large pebbles (rinsed to remove any dust or possible contaminants before they are put in place) may be added to create a gravelly beach. If you use gravel, make a small curb to keep the pebbles from slipping into the pool. For this purpose, use preformed concrete edgers and set them into the soil of the shelf toward the water. Cover with underlay, liner, and protective matting as described.

In ponds or pools built with a flexible membrane or rigid fiberglass liner, plants are grown in containers. I have seen it suggested that a thick fibrous mat be laid over and under the actual pool liner to create a sort of sandwich, with as few as 2 inches to as much as 6 to 8 inches of soil as the final topping. In reality, I think this would be troublesome. Both membrane and fiberglass have slick surfaces, and the matting would be difficult to keep anchored in place. Plants will root into the matting, and the regular maintenance necessary to prevent their rapid spread in such a pool would be very difficult. In contrast, fibrous mats and bundles are extremely functional in planting sites subject to erosion (see chapter 9 on planting techniques).

Filled plant containers must be lowered carefully into place, both for the safety of the plants and for the protection of the liner. Likewise, when you need to enter the pool — to groom the plants, for instance, or for seasonal cleaning — barefoot is better.

Earth-Bottom Ponds

Many ornamental ponds would better be called pools — relatively small scale, they are intended as an adjunct to a city or urban garden. Even in the suburbs they are rarely extensive projects. There are situations however, where a project is of such stature that "pond" is the only proper name. Stonecrop, the extensive garden of Frank and Anne Cabot in Cold Spring, New York, contains just such a pond. With six acres of garden on the forty-acre property, a water feature needed to be large scale if it were not to be insignificant. The garden contains several water features: a pond garden created from swampy low-lying ground; another whose water, gently cascading through a series of small rock pools is powered by a pump; and most majestic, a lagoon bulldozed out of the ground, lined with bentonite, and fed from a 20,000-gallon cistern and a recirculating water system. (The garden is open to the public by arrangement; an entrance fee is charged.)

Construction of an earth-bottom pond is a regulated activity. Governing statutes may be on a local level; state and federal regulations might also apply, depending on the scope of the project, the flow rate of any affected water course, and so on. Be prudent and check the local regulations in your community before construction begins, to avoid the possibility of legal action. While earth-bottom ponds can be successfully constructed, they are not as uncomplicated as might appear. Sydney Eddison's vernal pool (see pages 157–159) was built decades ago by the previous owners of her property. Deceived by the spring freshets, they had a basin scooped out which subsequently became a muddy buffalo wallow in summer. Another friend of mine built a pond that has resulted in a draw-down of the water level in the surrounding red maple swamp — an effect he had not anticipated.

If a pond or marsh was once filled in for farming and the land has now been taken out of agricultural production, then you might want to consider restoring the wetlands. *The New York Times* published an article ("The Mississippi Reclaims Its True Domain" in "This Week in Review," July 18, 1993) on the epochal flooding along the Mississippi River. In it, David Lanegran, Professor of Geography and Urban Studies at Macalester College in St. Paul, Minnesota, was quoted: "Now the river is taking back its old places. You can see the old marshes coming back in the farmers' fields, all the places where the duck ponds used to be. It's almost like a ghost. The water is saying, 'This is where I used to be. This used to be my place.'"

Many small pond construction and renovation projects in my town are handled on a local level. An application fee, surveying, and the services of the pond designer are up-front expenses before construction actually begins. Major projects can involve your state Department of Environmental Protection or Department of Natural Resources, or even the U.S. Army Corps of Engineers. It is always best to check your local regulations before the design phase of the project.

INLAND WETLAND REGULATIONS

As we have come to recognize the importance of wetlands, it has become important to protect them. The days when an individual property owner could fill in or drain marshes and swamps are gone. Current restrictions are a safeguard, making wetland alterations a matter for public scrutiny. Wetlands are regulated on federal, state, and local levels. In my own state of Connecticut, state wetland regulations were implemented in 1972. They not only define wetlands but also restrict activities within or adjacent to mapped wetlands, which are delineated based on soils and soil types. In other states, and by federal definitions, surface vegetation and hydrology may be included in deciding what is or is not wetland.

WORKING WITH A POND DESIGNER

If you work with a pond designer, ask to see examples of his or her work. Be sure that the firm or individual you select works in the appropriate idiom — that is, the style you envision for your pond-to-be. There is a world of difference between a naturalistic pond created as part of a wet meadow and a water garden in a more formal landscape.

Any activity that would be considered to affect a wetland negatively needs, *at a minimum,* an Inland Wetland Permit on a local level. If machinery — a dredge, dragline, or excavator — is needed to clean and/or dredge a pond, a permit is required. If there is an existing catch basin with a sump, you may be allowed to shovel it clean without further ado. (A catch basin "catches" water flowing into or out of the pond. The deeper portion, called a sump, allows debris — sand, twigs, leaves, old sneakers — to settle out of suspension in the water, thus making periodic removal of the debris somewhat easier. This removal keeps debris from entering the pond or its outflow.)

Creating a new pond requires a permit, and more information, than restoring an existing pond. Regulations vary from state to state, and different communities have different procedures. Before you begin, visit your local town hall to see what is required.

A New Pond

Where a pond with an earth bottom is being dug, remember that the more gradual the transition from open water through a shallow-water zone to a wet marginal zone, the more room you will have to plant a variety of marginal emergent plants. Additionally, the more gradual the slope, the more slowly silt and debris will slip and reach deeper water. If, for whatever reason, you need to make steeper sides at the construction phase, you can create a shallower planting area with some mechanical barrier offshore. Several large rocks or concrete blocks can be used under the water to make a retaining wall for a planting bed. Alternatively, if locust logs (or some other rot-resistant wood) are available, you can drive them in as pilings. This has an additional attraction: if the log ends project a few inches above the surface of the water, they can also function as stepping-stones.

One modern technique uses bentonite clay to line the pool. Fibrous matting is laid on the base of the excavation, impregnated with the bentonite clay, and then buried under soil or gravel. The bentonite swells when wet, creating an impermeable layer. Any minor punctures are usually self-healing. On the downside, the matting is expensive and not always available. Although a more successful technique than using bentonite clay alone (in a process called *puddling*), this method is not foolproof. If the clay dries out, it can crack and leak. This technique is generally used in a place that has a naturally high water table.

Pond Maintenance

If you have an existing pond, it makes sense to follow good management practices to maintain it in a healthy condition. Here are some suggestions:

- Limit pesticide and herbicide use in surrounding areas. If they are necessary, use only those that will not adversely affect groundwater.

- Create a *plunge pool* — a deeper area in an entering stream where sediment is deposited before it enters the pond.

- Empty catch basins on a regular basis: those with a sump to trap debris are preferred.

- To avoid soil's washing into the water, minimize land disturbance around the pond.

- Keep septic systems in good repair.

- Stabilize the pond edge by planting appropriate shrubs and herbaceous plants. Their roots stabilize the soil, and their uptake of

A SAMPLE WATER GARDEN

Imagine the following scene, which would be as appropriate for a small created pool as for a large natural pond: Emergent or marginal plants grow in shallow water. Those described in chapter 2 are suitable for pond margins, bordering deeper water. Further from the water are wet meadow plants, those that do not require standing water but are content with merely wet feet. With 2 to 3 feet of water above their roots, yellow lotus (*Nuphar luteum*), white water lily (*Nymphaea alba*), and pink water lily (*N. x marliacea* 'Rosea') float their leaves and flowers on the surface of the water. Lake rush (*Scirpus lacustris*) grows in 12 to 18 inches of water. As the pond becomes shallower, from 4 inches of water over the plants' roots to simply wet soil, a number of adaptable plants weave a tapestry of foliage along the shore: arrowhead (*Sagittaria latifolia*) and cattail (*Typha latifolia*) grow in 4 to 6 inches of water; then come marsh marigold (*Caltha palustris*), sweet flag (*Acorus calamus*), flowering rush (*Butomus umbellatus*), pickerel rush (*Pontederia cordata*), yellow flag iris (*Iris pseudacorus*), and swamp buttercup (*Ranunculus septentionalis*).

nutrients keeps it out of the water, slowing eutrophication. Native species are recommended.

∾ Avoid a broad sweep of lawn adjacent to a pond; this setting is attractive to Canada geese, which can be a serious nuisance.

∾ Avoid lawn fertilizers, which result in nutrient loss to the water, and mowing, which produces grass clippings that end up in the water. Both increase the growth of algae and speed the aging of the pond.

∾ Avoid planting willows around your pond. These messy trees drop branches and debris into the water, necessitating regular maintenance.

∾ Combat the overgrowth of vigorous water lilies, which can lead to siltation in shallow water at the pond's edge. Chemicals that kill

the lilies are generally ineffective, require state departments of environmental protection approval, and must be applied by a certified applicator. Mechanical removal is an annual task. One method of periodic control is to drain the pond partially in winter, allowing freezing temperatures to kill exposed roots.

Design Suggestions for Pools and Ponds

Whether you are choosing plants for a large pond or a small pool, it is important to select plants for the water's edge. Use nature as your guide. Notice the transition from upland to open water. Although a small area of turf at the margin of the pool is functional — it allows approach to the water's edge — it should not completely encircle it. Not only does a neatly mown lawn surrounding the water have a very manicured, artificial look, as was mentioned above, but excess nutrients leach into the water from runoff, and grass clippings in the water are difficult to avoid. Completely surrounding your pool with cattails, rushes, irises, and other plants is equally poor design. Although it is true that this situation exists in nature, it limits your view of the water and conveys a feeling of being shut out.

For leading the viewer to the pond, one of the most attractive designs I have seen was at the garden of Kurt and Hannah Bluemel in Baldwin, Maryland. A simple wooden boardwalk angles out from shore to put you literally over the water. When I visited in August, tall cattail foliage soughed in a light breeze; the pale pink buds, huge 12-inch-diameter rose-pink flowers, and warty-looking green seedpods (somewhat like the sprinkler on a watering can) of sacred lotus (*Nelumbo nucifera*) all nodded on their slender stems like a scene from some Egyptian fresco. Out on the surface of the water tranquilly floated the leaves and flowers of hardy water lilies. This very simple arrangement was elegant and satisfying.

Where wood is used near water it should be rot resistant. Locust and cedar are good examples of relatively affordable rot-resistant North American timber. Small local sawmills are likely sources for native wood, if it is available. Cypress and redwood also are rot resistant, but both of these species are being cut beyond their renewal rate. If only tropical woods such as Philippine or Honduras mahogany are available, ask at the lumberyard for material from managed plantations rather than that cut from the wild. It would be inconsistent to use old-growth cypress or redwood, or timber from endangered tropical forests, for a boardwalk in a natural water garden.

Aquatic Plants: The Water Lilies

When you first read the catalog from a nursery specializing in water lilies, the diversity is astonishing. How can you choose? Often the result is that too many are ordered, and the pool is overplanted. Crowded, the water lilies thrust their leaves up out of the water rather than float on the surface. The water disappears, choked with vegetation. Remember that the beauty of a pool or pond lies in the reflective mirror of its surface. If this is covered with plants, you have nullified an important aspect of the water garden. Plan to leave 30 to 40 percent of the water visible, and decide whether other plants with floating leaves, such as water snowflake, will be included.

HARDY WATER LILIES

Hardy water lilies (*Nymphaea* spp.) are native to North America, Europe, and Asia. They can be left outside year-round if their roots remain below the level of the ice. Where winters are severe and the pool is shallow, the roots must be lifted and stored over winter. These hardy water lilies are day-bloomers — their white, yellow, pink, or red flowers close at night. They do poorly in moving water, and the turbulence from fountains is bad for them. They do best in still water, ample space, and a warm, sunny position.

Some very small water lilies, such as *N. pygmaea* (*N. tetragona*), are suitable for the smallest of pools and are best grown in pots. They are discussed in chapter 7 on water gardening in containers. Other small-growing water lilies were raised by Marliac of France, possibly using *N. pygmaea* as one of the parents. When they are available, some cultivars that are ideal for tubs and small pools include the following: 'Laydekeri

Fulgens', with brilliant crimson-magenta flowers and fiery red stamens; 'Laydekeri Lilacea', with fragrant, soft lilac-rose flowers aging to vivid carmine and yellow stamens; 'Laydekeri Purpurea', rosy crimson, somewhat spotted and flecked with white, in bloom throughout the summer and free flowering, with dozens of flowers at one time on a well-established plant; and hard-to-find 'Laydekeri Rosea', with fragrant deep rose, perfect cup-shaped flowers.

White water lily (*N. alba*) is native to Europe, Asia, and North Africa. It grows best in 3 to 4½ feet of water but can accept depths up to 9 feet. From late May through August, it has fragrant, wide-open white flowers, 4 to 5 inches across. The crowded leaves can be as much as 12 inches in diameter. This species is vigorous and suitable only for earth-bottom ponds of suitably large scale. Another vigorous, robust variety suitable for large ponds and lakes is 'Gladstoniana', which grows in water 2 to 3 feet deep and spreads its strong deep green leaves to cover 5 to 12 square feet.

N. candida is much daintier. It is widely distributed throughout northern Europe, even extending into Arctic regions, and in Asia. In summer, it has small white flowers that do not open completely. It can be grown in 15 to more than 30 inches of water in earth-bottom ponds. This is an excellent choice in situations where there is cold water.

White water lily (*N. odorata*), from eastern North America and Mexico, is a parent of many hybrid water lilies. The species is very fragrant and passes this trait on to its offspring. It grows best in 2 feet of water, with starry white flowers that often stand 2 to 3 inches out of the water, from June until frost. It spreads its pale green leaves over 4 to 7 square feet. The tuberous roots form round or oval masses at the ends, which are easily harvested. The seeds may also be eaten.

White water lily (*N. tuberosa*) is a robust species suitable for large earth-bottom ponds, as it is able to grow with 6 feet of water over its roots. It has massive white flowers, 12 inches across, which stand clear of the water's surface. The wavy-edged, rounded leathery leaves cover 5 to 8 square feet.

A number of hybrids may be selected, based on the pragmatic considerations of depth of water and room to spread. The important aesthetic decision is flower color. Hybrid hardy water lilies are available with white, pink, red, or yellow flowers. There are even changeable water lilies that alter in color day by day as the flower ages, usually from yellow to copper or orange, deepening almost to red on the third day. All are day-blooming.

TROPICAL WATER LILIES

Tender water lilies need water warm enough to encourage growth; temperatures below 70°F are apt to set them back. They dislike cool spring weather and summer conditions in the Pacific Northwest and Alaska. In Texas and California, they can be planted outdoors in May, earlier in the Deep South, but not until June in the Northeast. Only in Zone 10 can they remain out of doors year-round. Their fragrant flowers stand above the water's surface. Some, called "day-blooming," open in midmorning and close in late afternoon. "Night-blooming" varieties open at sundown and remain open until midmorning of the following day. Like the hardy water lilies, flower colors are white, pink, red, and yellow. In addition, there are varieties with blue or purple flowers.

Some tropical water lilies are viviparous, with new plantlets forming on their leaves where they join the stem.

Night-blooming tropical water lilies add another dimension to the garden, especially for those who have only the evening hours or the weekend to enjoy their gardens.

Pond Lilies

Yellow waterlily, spatterdock, and **yellow pond lily** (*Nuphar* spp.) are robust plants considered inferior to hardy water lilies. Their size and vigor, coupled with their relatively small yellow flowers, limit their potential for garden use. They are suitable for water 3 to 6 feet deep and tolerant of shade and sluggish currents that are detrimental to *Nymphaea* species. These exceedingly vigorous, robust plants, with spreading 6-foot rootstocks, have invasive tendencies that lead to difficulties in earth-bottom ponds. Their vigor also renders most of them unsuitable for confinement in a container. Two dwarf pond lilies that *are* suitable, because they are smaller growing species, are discussed in chapter 7 on water gardening in containers: *N. pumilum,* from Europe and Asia, and *N. minimum,* which has tiny yellow flowers and small heart-shaped leaves. Both grow in 12 to 18 inches of water.

Yellow pond lily (*Nuphar variegatum*) is the most common species in the Northeast. It ranges across Canada, south to New England, Delaware, and Maryland, and west to Ohio, Illinois, Nebraska, and South Dakota. The heart-shaped leaves float on the water or stand above the surface, while submerged sagittate leaves are present in deep water. The yellow cuplike flowers, 1½ to 2½ inches across, appear from May to September along pond margins and slow-flowing streams.

୰ EDIBLE PLANTS. *The somewhat strongly flavored root of spatterdock (N. luteum) was eaten by American Indians. To prepare it, they brought it to a boil in two changes of water, then cooked it like any other starchy tuberous vegetable. The seed kernels were ground into a flour and used in breads or to thicken soups. They were also popped, like corn.*

Yellow pond lily, cow lily, or **common spatterdock** (*N. advena*) is very similar to spatterdock. **Yellow water lily** (*N. luteum*) is a vigorous species from Europe, Siberia, and the Near East.

Lotuses

Lotuses are always discussed in conjunction with water lilies. Like the latter, they grow in ponds, but rather than floating on the surface, lotuses raise their leaves and flowers high above the water. They are hardy and can be invasive in earth-bottom ponds.

American lotus, water lotus, or **chinquapin** (*Nelumbo lutea*) is a native species found in ponds and quiet streams; in oxbows, lakes, and sloughs in the big river floodplains of Missouri; and from Florida and Texas north. American lotus is not as common in the wild as water lilies or pond lilies. Along the Mississippi River though, especially between Wisconsin and Iowa, it forms extensive colonies in the quiet waters along the river's shores. It is hardy to Zone 4. Up to 2 feet in diameter, its large, round, shieldlike blue-green leaves are several feet above the water on long petioles, attached at the center rather than the edge of each leaf. In summer, many-petaled pale sulfur-yellow flowers — 6 inches across or larger, one to a stem — are also borne well above the water. Each is followed by an urn-shaped, flat-topped fruit covered with Swiss cheese-like holes, from which the partially exposed seeds peep out.

The thick rhizomes spread very quickly; a small group can spread 45 feet in one season, filling in a shallow 1-acre pond in just three or four years. Winter drawdown, which leaves the soil exposed to freezing temperatures for a month, offers some control of American lotus, as it does hardy water lily. Viable roots will remain, so this is a transient means of reducing overactive growth. Repeated cutting of the leaves, starting before the first flower buds open, also weakens the plants and helps to control its spread. Considering that the seeds have proven viable after a two-hundred-year dormancy, there need be little concern as to their continued survival.

✍ EDIBLE PLANTS. *American lotus was an important source of food for American Indians. Today the immature seeds may still be eaten, raw or cooked. They are easier to prepare when half ripe, before their covering has a chance to harden fully. Later, when they have matured, they need to be cracked before being boiled to extract the oil, or roasted and ground into a meal. Dried seeds can be ground and used together with flour to make bread. American Indians baked or boiled the starchy tuberous roots, then peeled them and used the glutinous sweet center in various dishes. They also peeled the fresh roots, cut them into thin slices, and dried them for winter use. Prepared in this manner, they can then be ground into a coarse meal and used to prepare a gruel, added to a stew, or used to thicken soups. In spring, the new leaves, gathered before they unroll, can be used as greens.*

Sacred lotus (*N. nucifera*) (color photo, page 133) is a more familiar denizen of aquatic gardens. From Asia, India, and China, it is similar to American lotus in appearance. Its platelike leaves also bear a waterproof waxy coating on their upper surface.

ANOTHER AQUATIC WITH FLOATING LEAVES

The naturalized European fringed water lily (*Nymphoides peltandra*) and our native floating heart (*N. aquatica*) are useful aquatic plants with floating leaves. These are discussed on page 140.

Sacred lotus is a vigorous plant, needing adequate root room. Smaller varieties, such as 'Momo Botan', 'Chawan Basu', and 'Tulip' ('Shirokunshi'), need at least a 10-inch-diameter container; other varieties need a container 3 feet square and 1 foot deep for satisfactory growth. Sacred lotus is slow to establish and usually produces only leaves the first year. Although not as hardy as our native species, sacred lotus can be grown out-of-doors year-round in Zone 5. Try it in Zone 4 if the water is deep enough to protect the tubers from freezing in winter. During the growing season, sacred lotuses prefer 12 inches of water or less above the soil.

✍ GROWING TIPS. *The banana-shaped tuberous roots of sacred lotus are easily damaged. Handle them gently. Place the tubers horizontally in the soil and leave the growing point exposed. Plant in spring when the water temperature has reached 65° F.*

Other Shallow-Water Aquatic Plants

Water clover or pepperwort (*Marsilea quadrifolia*) looks like a four-leaf clover, but in actuality it is a fern native to Europe and Asia. Hardy to Zone 5, it has naturalized throughout New England and into the Midwest after its escape from a pond called Bantam Lake in Litchfield County, Connecticut, where it was introduced in 1862. In 6- to 8-inch-deep water, the shamrocklike green leaves float on the surface; in shallower water, the leaves stand 3 to 6 inches above the surface. It can also be grown as a marsh plant, with its slender rhizomes growing in the muddy bottom of shallow, sunny pools and out into the adjacent saturated soil. The young leaflets fold up at night. A native species **of water clover** (*M. vestita; M. mucronata*), is found in the muddy shallows of ponds and lakes from Minnesota south to Texas and Florida.

Pondweeds (Potamogeton spp.), of which there are many species, are horrid weedy things, rapidly over-growing more desirable plants. They have small greenish flowers that are capable of producing copious amounts of seeds. They are too invasive for ornamental water gardens, but in wildlife ponds they are valuable plants: The seeds are an important food for waterfowl like ducks, geese, and shorebirds, as well as for beavers and moose; the underwater leaves provide an important spawning ground for fish; and the leaves are also habitats for many of the aquatic insects eaten by fish.

Potamogeton pulcher, a species native to the eastern half of North America, does have attractive foliage that provides an interesting contrast to that of hardy water lilies. Unless intended for a large earth-bottom naturalistic pond, however, it is more easily managed and kept under control by planting it in a container. Like many other species of pondweeds, this has two kinds of foliage: narrow, translucent submerged leaves scattered on long pliant stems and leathery, oval floating leaves from 1½ to 4½ inches long. Without some maintenance, the floating leaves can form a dense canopy, producing such heavy shade as to inhibit the growth of submerged aquatics. Depths of 12 to 18 inches of water are most suitable.

Common European pondweed (P. natans) is an extremely rampant plant. It has floating leaves that resemble those of **water hawthorn (Aponogeton distachyus),** a much better-behaved South African floating-leaved plant, which grows from edible starchy tubers the size of a chestnut. The dark green leaves, about 10 inches long and 2 inches wide, often have maroon splotches. Water hawthorne rarely flowers in the northern

United States, but where conditions are suitable, it blooms in late summer and into autumn. The strongly fragrant, vanilla-scented, waxy white flowers have contrasting black stamens and are forked. They appear from spring to late summer and on into early winter in the mildest climates. Their fragrance is most noticeable on still summer evenings. It will grow along with water lilies in 18 to 24 inches of water and is suitable for year-round cultivation only in Zones 9 and 10.

Wild rice (Zizania aquatica) is accorded gourmet status as a delectable food, its high price reflecting the fact that it prefers to grow wild and is not amenable to commercial cultivation. An attractive broad-leaved grass, it grows up to 10 feet tall. Its slender dark seeds are carried in a dense cluster at the top of the stem, each encased in a loose husk topped with a hairlike bristle. Once ripe, the seed shatters and quickly falls away from the plant.

Wild rice grows 6 to 10 feet tall, with nearly 2-inch-wide, flat, lance-shaped light green leaves on reedlike stems and foot-long terminal flower panicles. The flowers are followed by edible seeds on the uppermost broomlike portion. Wild rice is best grown in a natural pond where, if conditions are suitable, scattered seeds have an opportunity to eventually produce a self-sustaining colony.

❧ EDIBLE PLANTS. *The traditional method of harvesting wild rice was to pole a boat or canoe among the plants and use sticks to knock the kernels into the bottom of the boat. Some fell into the water, ensuring the next season's crop. Next, the kernels were spread on sheets of birch bark for a day to dry them, after which they were parched in a kettle or smoked over a slow fire on a hay-covered frame to loosen the husks. The dried kernels had to be pounded to loosen the husks, after which they would be winnowed to remove the chaff. Last, the rice grains were tread upon to remove the last fragments of husks.*

Manchurian rice *(Z. latifolia)* is a perennial species from Japan, China, Korea, eastern Siberia, and Indochina. It has 1-inch-wide, swordlike, somewhat arching leaves, 20 to 40 inches long, with an attractive autumnal color change. The culms reach 3 to 8 feet high.

∽ GROWING TIPS. *More commonly planted to attract waterfowl than as a decorative ornamental, this handsome annual grass should be sown in early spring in flats of muddy soil. Transplant like rice, setting small bunches in shallow water in May, in a site with deep, mucky ooze and gently circulating water.*

Free-Floating Aquatic Plants

Azolla *(Azolla caroliniana)*, water hyacinth *(Eichhornia crassipes)*, frog's-bit *(Hydrocharis morsus-ranae)*, and duckweed *(Lemna gibba)*, which are all free-floating aquatics, are discussed on pages 143–144. Both duckweed and water milfoil *(Myriophyllum spicatum)* can be a serious problem in shallow, still water; they completely cover the surface of the water and are difficult to eradicate.

Water soldier or **water aloe** *(Stratiotes aloides)* looks like a free-floating pineapple top, with 12-inch-diameter rosettes of narrow, sword-like, serrated green leaves. It floats from just under the surface of the water up to a couple of feet deep, bobbing to the surface to bloom in late summer. Small, dioecious creamy white flowers appear in the leaf axils in summer, with clustered male and solitary female blossoms on different plants. Water soldier also produces offsets attached to the parent plant on wiry stolons. These can be detached as a means of propagation. Native to Europe and western Siberia, it is hardy, surviving winter conditions by sinking to the bottom of the pond.

Chapter Six

Understanding Bogs and Their Garden Potential

My first visit to a bog was with Linc Foster, doyen of rock gardeners and extraordinarily knowledgeable about our native plants. Located near his home in Falls Village, Connecticut, this bog is privately owned. We had permission to enter and explore this unique habitat. At Linc's suggestion, I wore an old pair of sneakers, and as we ventured into the bog, I found out why — it was impossible to walk without getting my feet wet. Although most of the water in this bog came from rainfall (making it an *ombrogenous peatland*) rather than from surrounding streams or groundwater, it was saturated with water lurking below the surface vegetation; the water was more visible in small, open pools and an inner pond at its center. The dense, thick carpet of sphagnum mosses growing in bogs creates a water-filled sponge. Just as squeezing a kitchen sponge releases the water it contains, walking on the mossy mat frees the water, creating foot-shaped pools and quickly soaking one's feet. Black spruce (*Picea mariana*) was the dominant tree in the Connecticut bog, dwarfed by a parasitic mistletoe. Bog rosemary and bog laurel formed the shrub layer. Buckbean, wild calla, and other, more specialized plants flourished: carnivorous insect-eating plants like northern pitcher plant (*Sarracenia purpurea*) and sundew (*Drosera rotundifolia*), as well as bog orchids, though it was too early in the season for any bloom. This was a very different place from any other wetland — marsh, swamp, or pond — that I had ever seen.

Building a Bog

If you have a healthy natural bog on your property, the best thing you can do is leave it alone. Tampering with a bog — affecting the balance of water in/water out or disturbing the vegetation on any significant level — is deleterious to its continued health and well-being. For those fascinated by the specialized flora of such wetlands, building a bog garden offers an opportunity to cultivate plants that require very specialized

THE BOG

Bogs *are* unique, the consequence of slow-moving, oxygen-poor water, which results in slowed decomposition of dead plants. Slowly moving water does not carry away organic matter, as swifter currents do. As the plants decay, the oxygen in the water is depleted. Since the water is not agitated, the oxygen is not replaced. This can happen where outflow is limited, such as in a basin where there is heavy precipitation during the growing season, where groundwater is close to the surface, and where humidity is high. The incompletely decayed vegetation accumulates, forming the residue that is peat. A bog is the result, perhaps because of a filling-in process. A glacial depression collects water if the groundwater is higher than the bottom of the basin. Algae colonize the water, die, and sink to the bottom. Sedges and other emergent plants grow along the edges; submergent and floating-leaved plants grow in deeper water. In some cases, a floating mat of shoreline growth extends over the open water. Where nutrients are limited, acid-loving plants take hold. In the Northeast, these typically would be trees such as black spruce (*Picea mariana*), Atlantic white cedar (*Chamaecyparis thyoides*), and larch (*Larix laricina*). The most familiar bog shrub is cranberry (*Vaccinium oxycoccos*). Others include bog laurel (*Kalmia poliifolia*), Labrador tea (*Ledum groenlandicum*), leatherleaf (*Chamaedaphne calyculata*), dwarf huckleberry (*Gaylussacia dumosa*), and black crowberry (*Empetrum nigrum*). Sphagnum mosses — and there are up to fifty different species — are the most abundant plant. Herbaceous plants adapted to the nutrient-poor, low-pH, water-logged conditions are typified by carnivorous plants and bog orchids.

Sphagnum mosses die from the bottom and grow from the top. The living portion extends above the water level, while the submerged portion begins to decay, directly contributing to the accumulation of peat. Some species of sphagnum mosses can hold up to twenty-five times their weight in water. Adapted to constant moisture and high humidity, living sphagnum is susceptible to drought: if they dry out, they die. Some species, those that accumulate into dense hummocks, are more tolerant of temporary brief dry spells than other species that grow in thinner, more open mats in constant contact with water.

conditions. It is possible to create these conditions on a small scale in your own backyard. Or, if you want to try just a few plants, you might grow them in containers (see chapter 7, pages 145–146).

A created bog can look appropriate in a garden if it is placed in conjunction with a garden pool. A primary consideration is that it be a sunny site — at least six hours of sunlight daily, although some shade in the middle of the day can reduce evaporative losses. It is equally important to have a source of lime-free, untreated water (well water low in minerals or pond or pool water), as sphagnum is sensitive to alkalinity, chlorinated water, and water containing metal ions or garden chemicals — including insecticides and fertilizers as well as herbicides. Because the most satisfactory growing medium for carnivorous plants and bog orchids is living sphagnum, it follows that your bog must be designed with suitable conditions for the sphagnum. The planting medium for the moss needs to be kept saturated, and there must be sufficient surface area to maintain humidity. Gardeners in the eastern United States or the Pacific Northwest have an easier time maintaining humidity than those living in the arid Southwest (where, at any rate, a bog would be an artificial-looking addition).

These requirements help determine how deep, how long, and how wide the shell of your bog must be. The minimum finished depth is 12 inches; 18 inches is better. The minimum surface area is 10 square feet; larger is better. You might want to consider 12 or 15 square feet as a lower limit.

Excavate for your bog garden as described in techniques for an open water pond (pages 96–97). Line the excavation with a watertight liner or fiberglass pool. You can use an inexpensive child's wading pool, but arrange two nested together, as their thin-walled construction makes them fragile. Install the liner as for the pool. The only exception to those directions is that you must drill a ⅜-inch-diameter hole in the side of the rigid container approximately 6 inches down from the top before you install it. If you are using nested wading pools, run a short length of aquarium tubing through the hole to keep water from leaking between the layers. A length of tubing will also keep the tiny hole through a membrane liner open. This underground drainage hole allows excess water to drain off slowly after a heavy rain, thus preventing flooding. The idea is to keep the sphagnum moist, not submerged. Fasten a small square of plastic window screen over the drain hole to keep the sand substrate from clogging the opening.

Fill the lined excavation to just below the level of the drain hole with coarse silica quartz sand. This material is used by sandblasting companies for paint removal.

Once the sand is in place, fill the remainder of the bog with sphagnum. There are two basic types of sphagnum: coarse, rapidly growing species that are too robust for any herbaceous bog plants other than *Sarracenia,* and more compact, smaller, slower-growing species, which are more desirable. Since sphagnum grows from the top and dies from the bottom, it is important that you orient the strands properly.

Dry baled sphagnum, with long fibrous strands, can be used for the lower layer. (Milled brown sphagnum, the sort used as a soil amendment in gardens, is not suitable.) Before putting the dry sphagnum in place, you must wet it, a slow, tedious process often taking several days. Tie a length of panty hose over the end of the hose to break the force of the water and let it trickle out. Soak the dry sphagnum in its bag or bale before shifting it into the bog. Wet sphagnum is exceedingly heavy, so I suggest you wet it down near the bog site.

A bog garden next to a small manmade pool, with drainage hole kept open with a short length of tubing.

Place the moistened sphagnum on top of the sand, and arrange it to create an uneven surface, with some high/low variation to create hummocks and hollows. Spray the surface with water. When this layer is satisfactorily moist, add the important final layering — a topping with green living sphagnum.

If you have only a limited quantity of live sphagnum, it can be propagated: Force the strands through a coarse screen or, using scissors or garden shears, coarsely cut them up. Scatter the pieces over the surface of the brown sphagnum strands and firmly press them into close contact. If you keep the green sphagnum moist, it should grow, knitting together to fill in and cover the surface. If you wish, landscape the site with the addition of a hollow mossy stump or lichen-covered log.

WATERING YOUR BOG GARDEN

Roberta Case of Michigan described a clever method of using an adjacent pool to water a bog in *The Bulletin of the American Rock Garden Society* (Volume 50, Number 1, Winter 1992). Drill numerous small holes in the sides and bottom of a deep plastic flowerpot wide enough so that you can fit your hand in. Sink the pot into the sand in the corner of the bog garden closest to the pool. Use a short length of garden hose as a permanently installed siphon. Fill the hose with water, stopper both ends, and place the hose in position with both ends below the water level of the pond. When unstoppered, the water flows into the pot and seeps out into the sand, maintaining the water at the same level.

An alternative method uses a soaker hose laid in the fibrous brown sphagnum strands, with the end brought up to the surface. A small piece of narrow, perforated PVC (polyvinyl chloride) pipe on end in a corner of the bog allows you to check the water level easily — stick a wooden dowel in and see how high the water is. As necessary, connect the hose and allow water to seep out and soak in. This is a very gentle method that waters from below rather than sprinkling from above. Be sure to use only untreated water supplied from an artesian well; treated water from a municipal system or a home water softener will kill sphagnum.

BOG MAINTENANCE

The final layer of sphagnum must remain constantly moist but not soggy. If it is too wet, you can always add more fibrous brown sphagnum under the living layer to raise it up. This will need to be done every two or three years as the bog compacts and subsides. Pry up the mat of vegetation at the edges with a long-handled shovel. Stuff a bolster of well-soaked long-fiber sphagnum under the shovel's blade. Withdraw the shovel, and gently pat the living cover into contact with the new material, adjusting the contours as necessary.

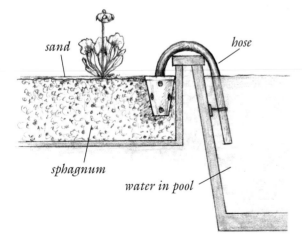

To water your bog garden, siphon water from a small pool into a perforated plastic flowerpot set in the sand of the bog garden.

PLANTING YOUR BOG GARDEN

Be sure to select plants suitable to your climate. Small shrubs from Arctic regions are an excellent choice for bog gardens in cold climates but many of these are unsuitable for mild-winter areas. Carnivorous plants from the coastal plains of the southeastern United States cannot survive bitter weather for extended periods.

Set plants at the same depth they were growing and provide shade for the first few days. If the potting medium is very different from that which occurs in your bog, you might want to remove most of it from around the roots. A soil-based mix in which a willow might be growing would be too different from a sphagnum substrate, for instance. Removing its soil, however, creates more stress on the plant. Where extended freezing weather is normal, a winter mulch of evergreen boughs can shelter plants from desiccating winds and help trap insulating snow.

Responsible Appreciation of Bog Plants

I feel it necessary to emphasize again that bog orchids and carnivorous plants are *not* for the novice or casual gardener. Furthermore, do not rationalize collection from the wild on the ground that the area might be threatened sometime in the future.

It is always better to buy propagated, rather than collected plants. Pragmatically, propagated plants have received better care, have a sturdier root system, and are more likely to survive transplanting shock, grow and thrive in your garden. Ethically, respect for the survival of plants in the wild mandates that concerned gardeners purchase **only** propagated plants. Rare and endangered plants such as bog orchids or carnivorous

A BOG FOR TURTLES

Most people install a bog garden so they can grow the specialized plants that live nowhere else. Jim Warner builds his bogs in Connecticut for his turtles. These outdoor pens, framed in wood and covered, sides and top, with chicken wire to deter raccoons, have wetlands as part of their landscaping. He uses wading pools and says he has no problems with their longevity — in fact, one has been in place for fifteen years. His most recent installation is 8 feet square and 18 inches deep, filled with 36 cubic feet of sphagnum (the measurement of the compressed bales he bought at the nursery). The drain is near the top to allow flushing action in periods of heavy rain. Since the bog is intended as a home for the turtles, he has not used small plants that would be readily damaged. Rather, live sphagnum, cinnamon fern, and some mature sedge tussocks make up the decor. The turtles happily burrow into the moss, come up on the sedge clumps to bask, and in general seem to feel right at home.

plants should not be purchased unless you are **sure** your source is providing propagated plants. When institutions such as the New England Wildflower Society offer insectivorous plants or terrestrial orchids, the plants are almost certain to be propagated. Such sources offer few, and you won't be able to mail-order. Some nurseries offer dozens or hundreds and may provide mail-order service. If prices seem too good to be true, the plants are probably collected, a less expensive means of acquisition for the nursery than propagation. Certainly, hybrid pitcher plants are more likely to be of propagated origin than the species. To the best of my knowledge, those nurseries listed as mail-order sources on pages 173–174 are selling only propagated plants. However, as a responsible consumer, you should check with the nursery before any purchase is made, to be sure that the material is propagated, not wild collected.

Undoubtedly, the best way to enjoy rare plants such as bog orchids and carnivorous plants is to visit some public or privately owned protected bog site.

Small Shrubs for the Bog Garden

Bog rosemary (*Andromeda glaucophylla*) is native to cold peat moors in northern North America. Popular with rock gardeners, it is sometimes available from nurseries that cater to their trade. It has small blue-green evergreen leaves, glaucous on the underside, on thin, twiggy branchlets that reach perhaps 12 to 18 inches tall. It needs full sun, acid, peaty soil, and constant moisture in early spring. It produces clusters of small, plump, bell-shaped pink and white flowers at the tips of the twigs.

Another **bog rosemary (*A. polifolia*)** is very similar in appearance. It is found in sphagnum bogs of north-central Europe, Asia, and North America. The leaves are dark green above and light blue-green beneath. In late spring, each thin twig produces clusters of four or five small, bell-shaped pale pink flowers. It needs a partially sunny site with moist, acid, peaty soil and high humidity. Both species of bog rosemary are hardy in Zones 2 to 6.

∾ DESIGN TIPS. *Bog rosemarys combine well with cranberry, Labrador tea, dwarf birch, and leatherleaf to create a richly textured, low-growing landscape of miniature shrubs and trees.*

Dwarf Arctic willow (*Betula nana*) has a circumpolar distribution, equally at home in the high moors of Europe and in northern Canada, growing naturally with bog rosemary, cranberry, crowberry, cotton grass, sedges, and sundews, among other plants. Like these, it thrives in moist, nutrient-poor, sunny sites, where it makes a dense, twiggy mound of procumbent branches, eventually reaching 20 to 24 inches tall. During the growing season, it clothes itself with small leaves; in winter, it is bare, exposing blackish gray bark on older branches. Outside Arctic or alpine regions, some judicious pruning will improve its appearance; it is overly lush in more clement climates.

Leatherleaf (*Chamaedaphne calyculata* var. *nana*) is another small shrub characteristic of high mountain moors and bogs in northern temperate and Arctic regions. It has small, leathery, evergreen greenish brown leaves on a dense, tight-growing dwarf shrub. In bloom in early spring, small, bell-shaped white flowers dangle near the tips of the arching shoots. Able to grow in Zones 3 to 7, it prefers full sun if temperatures are cool and humidity is high. Where summers are warmer, partial shade is better.

Crowberry (*Empetrum nigrum*) is found in high mountain regions, growing in acid, impoverished, infertile soils where it receives winter snow cover and ample moisture during the growing season. This species is more tolerant of cold than of heat, able to grow in Zones 2 to 6 and going into a terminal decline in regions with hot summers. It has a prostrate habit, making a dense, low, twiggy evergreen mat of needlelike foliage, with branches curved up at the ends.

Its inconspicuous flowers are followed by large, round, glossy black fruits, which give it its common name. In overall appearance it is similar to a heath.

Creeping snowberry (*Gaultheria hispidula*) is a dainty ground cover for cool, shaded, very moist sites. Native to most of northern North America, it is suitable in Zones 4 to 6. In a bog, it scrambles over sphagnum to make sizable carpets of fine stems. The small, urn-shaped white flowers nestle among the tiny (less than 1 inch long), rounded evergreen leaves and are followed by ¼-inch-diameter pure white wintergreen-flavored berries.

Bog laurel (*Kalmia poliifolia*) is a dwarf relative of the more familiar mountain laurel (*K. latifolia*). Native to cold moors and peat bogs of North America from Newfoundland west to British Columbia and south to Pennsylvania, Minnesota, and the Pacific Northwest, it naturally associates with Labrador tea. It is a low, loose-growing shrub about 20 inches tall. The evergreen leaves, about 1½ inches long, are narrow and leathery, with the edges rolled under. They are bluish green above and almost white on the underside. The small rose-purple flowers, ½-inch-diameter miniatures of mountain laurel's blossoms, open in clusters on the tips of branches in late spring. It grows best in infertile, sharply acid, moist soil, in full sun if temperatures are cool and humidity is high; where summers are warmer, partial shade is better. It is useful in Zones 2 to 6. A dwarf variety of bog laurel, *K. poliifolia* var. *microphylla,* grows only 8 inches tall, forming a short, wide mat of foliage.

Labrador tea (*Ledum groenlandicum*) needs full sun and acid, peaty, moist soil. Leathery, narrow, wrinkled medium green evergreen leaves, 1 to 2 inches long, have a dense, rusty indumentum on the lower surface. In late spring and early summer, flat-topped clusters of small white flowers appear at the tips of shoots. The twiggy shrubs grow 2½ feet tall, making them suitable for the large bog garden. Unhappy in hot weather, Labrador tea grows well in Zones 2 to 6. **Wild rosemary (*L. palustre*)** is the Eurasian counterpart of the North American species. Wild rosemary is found on sphagnum hummocks with bog rosemary, cranberry, cotton grass, and sundews.

Twinflower (*Linnaea borealis*) is the one plant Carolus Linnaeus chose to name for himself. It grows in northern coniferous forests, weaving its yard-long prostrate stems among the mosses that carpet the ground. Pairs of small dark green evergreen leaves outfit these runners. In summer, pairs of small, intensely fragrant apple-blossom-pink flowers grow from 2-inch stems at the leaf axils. In more open situations, it grows in tundra, shrubby heaths, and high mountain circumpolar boreal regions. A facultative plant, it rambles over old stumps and logs projecting from the sphagnum mat in cool, shady bogs. It is useful in Zones 2 to 6, perhaps in cooler microclimates in the next warmer zone (Zone 7).

Cranberry (*Vaccinium macrocarpon*) is a native of North America, from Newfoundland to North Carolina, Indiana, and Ohio. The cranberry of Thanksgiving holiday meals, it is evergreen, forming large, flat mats of prostrate trailing vines that root as they spread. Pink flowers appear in early summer, to be followed by ½-inch-diameter, edible red berries. It needs infertile, sandy, peaty, acid, wet conditions and full sun.

Also called **cranberry, *V. oxycoccus,*** is native to Europe, Siberia, northern and central Japan, and North America. It has somewhat smaller fruits than *V. macrocarpon.* Both make a good ground cover for the bog garden, scrambling over sphagnum mats and mossy tree stumps.

Cowberry, lingonberry, or mountain cranberry (*V. vitis-idaea*) is a stoloniferous plant with leathery, oval, glossy evergreen leaves, small white to pink flowers in late spring and early summer, and sealing-wax-red berries. Circumpolar in distribution, it is native to northern Asia, Europe, and North America, and south to British Columbia and Massachusetts. Eurasian varieties, usually referred to as *V. vitisidaea* var. *majus,* grow 8 to 10 inches tall and are somewhat less cold tolerant. They are most useful in Zones 5 and 6, with perhaps a zone each way in protected microclimates. *V. vitisidaea* var. *minor* is the Arctic form, growing half as tall. More cold tolerant, it is useful in Zones 2 to 4 and mild-summer areas of Zones 5 and 6. Slow growing, this is a superb small-scale ground cover.

WILLOWS

Willows (*Salix* spp.). A number of prostrate or shrubby alpine and Arctic willows grow in these unfavorable climates, with their short growing season and cold, windswept stretches. Many of these willows, though low-growing, spread too widely for the limited confines of a bog garden, although pruning will help keep the less rampant within bounds. All want full sun and moist conditions.

❧ DESIGN IDEAS. *Willows' natural association with dwarf birch, leatherleaf, Labrador tea, crowberry, and cranberry suggests similar associations in the garden.*

S. hastata, at 3 to 6 feet tall, is perhaps too large for a bog garden, but it is a very attractive willow that might be considered for an adjacent swampy, wet meadow site next to the bog garden. Native to forest tundra and wet meadows, as well as along swift-flowing streams in circumpolar regions, it forms a well-branched shrub with dark gray twigs and large buds in winter, opening to 1-

to 3-inch-long leaves. Just before the leaves appear, very large ball-shaped catkins open.

S. lanata is native to stream banks and gravel bars from southern Scandinavia to below the polar circle and northern Asia. It makes a low, compact, wide-spreading shrub with densely woolly yellow branches. Even the flower buds are woolly, as are the young leaves, which are gray when they mature. Large golden yellow catkins appear before the leaves.

S. myrsinites is a low-growing upright willow reaching 15 inches tall. Found in swampy, wet, grassy moors and forest tundra sites in the high mountains of Scandinavia and the northern Urals, it makes an attractive addition to the cool-climate bog garden. Short, glossy reddish brown bark on the branches, persistent small oval green leaves, and small, cylindrical catkins with violet anthers before the leaves appear combine to make this an especially decorative species.

S. reticulata, from the high mountains and Arctic regions of Europe, Asia, and North America, has sparse foliage. Its large, round, rough, netted deep green leaves are silvery on the underside. The prostrate branches root down as they grow, creating a large, congested cushion of branches only a few inches high. Its large buds are decorative in winter and dressed with long, narrow catkins at the ends of leafy twigs in spring.

S. serpyllifolia is native to the Alps, where it grows above the timberline in rocky soil with its roots bathed in melting snow. It has short, prostrate branches that make a dense mat of wiry stems. The small yellow catkins appear at the same time as the small, rounded, glossy, dark green leaves. This species is most suitable for moraine conditions.

Bearberry willow (*S. uva-ursi*) is found in subarctic circumpolar regions of North America and Eurasia. A low-growing species, it has bright green lustrous leaves, ¼ to 1 inch long, and upright reddish catkins. Intolerant of heat, it is useful in Zones 1 to 4.

Herbaceous Bog Plants

Some plants suitable for bogs are discussed elsewhere. These include calla lily (*Calla palustris*), cotton grass (*Eriophorum* spp.), golden-club (*Orontium aquaticum*), and sedges (*Carex* spp.) (see index). In addition to these, consider the following typical species.

Goldthread (*Coptis groenlandica*) is an attractive plant, useful for a refined ground cover. Named for its creeping yellow roots, its stems are only a few inches tall, with glossy three-part leaves. In May and June, a few white buttercup-like flowers appear, solitary on slender low stems. Native from Greenland and Manitoba in Canada, south to New Jersey and at higher elevations in North Carolina and Tennessee, it is a plant for cool, shaded conditions where it can scramble over sphagnum mats in bogs or ramble over moss in wet woodlands.

∾ Growing Tips. *Goldthread can be difficult to transplant. When taking cuttings or dividing an existing mat, pot them in an acid, sandy, peaty mix. Keep the plant well watered and shaded until a sturdy root system develops. Remember that it is illegal to dig any plant, even those not necessarily endangered, from public or conservancy land or from private land without the owner's permission.*

Bogbean or buckbean (*Menyanthes trifoliata*) has large, bean-plant-like, three-part, dark green leaves on plants growing 8 to 12 inches above the water. Pink in bud, the short racemes of attractive white flowers are charmingly fringed along the edges of the petals. They appear in May and June. Found in boreal North America south to New Jersey, Virginia, Indiana,

and Missouri, bogbean prefers permanent shallow-water situations in bogs and marshes, but it will grow in up to 12 inches of water, sending its rhizomes creeping through the mucky soil of a pond. It is equally at home in wet mud as in shallow water, so it can be useful in disguising the edges of a bog or pond. It is one of the few plants that has functioning roots deep in the oxygen-deficient peat. Most herbaceous plants have live roots only in the upper, more oxygenated layers. Trees and shrubs like black spruce, northern white cedar, and willows that grow in bogs usually develop adventitious roots in the event the water levels rise.

Yellow-eyed grass (*Xyris* spp.) has a tuft of grasslike basal leaves that is easily overlooked when out of bloom. In summer, a leafless scape 18 inches tall is topped with a tiny pinecone-shaped spike. Small butter-yellow flowers open in the afternoon. Although only one or two flowers are open on each plant at a time and they quickly wither, the sheer number of plants growing together creates an attractive display, shedding a soft yellow haze over bogs, swamps, and wet roadside ditches from July to September. Several species are native to eastern North America: *X. flexuosa* is found from New Jersey south to Florida and west to Texas; *X. montana* occurs from Newfoundland west to Ontario and south to New Jersey and Michigan. These two are difficult to tell apart; it is often necessary to use a hand lens to check the details. Whichever you acquire, plant a group rather than just one or two, and provide wet, mucky, acid soil and full sun for the reward of these sunshine-yellow flowers.

Carnivorous Plants

The concept of plants that trap their food — even when that food consists of small midges, gnats, flies, spiders, and ants — fascinates people. It is one way by which these highly specialized plants have adapted to their nutrient-poor environment: the insects provide nitrogen that the immobile plants cannot wander off to find. Unable to search for insects any more than they can for nutrients, the plants lure insects to them in various ways. Some have a sweet nectarlike aroma, attractive to ants, bees, and flies. Others smell like carrion. Most carnivorous plants are passive hunters. Some, like cobra lily and pitcher plants, have hollow leaves that

A native of the Pacific Northwest, cobra lily (Darlingtonia californica) is an insectivorous plant that traps its prey in specialized, modified leaves.

function as pitfalls, wherein the insects become trapped and drown. Others, like sundews and butterworts, snare the insects with small sticky glands, like tacky-surfaced flypaper. Most fascinating is the active trapping system of Venus's-flytrap. However they hunt, these plants are adapted to low nutrient levels. Do not go out catching flies for them, drop a crumb of raw hamburger into their maw, or even use liquid fertilizers. Such misguided kindness leads to terminal indigestion for the plants.

Because these plants are fascinating, indiscriminate collection from the wild has become a problem. This fact, coupled with habitat destruction, has resulted in serious declines — in some instances, to the point where they have become endangered species. However, in a few instances, some species are being successfully propagated by commercial nurseries. An article by Larry Mellichamp in the March 1986 issue of the *Carnivorous Plant Newsletter* (published by the International Carnivorous Plant Society) discusses commercial propagation of carnivorous plants in Holland. Venus's-flytrap and fifteen varieties of *Sarracenia* were being propagated by tissue culture and then sold wholesale to mostly European and Asian buyers.

Currently, some American nurseries are sources of some propagated insectivorous plants, but you should take necessary care to avoid purchase of wild collected specimens. If you are not sure, ask the nursery *before* you purchase. This can even apply to seeds: The U.S. Fish and Wildlife Service does not permit the distribution of either wild-collected or cultivated seed of *Sarracenia oreophila* or *S. rubra* ssp. *jonesii* (*S. jonesii*) without a special permit.

Pitcher plants (*Sarracenia* spp.). There are about ten species of pitcher plants, and a number of natural and man-made hybrids between the species. These native plants are considered threatened in their natural range, endangered by habitat destruction. I have seen the pitchers of white-topped pitcher plant offered for sale as a cut "flower" in florists' shops in the Northeast. Often collected from the wild, sometimes these varieties are harvested from managed plantations of wild plants. As long as the harvest is kept at sustainable levels, this practice probably will help protect the boggy sites and savannas that might otherwise be drained. Finding a commercial use for what some

NORTH CAROLINA PITCHER PLANTS

When I had the opportunity to visit the Green Swamp, a Nature Conservancy reserve in North Carolina, in 1984, I knew it would be a special place. The diversity of little bog orchids and carnivorous plants was incredible. I found and photographed a superior clump of *Sarracenia*, yet one even better was revealed when I turned around. The occasion was a preconference tour for the annual meeting of the American Rock Garden Society. T. Lawrence Mellichamp, who was leading the busload I was in, seemed to know each and every plant in the area.

For those reluctant to venture unaccompanied into these areas, a visit to the University of North Carolina Botanic Garden at Chapel Hill will provide a more cultivated alternative. Here is re-created a bog that was threatened with destruction. For this undertaking, each piece of sod was numbered, dug in sequence, and replanted in its new home in precisely the same relationship and orientation as it was growing in the wild. Labels make identification a cinch.

At the University of North Carolina Botanic Garden at Charlotte, Dr. Mellichamp is cultivating, in pots, a number of *Sarracenia* hybrids he has created. Eventually, he hopes to select the superior forms, develop a method of propagation in commercial quantities, and make them available to the gardening public.

consider "waste ground" can help to maintain this habitat.

In Europe, the cut pitchers are produced from commercially cultivated plants, primarily raised in Holland. Certainly you can occasionally cut a few from your own plants. Remember, though, that as well as trapping insects, these pitchers are leaves, the chlorophyll factories that help the plants metabolize their nutrients. If you cut too many, you'll do more than spoil the garden landscape — you'll seriously weaken the plant. This is different from trimming spent foliage. Removing dead leaves by cutting them off at the base with scissors, for both appearance and hygiene, is good garden cultural practice.

As well as their bizarre foliage, pitcher plants have lovely flowers — nodding and solitary, one to each tall, upright stem, some over 3 inches in diameter. Five shorter petal-like sepals are fastened above five longer drooping petals, which encircle a curious pistil resembling an upside-down open umbrella. The flowers may be pale sulfur yellow to pink to deep garnet red; some are sweetly scented. They make excellent, long-lasting cut flowers.

Pale pitcher plant (*Sarracenia alata*) is an easily cultivated species with yellow flowers and upright, 2½-foot tall green to reddish pitchers in spring and fall. It is native to southern Alabama, Mississippi, and Louisiana and eastern Texas.

Yellow huntsman's-horn (*S. flava*), native from Virginia to Alabama, is a robust species with large yellow flowers and upright, 3-foot-tall pale green to golden yellow pitchers marked with red veins in spring. It is easy to cultivate and unfussy in its requirements, and it produces its decorative pitchers from spring until late summer. Clear yellow flowers with a faint bittersweet scent appear early in spring. Yellow huntsman's-horn produces phyllodia — thick, flat, irislike leaves — which remain green all winter and into spring.

White-topped pitcher plant (*S. leucophylla*) (color photo, page 134) has sweetly fragrant red flowers. As showy as many flowers, the hood and upper portion of the 3-foot-tall, green to reddish pitchers is white, distinctively veined with pink, crimson, or reddish purple. The pitchers are tremendously variable, with one plant being blotched almost pure white without any veination, the next almost completely red, and every possible combination between. It is native from northwestern Florida and southwestern Georgia west to southern Alabama and Mississippi.

Hooded pitcher plant (*S. minor*), a very common species in the Southeast, is native from North Carolina to Florida. It has yellow flowers and green to reddish pitchers, 9 to 12 inches tall. Its hood so closely covers the mouth of the pitcher that rain cannot enter. Like other pitcher plants, it secretes its own liquid to drown the midges, gnats, and flies that enter the pitcher. These insects mistake translucent spots at the rear of the hood for another opening. Consequently, unable to exit, they are trapped. Plants growing in wet sphagnum bogs, such as the Okefenokee Swamp, are often twice as large as those growing in moist soil.

Green pitcher plant (*S. oreophila*), listed on the Federal Endangered Species list, is known to exist only in a few locations in northeastern Alabama, adjacent Georgia, and North Carolina. A permit is required even for possession of seed.

Parrot pitcher plant (*S. psittacina*) is a very low-growing species with short green or red pitchers only 8 inches long. These pitchers lie flat on the ground, forming a wagon-wheel rosette.

New pitchers are produced all summer long. The sweetly scented flowers are deep red. This species is native from Georgia to Mississippi, where it grows in wet, sandy, low-lying areas subject to periodic flooding. This factor, coupled with its decumbent growth, allows it to trap tiny aquatic insects such as water fleas (*Daphnia* spp.). It also traps more typical insects, like midges and flies, when conditions are drier.

Northern pitcher plant or huntsman's-cup (*S. purpurea*) has the widest distribution and is thus probably the most familiar species, as it is native to the eastern United States and Canada. Readily available, it is probably the best species to start with. The dark red or crimson-maroon pitchers, 12 to 18 inches long, are somewhat lax and lie on the ground, with the open mouth facing upward. Occasional plants lack the anthocyanin pigments and thus are chartreuse shading to pure yellow at the edges of the hood. Northern pitcher plant prefers very wet conditions, usually growing in saturated, sometimes flooded hollows in sphagnum bogs. New pitchers are produced in spring, summer, and fall, with each pitcher lasting a year, sometimes more. Northern pitcher plant has red flowers. It is the most cold tolerant of the pitcher plants, naturally occurring as far north as Labrador. Adaptable, it has even been purposely naturalized in Scotland, Ireland, and Switzerland.

Sweet pitcher plant (*S. rubra*) is the smallest species, with upright olive-green or coppery red pitchers that are veined maroon and grow 6 to 12 inches tall. The small dark red flowers, on stems taller than the pitchers, have a sweet rose or violet fragrance. Sweet pitcher is native from North Carolina to Florida. In the wild, it grows in moist soil together with tall grasses, other herbaceous plants, and even in somewhat shaded scrub communities. It is especially efficient at trapping ants, which are attracted by the nectar it secretes.

The especially rare subspecies *jonesii*, is listed on the Federal Endangered Species register.

Venus's-flytrap (*Dionaea muscipula*) is the only plant in its genus. Like *Sarracenia*, it is considered threatened in its natural range. Native to an extremely limited area, Venus's-flytrap is found growing only in scattered longleaf pine savannas on the coastal plain of southeastern North Carolina and nearby eastern South Carolina. Its natural habitat is thus a half circle bounded by the coast, with Wilmington, North Carolina, at the center of its 150-mile diameter. Unfortunately, I have seen tin cans planted with recently collected flytraps lined up for sale at gasoline stations along the roads in that area. The Green Swamp has been overcollected, even though Venus's-flytrap is protected by state law in North Carolina. In addition to this irresponsible wild collection, loss of habitat is reducing the native populations. Ditching and drainage to dry the land and suppression of fire that clears away the overburden of trees and shrubs, resulting in too much shade for both flytraps and pitcher plants, are equally destructive. It is easy to understand why these are endangered plants.

The highly modified leaves of Venus's-flytrap grow in a rosette. The mechanism is very sophisticated. At the end of each broad petiole is a leaf blade with two lobes, each about 1 inch long. The inner surface is red, and along the outer edge of each lobe are stiff bristles. The inner surface of each lobe has three triangularly spaced hairs that trigger the plant's closing mechanism. If the wind blows the tip of a grass blade over a trigger, nothing happens. But if one trigger is touched twice in a row, or if two of the hairs are touched, the two halves swiftly close, like a clamshell. The pointed bristles on the outer edge of each portion mesh together like the fingers of your clasped hands, and the fly is trapped. In a week to a week and a half, the softer parts of the insect have been dissolved and digested. The trap opens, releasing any hard chitinous parts that remain, and it is ready to be sprung again. On average, a trap can catch and digest three insects before it ages and dies. New traps are produced continuously throughout the growing season.

These flat leaflike petioles and traps are produced in spring. The plants flower from late May through early June, with three to ten attractive five-petaled white flowers on 6- to 18-inch-tall stems that reach above the grasses, sedges, and many native orchids amid which Venus's-flytrap grows. Often leaves produced after the flowering season have a different type of petiole — longer, narrower, and more upright.

Venus's-flytrap is much hardier than its natural range suggests, with some experimental plantings thriving as far north as Pennsylvania and New Jersey. Winter temperatures of 20°F are probably as low as it can take.

∾ GROWING TIPS. *Because the natural habitat of Venus's-flytrap is one with moist, acid, sandy-peaty soils, similar conditions are necessary if they are to thrive in cultivation. In fact, a sand-sphagnum medium is better for Venus's-flytrap than live sphagnum. A winter resting period with complete dormancy is required; without it the plants die. A common cause of failure with the plastic-bubble-encased versions sold as houseplants is the lack of information provided about the need for a dormant period. The seller is at fault for offering endangered plants with precise growing requirements as a houseplant, implying it is as easy as a philodendron. The purchaser is, from ignorance, accepting an endangered plant almost guaranteed to die in short order. If you do buy an unfamiliar plant, whether Venus's-flytrap or tropical orchid, it is only sensible to look for information about its cultural needs **before** it dies.*

Not as large as *Sarracenia*, nor as notorious as Venus's-flytrap, **Sundew or catchfly (*Drosera spp.*)** is a third kind of carnivorous plant. This is nature's flypaper, trapping insects by means of sticky hairs. These glands are usually bright red and tipped with a drop of sweet nectar like a glistening dewdrop. Attracted by the color and secretions, small midges and gnats become stuck on the sticky hairs. The longer-stalked glandular hairs at the edges of the leaf bend over the prey, which is then digested.

In **round-leaved sundew (*D. rotundifolia*)** the leaves very slowly fold over, too, holding the insect even more firmly. These are pretty little plants, with the entire leaf glistening in sunlight and attractive white to rose-pink flowers, five to thirty in a spike. Several northern or high-mountain species have a winter dormancy. Winter-resting buds, called *hibernacula*, form in autumn, and the leaves and even the roots die. In spring, the plant awakens and begins to grow again. Southeastern species do not form hibernacula. Round-leaved sundew (*D. rotundifolia*) sometimes arrives in a bog on its own, arising from seed transported in live sphagnum or as hibernacula. The rosette of spathulate leaves in spring and summer is only 3 to 5 inches across. The flowers, usually white, appear from June to September. This is a very widespread species. In North America, it is native from coast to coast — Alaska, British Columbia, and northern California east to Labrador and Newfoundland and south into the Appalachian Mountains. It is also native in Europe.

Narrow-leaved sundew (*D. linearis*) has elongated leaves, usually held upright rather than wide-spreading like those of round-leaved sundew. Though frequently found in the wild in alkaline marl bogs, it can grow in acid soil. (A marl is a loose or crumbling earthy deposit — sand, silt, or clay — that contains a substantial amount of calcium carbonate.) Native to the southern part of Canada and northern regions of the United States, it is found from the Great Lakes east to Labrador and as far south as Michigan. It usually has white flowers and is another species forming winter hibernacula.

Thread-leaved sundew (*D. filiformis*) has upright, even narrower leaves, 10 to 20 inches long. The smaller plants, which are found from Cape Cod south to the Pine Barrens of New Jersey and occasionally in the southeastern states, have bright red or purple glands. The larger plants, native to the southern coastal plain into southern Mississippi, have green glands. Thread-leaved sundew is adaptable and can grow in sandy, peaty, moist soils. It has pink flowers, which appear in June, and forms winter hibernacula.

❧ GROWING TIPS. *Cultivation of sundew is fairly easy if the smaller-growing varieties of sphagnum are available. Hummock-forming species of sphagnum tend to overgrow the small sundews. In containers, use the same mixture of silica sand, sphagnum, and vermiculite suggested on page {00}.*

California pitcher plant or **cobra lily (*Darlingtonia californica*)** is a demanding, difficult plant to cultivate. Superficially it resembles the more familiar pitchers of *Sarracenia* species. The openings of cobra lily's pitchers all face outward; in Sarracenia, they tend to face the center of the rosette. Like a drooping mustache, cobra lily's two appendages trail down from the outside edge of the opening.

Native from Oregon to northern California, this carnivorous plant grows in coastal bogs and mountain slopes to about 9,000 feet elevation. The pitchers are pale yellow-green shading to darker green at the base, often with some reddish color on the top of the hood if the plants are growing in full sunlight. The hood also has many small, translucent light-admitting patches at the back, misleading insects that prefer not to fly into dark places. This is a plant of spring-fed (geogenous) sphagnum bogs rather than standing-water (ombrotrophic) bogs. In all instances, they seem to be associated with cool, moving water, about 68°F, even growing in peat and gravel seepage bog areas near cool mountain streams. It is this need for cool water at the roots and comfortably cool night temperatures (below 70°F) that makes this plant difficult to grow.

❧ GROWING TIPS. *Plant California pitcher plant in a porous clay pot containing an open, coarse gravel substrate topped with live sphagnum. Flush with lots of cold water (50°F), every day. In summer, keep the plant in a partially shaded site and water two, or even three, times a day. In winter, watering is necessary only once or twice a week. If you cannot provide the daily attention, do not even try this plant.*

Yellow butterwort (*Pinguicula lutea*) is native to the southeastern United States, in the coastal plain from North Carolina to Louisiana. It makes pale green rosettes, 2 to 6 inches across, with sharply inward-rolled leaf margins. As with sundews, small insects that land on the upper surface of the leaves become trapped and are digested and absorbed. Butterworts have such small, stalkless glands that they are practically microscopic. But if you rub your finger over the leaf, it feels slippery and greasy; this is caused by the glands. The buttery yellow flowers — one to a stem but with several stems produced in succession — appear in early spring; they are 1 to 1½ inches across.

❧ GROWING TIPS. *As growth is beginning in spring, full sunlight and ample water are necessary for yellow butterwort. Later in the growing season, the plants should be shaded by taller plants such as grasses and sedges, as strong midday summer sun is harmful. At this time of year, the soil often dries to barely damp. Growing yellow butterwort on a raised mound in a bog garden will help provide less wet conditions than on the flat or in a hollow.*

Bog Orchids

Everything said about the conservation issues that surround carnivorous plants should be doubled for temperate-climate terrestrial orchids. Bill Brumback, Conservation Director of the New England Wildflower Society, wrote me that to his knowledge there are no cultivated sources for *Arethusa*, *Calopogon*, or *Platanthera*.

In fact, the vast majority of temperate terrestrial orchids offered for sale are wild collected plants. If these plants are so threatened that the international community recognizes their endangered status (see box on page 124), how can we rationalize our purchase of any collected from the wild? Sites about to be destroyed for highways, shopping malls, or agriculture are a source for research material. These plants may be propagated and offered for sale by certain botanic gardens or wildflower/native plant societies. Unless you are certain of the propagated source of the orchids you intend to purchase, ethics suggest that you not buy them.

On a positive note, research continues in an attempt to discover how to propagate these plants. Perhaps some day they will become available, appropriately, as commercially propagated plants.

The first important criteria to growing these plants is that you not buy any bog orchids unless you are certain of the propagated source of the plants you intend to purchase. A second consideration is whether you fully understand, and can provide, suitable growing conditions? For example, unless you have previously prepared a suitable boggy home for them, you are wasting your money on their purchase. Unless climatic

THE CONVENTION ON INTERNATIONAL TRADE ON ENDANGERED SPECIES

All orchids are under the Convention on International Trade in Endangered Species of Wild Fauna and Flora (CITES), which regulates international trade in plant and animal species that the signatory nations have agreed are possibly threatened by over-exploitation. A listing in Appendix II limits trade of all species of orchids, cacti, cycads, and certain other plants to levels that the species can support. The trade in some species is so large that it raises concern about long-term survival. Heavily traded Venus's-flytrap was only included in CITES in 1992. The more restrictive Appendix I classification, contains those plants believed to be threatened now with extinction. Green pitcher plant *(Sarracenia oreophila)* is so listed, and only noncommercial trade for research and propagation that will benefit the species' survival in the wild is permited.

This has nothing to do with shipment within the United States, where these plants are native. In the United States, the Endangered Species Act prohibits interstate sale, export, or import, of any plant species listed as endangered or threatened. It also prohibits the collecting of any such plants from federally owned land. A permit can be issued, which authorizes trade in propagated specimens. A second federal law, the Lacey Act, prohibits interstate trade or export, protecting CITES-listed and certain other plants, collected or possesed in violation of the law of the state of origin. *The Gardener's Guide to Plant Conservation* by Nina T. Marshall is a good source of information on whether a plant is likely to be propagated or collected.

conditions in your garden — summer highs and winter lows — are within the acceptable range for the plant, it will die.

At this point in time it is easier to address the second part of the situation. Hopefully, the day will come when the first criterion is also met.

In general, bog orchids may be cultivated under the same conditions as the carnivorous plants, some in sphagnum and others in a sandy bog. Orchids are noncompetitive plants, often found in impoverished conditions where poor nutrient levels limit the jostling by other, more vigorous plants. Certainly this is true for bog orchids. Where they grow, they thrive, but they have a narrow range of acceptable conditions. A few are relatively easy to grow if these conditions

are met, but you must weigh other considerations before you decide to cultivate them.

Ladies'-tresses (*Spiranthes cernua*) is one of our daintiest native orchids. Up to sixty small white flowers are arranged in a tight, multiranked spiral with a fanciful resemblance to braided hair. One of the last orchids, indeed, among the last flowers, to bloom in autumn, it flowers from September to November. It is native in Nova Scotia, Quebec, and Ontario in Canada and across the eastern half of the United States. It may be found in bogs, wet meadows, marshes, and swamps; in peaty, gravelly soil on lakeshores and stream banks; and in saturated drainage ditches. The number of spiraling rows of flowers varies, as does the intensity of its vanilla-like perfume and even its habitat requirements. Some grow in drier, neutral pH sites; others are semiaquatic, preferring wet, acid sphagnum bogs. A plant from a bog is **not** adaptable to drier, circumneutral conditions, and vice versa. Many fleshy roots produce a stem 8 to 20 inches tall with three to six basal leaves. Numerous other species of ladies'-tresses grow in eastern North America, a few in Europe, and one in Japan.

Fragrant ladies'-tresses (*Spiranthes odora*) is sometimes considered a variety of *S. cernua*. One particularly vigorous clone, given the name 'Chadds Ford' has survived in cultivation since the late 1960s. Confusingly, although the clone originated near Bear, Delaware, it was named for an area of southeastern Pennsylvania. It has been successfully grown in gardens, provided it has a moist but not constantly soggy situation. Under

A STORY OF DEVELOPMENT

Two friends and I used to visit a pond in Guilford, Connecticut, each July. Where the road ended, we would park the car and hike in. It was sort of a summer ritual, as we met and companionably rambled through the woods. The pond was not very large, but it sparkled in the sunlight. Dragonflies performed acrobatic aerial maneuvers, bullfrogs provided the bass background for a chorus of smaller, shriller frogs, and typical wetland plants such as buttonbush grew there. It was not a classic sphagnum bog, but on the sandy, gently sloping pond banks grew sundews, yellow star grass (*Xyris* spp.), and numerous rose pogonias (*Pogonia ophioglossoides*). The last time we hiked in, we found a dragline parked in the muddy middle of what used to be the pond, while a large sign proclaimed the opening phases of construction for Pond View Condominiums. All the original inhabitants had been dispossessed. We walked the spoil banks looking for anything to salvage, but it was too late. If notification is received in time, the one compensating factor of a situation might be a rescue operation — with permission.

In happier days, the three of us would stop off to visit a fourth friend in Guilford, the late Howard Porter. He grew a number of rare and difficult plants with such ease that you would have thought them the equivalent of marigolds and impatiens. What always fascinated me was a large cylindrical tank, at least 3 feet in diameter, set on his back terrace. It had a square lid of gray slate, with a circular cutout that matched the dimensions of the tank. The side was concealed behind a freestanding wall of granite blocks. In the tank grew sphagnum and rose pogonia, nothing more. When the three of us would stop by for some refreshment — lemonade or iced tea — more than a hundred of the little rose pogonia orchids would be in bloom. Given the constant moisture and competition-free conditions this orchid required, his original planting had flourished. Few people would be willing to devote that much space and effort to a brief seasonal display of this nature. Howard Porter did, and the memory stays with me.

cool greenhouse conditions this clone can be multiplied rather rapidily. It has been suggested that one stock plant, from an 8-inch-diameter pot, could produce upward of 100 saleable plants in two years. Although I have not seen the results of further studies, the clone is known to self-sow, and approximately 75 seedlings volunteered in the live sphagnum on the top of the pot.

Rose pogonia (*Pogonia ophioglossoides*) (color photo, page 135) is a charming small orchid, quite amenable to cultivation if it is given appropriate growing conditions. Native across most of eastern North America, from Newfoundland to Florida, it is one of the most abundant bog orchids, common in sphagnum bogs, wet meadows, boggy savannas, pocosins (evergreen shrub bogs), sandy lakeshores and pond shores, and even seepage areas such as saturated roadside ditches. Tiny, it grows a scant 3 to 12 inches tall, with one leaf (or, rarely, two) halfway up the stem. Somewhat reminiscent of arethusa, the rose-pink flower has a deeply fringed darker lip with a yellow beard down its center. In the southern portion of its range, the plant blooms in March with two or three flowers; in Connecticut, it bears one or two flowers in midsummer; and in its northern Canadian range, it has solitary flowers in August. It has fibrous roots that grow just beneath the surface, be it sphagnum or sandy, peaty soil. These stoloniferous roots are a significant means of increase, readily producing new plantlets. Their shallow placement also makes this plant very susceptible to drought: it dies rather rapidly when conditions become even briefly dry, more promptly than grass pink, with its underground corm. In cultivation, it thrives in sandy, peaty, acid conditions with a constant supply of water. It seems indifferent to summer heat. A very similar species from Japan is *P. japonica*.

Chapter Seven

WATER GARDENS IN CONTAINERS

The longer I garden, the more I appreciate what plants in containers can do for the landscape. They serve as focal points, adding emphasis to the herbaceous border, terrace, or patio. Brought into more prominent display, the plants gain in importance. Although we often see annuals, bulbs, perennials, conifers, and shrubs grown in this fashion, aquatic and marginal plants are equally suitable for this type of display.

Several good reasons argue growing plants for wet places in containers, not the least of which is abolishing the question of when to water — unlike other plants, you just keep them wet all the time! Perhaps your home has no space for a large-scale garden, only a townhouse patio or apartment terrace; with a container, you can have the water garden you are dreaming about. Perhaps you have always thought water lilies romantic. But your garden is a shaded woodland, without a pond, and definitely not sunny enough to grow water lilies. If you have a sunny terrace or deck, a container can satisfy your craving.

Perhaps there is some plant, like variegated sweet or manna grass, the elegantly striped *Glyceria aquatica* 'Variegata', that is too invasive to turn loose on your property. In a container, it is confined, restrained to a limited area. Or you can fill a container with the precise type of soil needed by some fussy plant. Many choice but difficult bog plants can be cultivated more easily as container plants than in the garden.

In some situations, aquatic plants are, quite simply, more appropriate than an alternative choice. Every in-ground swimming pool in the United States seems to have some decorative planters set on the pool apron to add summer color. Almost always the plants in these containers are geraniums (*Pelargonium* × *cultorum*), drought-tolerant, semi-succulent plants from South Africa. It would be more logical to use plants that strengthen the aquatic connection. Instead of a flash-in-the-pan annual, expand your horticultural horizons and grow papyrus, water canna, or miniature water lily.

If the plants for which you yearn are not hardy under local conditions, try growing crinum or calla lily in containers that can be brought indoors for protection through chilly northern winters. After all, unlike an in-ground garden, containers are portable.

Not all wetland plants are appropriate for container cultivation. Certainly it is obvious that trees, most shrubs, and larger herbaceous perennials can be awkward if not impossible to deal with as container plants. It is important to choose suitable plants, as well as harmonious containers. Remember that even a small water lily suitable for container gardening will need at least a 2-foot-diameter space to spread out its leaves on the water's surface.

Containers for Water Gardens

If the plants need merely moist conditions, use any type of ceramic, clay, or plastic pot. Fill a waterproof saucer and place it beneath the pot to keep the soil wet. Plastic pots work quite well for the plants. Most satisfactory are rigid-sided, sturdy pots of an appropriate size for the plant, but at least 5 inches in diameter. For larger gardens, galvanized stock watering tubs are available from stable supply stores or feed and grain stores. They come in several useful sizes. You could even use an old claw-footed bathtub for a funky, playful display of water plants.

A BRITISH CONTAINER GARDEN

My friend Roger Hammond in England grows water lilies in containers. It is not that he has nowhere else to grow them, for The Magnolias, his small urban Brentwood garden, has two koi ponds that he built, and one of the three glasshouses has an in-ground pool with aquatic plants, turtles, fish, and frogs. It is simply that he finds growing container aquatics an interesting process. And he is not alone in his opinion. When British television's Channel Four "Gardening Club" visited his garden, this was the aspect they chose to film, rather than the magnolias that give the garden its name.

Roger creates these miniature water features in ceramic pots. He first fills the hole at the bottom with fiberglass and other materials sold to repair automobile bodies. He then paints the inside with G4 concrete sealant (an equivalent available in the United States is Drylock double-duty sealer, an oil-base paint with portland cement in it). He plants smaller-growing water lilies, especially selections of *Nymphaea tetragona,* and marginal aquatics to create varied and interesting displays. In honor of his television debut in 1993, he bought "three rather nice Malay pots with dragons, not painted on, but moulded onto the surface in a lighter-coloured clay."

The tropical water lily Nymphaea 'Albert Greenberg' has interesting variegated foliage.

© DENCY KANE

© DEREK FELL

The water lily Nymphaea 'Escarboucle' shares this half-whiskey barrel with water hyacinth (Eichhornia crassipes, p. 143), water lettuce (Pistia stratiotes, p. 44) and duckweed (Lemna minor, p. 144).

More care in selecting containers is necessary when the plants are true aquatics, like water lilies, or they can be grown as facultative aquatics, like the Longwood water cannas. The containers must not only be watertight, but they must be made of material that is able to tolerate constant moisture. Some terra rossa (unglazed, fired clay pots of a brownish orange color) pots will crack if they are kept filled with water over a long period of time, even when temperatures remain above freezing. That is why Roger Hammond paints his with a sealant (see box, page 128).

If the container you select has drainage holes, their presence is not grounds for rejection. With silicone caulking and/or a flexible liner, almost any pot can be made leakproof. Many nurseries like Lilypons that carry aquatic plants and supplies sell 5-foot-square pieces of 20-mil PVC (polyvinyl chloride) or 45-mil rubber liner intended for use as a barrel liner.

PREPARING A HALF WHISKEY BARREL FOR A WATER GARDEN

When you choose a wooden half whiskey barrel, look for one that has been cut in half neatly rather than unevenly. Make sure the bottom is not warped, or the barrel will be unsteady. The hoops should be tight to the barrel.

After you have selected the barrel, you will need to clean and seal it. Brush the outside free of loose dirt and use a wire brush to remove flaking rust from the metal hoops. Paint the metal with a rust-inhibiting enamel. A dark forest green or soft French blue will complement the plants nicely. Next use a marine-quality polyurethane to protect the outside of the barrel staves. This type of finish has inhibitors that protect against breakdown when exposed to ultraviolet rays in sunlight. A matte finish seals the surface without leaving an artificially shiny appearance, as a gloss polyurethane does.

© GAY BAUMGARNER-PHOTO/NATS

A more formal container water garden, with water flowing over the rocks at the back.

The starry white blossoms of hardy white water lily Nymphaea odorata 'Minor' are quite fragrant.

I like to drill a ½- or ¾-inch hole an inch or so down from the rim through one of the widest staves. When it rains, excess water can drain out through this hole, keeping the pool water at a constant level.

The inside of the whiskey barrel will have been charred to age the whiskey that was originally kept in it. Wood shrinks as it dries, however, and your half barrel will not be watertight. To correct this, fill the barrel with water and let it stand, topping it up periodically until the staves have swollen to a tight fit. A side benefit of this filling, soaking, and emptying of water is that you will flush some of the residues left inside the cask. Complete the cleaning by scrubbing the inside with a mild detergent applied with a stiff-bristled brush. Rinse thoroughly. While you are adding and draining off water from the barrel during this cleaning process, do not stress the integrity of the barrel by tipping the container to empty it. This

The air-filled stems of water hyacinth (Eichhornia crassipes, p. 143) give it the buoyancy it needs to float on the top of water.

puts undue pressure on the staves. Instead, use simple physics and atmospheric pressure to siphon off the water. Fill a short length of hose with water by submerging it in the container. Put your thumb over one end and hold it near the bottom. Lift the other end out and place it lower than the bottom of the container. Take your thumb off the submerged end of the hose, and as long as it is under water, it will siphon to the lower level.

Many people prefer to line the half barrel with a flexible membrane to avoid any possibility of toxic residues from the barrel leaching into the water and harming plants or fish. Note that if the half barrel is lined, the staves will again dry out and shrink. In this case, avoid the likelihood of the metal hoops slipping out of place by fastening each band with five screws or short, broad-headed galvanized nails before painting the hoops.

If you use a liner, there are several ways to fasten it to the top of the barrel. One method is to bring the liner up over the rim of the barrel and staple it to the outside about an inch below the rim. The disadvantages of this technique are that the liner degrades when it is exposed to sunlight, and it is not especially attractive. A second method,

caulking

A half-whiskey barrel, with liner stapled to side just below water level. Two rows of silicone aquarium caulking between liner and barrel help seal the top edge.

Most sacred lotus (Nelumbo nucifera) are large stately plants, but some cultivars are available for containers (see pages 106 and 140).

© LARRY MELLICHAMP

© DEREK FELL

The hardy water lily Nymphaea 'James Brydon' (p. 139)
will flower in light shade.

effective but more difficult, is to seal it to the wood just below the rim on the inside. To do this, after the liner is in the barrel, partially fill it with water. At this point, the whole affair will resemble a muffin pan (half barrel) with a cupcake liner (membrane) half filled with batter (water). Run a bead of silicone aquarium caulking in two parallel rows about an inch apart, with the upper band just below where the liner will end. Staple the edge of the liner into place. Trim the liner, then cover the edge and staples with patching or splicing tape sold for seaming or repairing the type liner you are using.

A pint of water weighs 1 pound, a gallon weighs 8 pounds — and a filled half whiskey barrel is a weighty object! Decide where you want it *before* you fill it with water. Remember, for instance, that water lilies prefer full sun, although a few flower with as little as six hours of sunlight. Make sure the container is level. Allow the water in the container to sit for a day or so before planting, to permit it to warm to ambient temperature. If your water is chlorinated, this also allows the chlorine (harmful to fish) to escape.

OTHER TYPES OF CONTAINERS SOLD FOR WATER GARDENS

Nurseries that specialize in aquatic plants and supplies offer high-density polyethylene tubs specifically designed for use as tub gardens. A large tub shown in the Waterford Gardens catalog is 35 inches in diameter and 12 inches deep, with three shelves on which to set plants. It is available in

Pitcher plants (Sarracenia spp.), like these in a half-whiskey barrel, can be groomed at any time. Inset shows leucophylla, p. 120.

Mesh baskets are used to plant water lilies and other aquatics in pools and ponds; the solid containers are for water gardens.

black or terra-cotta. William Tricker, Inc., has a similar large tub that is 34 inches wide by 16 inches deep. These tubs hold approximately 40 gallons of water. Maryland Aquatic Nurseries has several "patio pool garden" planters in terra-cotta–colored plastic. These vary in size from 26 inches wide by 15 inches high to 54 inches wide by 18 inches high, both with a decorative rolled rim. An intermediate-size container with a plain side measures 39 inches wide by 17 inches high. Maryland Aquatic also sells small containers 8 to 10 inches high, but use caution with containers this small, as overheating might be a problem. (Nursery addresses are listed in Mail-Order Sources, pages 173–174.)

PLANTING IN YOUR WATER GARDEN

You have two choices when it comes to planting. Either you can place the soil directly in the bottom of the container and plant directly into it, or you can keep the plants in pots that are submerged in the larger container. I think the second method is better, since it allows flexibility in how deep each individual plant is under water. It is also easier to keep the water clean. If you intend to keep the plants over the winter, it is simpler to move several smaller pots than to shift the more massive containers.

© JUDY GLATTSTEIN

Rose pogonia (Pogonia ophioglossoides, p. 126) is one of the most abundant bog orchids. It is grown here in a container in the late Howard Porter's garden.

Do not use regular potting soil, manure, or compost in potting mixes for water plants, as they tend to increase algal growth. Also, avoid peat moss, which may work its way out of the soil and float around. I like sedge peat. It comes in 40-pound bags and costs only a few dollars. Agway (a chain of farm-oriented garden-supply stores) is usually my best source. Sedge peat is a black, sticky muck, very different from fibrous brown peat moss.

The shelf built into the side of this container, as well as props under individual pots, raise these water plants to whatever level they need to thrive. See text for recommendations for specific plants.

Fertilize at planting time, using specially prepared tablets intended for water plants. If these are not available, use a granular fertilizer with 5–10–5 or 6–10–4 analysis, mixed into the soil before planting. If you use granular fertilizer, be sure the amended soil is in the bottom two-thirds of the container, to reduce nutrient loss to the water. Excess nutrients in the water produce an overabundance of algal growth.

After planting, top off with a ½-inch-thick mulch of small stones or pea gravel. I use traprock, a blue-gray crushed stone generally available at masons supply yards, which can be found in the yellow pages of your phone book. Limestone is too clearly visible and adds alkalinity.

When the container is ready, water your plant thoroughly. With the hose at a trickle or using a watering can with a rose, slowly soak the newly planted pot until water drains out the bottom; this will eliminate air pockets. Lower the pot slowly into the water, gradually enough for any air remaining in the soil to gently dissipate. If you drop the pot in quickly, air bubbles may gush up and blow soil into the water.

Maintenance

As you view your container water garden, notice any maintenance and take care of it. Remove yellowing foliage and old water lily flowers (they will sink under water after three days and should be removed). Fertilize about once a month during the active growing season, as described on page 170. For the most part, just enjoy it.

Fish in Container Gardens

As is mentioned in chapter 8, mosquitoes lay eggs in the water, and fish are the best means of control. Goldfish are more suited to cooler water, and koi need highly oxygenated moving water. Guppies (*Lebistes reticulatus*) or mosquito fish (*Gambusia affinis*) are a better choice for container gardens. Mosquito fish grow up to 3 inches long and have silvery dark-edged scales. Native to the southeastern United States, they range from New Jersey south to Florida and west to Texas. Prolific live breeders, they give birth to as many as two hundred fry every three weeks through the summer. In natural marshes and ponds, mosquito fish are food for other, larger fish, such as sunfish. In containers, the adult mosquito fish eat the fry.

At Jin-dai Botanic Garden in Tokyo water lilies are displayed in exquisite polychrome ceramic pots.

Winter Care

In cold-winter climates, water in the relatively small container used for aboveground water gardens will freeze solid. Hardy water lilies and bog plants should be lifted, trimmed of all foliage, and put in a plastic bag. Set the pots upright in a box, then insulate under, between, and over their tops with buckwheat hulls, straw, or pine needles. Store the box where temperatures will remain cool but will not freeze, such as an attached unheated garage. Tropical water lilies are more demanding. Remove them from their pots, rinse off the soil, and store them in damp sand at 55°F. Some gardeners treat these as annuals and discard them, but I find them too expensive to replace each year. Fish and tropical marginal plants should be kept in an aquarium. The plants may die back somewhat in the lower light levels found in a house.

Before storing your container over the winter, empty it, remove any debris, and use a scrub brush to clean off any algae growing on the sides and bottom. If you have a lined half barrel, use a plastic-net-covered sponge to remove the algae. Unlined half barrels should be refilled with water to prevent wood shrinkage; these can remain outdoors. Other containers should be stored, empty, in a toolshed, garage, or basement.

A Submerged Half Barrel

There is another way to use half barrels in the garden — sink them in the ground as minipools. Although the wood will rot in a few years, you can slow, though not prevent, this deterioration by treating the outside of the barrel with a wood preservative. If the half barrel is to be lined, do so before setting it in place. To install, dig a hole a little larger and deeper than the half barrel, then set the barrel in place using the same care to see that it is level as you would with a larger pool.

Keep the container filled with water to the rim to create a wet soil area adjacent to the minipool. To create a natural transition from the pond to the garden around it, excavate an area approximately 1 foot deep by the side of the container, then let the excavation slope gradually upward away from the container to about a 6-inch depth. Line the excavation with a PVC or rubber membrane, and fill it with a moisture-retentive soil mix. Drill a hole right at the rim-edge

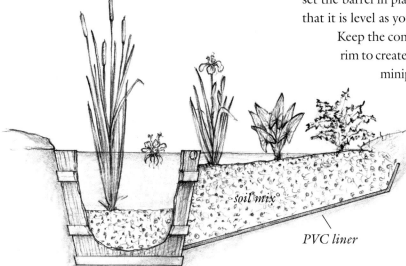

soil mix

PVC liner

For a natural-looking small in-ground container water garden, create a marshy area next to it, sloping up from the pool, lined with PVC liner, filled with soil mix, and planted with wet meadow and marsh plants.

of a stave to allow water to seep into this adjoining marshy area you have created. To plant, select wet meadow and marsh plants that will be in scale with your small pool — swamp milkweed rather than towering Joe-Pye weed, for example.

Planting Container Water Gardens

Contain your enthusiasm, as well as the plants — do not overplant containers. One water lily, a couple of marginal plants, and an oxygenating plant are plenty for a 24-inch-diameter container. If you select only one marginal plant, you can add a floating plant. For containers smaller than 2 feet in diameter, leave out the water lily.

An attractive, cool-looking combination might begin with a miniature water lily with white flowers, such as *Nymphaea tetragona* 'Alba'. The small white-flowered calla lily *(Zantedeschia albomaculata)* has a bonus of silver-spotted leaves, which contrast nicely with the grasslike, green-and-cream-variegated foliage of Japanese sweet flag *(Acorus gramineus* 'Variegatus'). Or, for a sunnier variation, select a yellow water lily, such as 'Helvola' or 'Chromatella', and put it together with yellow-flowered calla lily *(Zantedeschia elliottiana)* and a dwarf papyrus for foliage interest. If blue is your favorite color, some good choices are a dainty blue-flowered water lily, perhaps 'Dauben', together with violet-blue pickerel rush *(Pontederia paniculata)* and monkey flower *(Mimulus ringens)*. Match a soft pink water lily such as 'Pink Opal', with a rosy pink calla lily *(Zantedeschia rehmannii)*; dwarf cattail *(Typha minima)*, with its grasslike foliage and miniature brown poker heads might supply an effective contrast in color. Parrot's-feather is a good choice as an underwater oxygenating plant.

HARDY WATER LILIES FOR CONTAINERS

At the Jin-dai Botanic Garden in Tokyo, I saw beautiful water lilies growing in exquisitely glazed containers. The containers had lovely flowers and leaves painted on a white background, and with the water lilies in blossom, the overall effect of flowers both on and in the containers was especially lovely. (See page 136.)

Naturally, suitable water lilies for container gardens are those that have a relatively restrained habit and mature to a smaller size. The container itself often has a dwarfing effect on the plant. A small water lily grown in the confined space and shallows of a container is often less vigorous than the same species grown in a pond with more room for it to spread out and deeper water. When assessing water lilies for potential container use, a rule of thumb is as follows: their spread is equal to or half again greater than their suitable depth. A plant that typically grows in 12 inches of water, for example, will spread 12 to 18 inches; one growing in 36 inches of water can spread 36 to 48 inches. Obviously, a water lily naturally suited to a 12-inch depth is more appropriate for container cultivation.

Pygmy water lily *(Nymphaea tetragona; N. pygmaea)* is native to eastern Siberia, Manchuria, China, Japan, Korea, India, and North America. The daintiest water lily of all, it has small fragrant flowers and rounded leaves that are green with a red underside and measure only 2 to 5 inches long and 3 to 6 inches wide. It grows best in fairly shallow water, 6 to 12 inches deep. Early in the season, care must be taken to make sure that the water does not overheat; later, the expanding foliage helps shade the surface. 'Alba' has white flowers only an inch in diameter and blooms from June until late autumn. It has small, oval dark green leaves that are purple underneath. It will grow in as little as 6 inches of water. This water lily grows well from seed, or mature plants can be divided in spring. 'Helvola' is arguably the most popular dwarf water lily, with golden yellow flowers nearly 2 inches across. Its small olive-green leaves are heavily mottled with purple and brown and spread up to 16 inches. 'Rubra' has tiny blood-red flowers and rounded purplish green leaves with a reddish underside — still small but larger than the other two cultivars.

The small flowers of N. 'Aurora' change from creamy soft yellow to orange to deep blood red on successive days. The small olive-green leaves are attractively mottled with purple and spread to about 2 feet. It grows in 12 inches of water, and needs full sun to flower well.

N. x *marliacea* 'Chromatella' is a hardy water lily with soft creamy yellow flowers. Relatively restrained in growth, its leaves spread 1 to 2 feet, somewhat less in a confined situation.

N. 'Chrysantha' has small orange-yellow flowers that fade to yellow.

N. 'Gloriosa' is a free-blooming small water lily with very fragrant deep cranberry-red flowers up to 6 inches across. In a pond, the rounded dull bronze leaves spread to 3 feet or more across. In the confined quarters of a large container, the plant will be more dwarfed.

N. 'Graziella' is a free-flowering water lily with small (2 inch diameter) orange-red flowers. Small olive-green leaves are blotched with brown and purple. A good choice for container minipools, it thrives in 10 to 15 inches of water, with tidy foliage spreading 1 to 2½ feet.

N. 'James Brydon' (color photo, page 133) has lovely rose-pink flowers with a deep orange center. It will flower in light shade. The dark, circular leaves normally spread 2 to 4 feet, but will be constrained in a container. It grows well in 9 to 18 inches of water.

N. *odorata* 'Minor' (color photo, page 131) is a smaller-growing cultivar of the species, with fragrant, star-shaped white flowers about 3 inches in diameter. Its soft green leaves are red on the underside, and spread 1 to 2 feet.

N. 'Paul Hariot' has changeable flowers. They open a rich yellow, change to apricot, and then age to a deep orange-red. It grows and flowers well in partial shade. The mottled leaves spread 1 to 2 feet over the surface, less in a confined situation.

N. 'Pink Opal' has small dark pink flowers.

N. 'Sioux' has changeable flowers, on successive days changing from pale yellow through orange to crimson. The dark green leaves are mottled with purple and spread 1 to 2 feet.

N. 'Sulphurea' is a free-blooming yellow-flowered water lily.

TROPICAL WATER LILIES FOR CONTAINERS

Nymphaea 'Colorata' is a day-blooming blue-flowered water lily. Its green leaves cover 1 to 2 feet. It also flowers well in semishade.

N. 'Dauben' ('Daubeniana') is the most suitable tropical water lily for containers, able to grow in a scanty 6 inches of water. Its flowers, which are a lovely soft blue and about 2 inches across, open in the daytime and have a sweet, spicy scent. The speckled leaves spread 1 to 2 feet, less in tight quarters. It is a viviparous water lily, producing new plantlets on the somewhat arrowlike leaves, which are brownish green splashed with chocolate. It flowers well with six hours of sunlight.

N. 'Panama Pacific' is a viviparous water lily with speckled leaves. Its flowers are purplish blue when they first open, then turn a rich reddish purple when they unfold fully. It will bloom in semishade, opening its flowers during the day. Expect it to spread to 1½ to 2½ square feet.

Pond Lilies, Lotuses, and Other Hardy Container Plants

Most species of *Nuphar* and *Nelumbo* are too large, vigorous, and rampant for container gardening. The strong, creeping 4-inch-thick rootstocks of *Nuphar* can reach 6 feet long. The edible rootstocks of *Nelumbo*, thinly sliced and looking rather like a lace doily, are a familiar item in Oriental cuisine. Those discussed here grow best if given a container of their own, perhaps shared only with a submerged oxygenating plant (see pages 144–145).

Yellow pond lily *(Nuphar pumilum)*, native to Asia and Europe, is perhaps the best choice among pond lilies for containers. Smaller than the other species and cultivars, it needs cool conditions with dappled shade and water 18 to 40 inches deep. It has rather dainty leaves only 5 inches in diameter and pale yellow to reddish cuplike flowers in July and August. **Small pond lily *(N. microphyllum)*** occurs in Canada south to New Jersey. It has 2- to 4-inch-long leaves and 1-inch-wide yellow flowers. It is a good choice for regions with cool summers, if you can find it. With coarser, sagittate foliage, *N. japonicum,* is a native of Japan, where it is common in ponds, lakes, and shallow streams. It grows in 1½ to 2½ feet of water, with 2-inch-wide yellow flowers. It has both submerged and floating arrowhead-shaped leaves up to 10 inches long and 3 to 5 inches across at the widest point. Unlike other pond lilies, most of which prefer slowly flowing water, Japanese pond lily thrives in relatively still water. **Arrow-leaf pond lily *(N. sagittifolium)*** is quite similar to the preceding species with leaves three times as long as they are wide, but much coarser in growth.

Sacred lotus *(Nelumbo nucifera)* is a large, stately plant discussed in chapter 5. The best choices for container cultivation are 'Momo Botan', a miniature plant with large, double carmine-red flowers whose leaves range in size from 10 to 18 inches across; 'Pygmaea Alba', a miniature cultivar with leaves standing 12 inches above the water and pure white flowers 4-inches across; and 'Baby Doll', a dwarf lotus with single white flowers.

Fairy water lily, banana plant, or **floating hearts *(Nymphoides aquatica)*** has dainty, fringed white flowers and 6-inch-diameter green leaves. It is native from southern New Jersey to Florida and west to Texas. A different **floating hearts *(N. cordata)*,** with smaller (2½ inch diameter) leaves is native across eastern North America from Newfoundland south to Florida and west to Ontario and Louisiana. A third **floating heart** or **water fringe *(N. peltata)*** native to Europe, Siberia, Japan, and China, has green foliage and small bright yellow flowers from midsummer until early autumn. It has become naturalized in the United States. Catalogs also list **fringed yellow snowflake *(N. crenata)*,** with yellow flowers and rounded, serrated floating leaves, and *N. cristatum,* with red-and-green variegated leaves and small clusters of white flowers. They all can be grown in 12 inches of water in a container, deeper in a pond. Sun or light shade is suitable. Ruthlessly invasive, they can be a problem in a pool and need pruning in a container.

Tender Plants with Floating Leaves for Containers

Water poppy *(Hydrocleys nymphoides)*, from South America, has clusters of large, showy, three-petaled yellow poppylike flowers, 2 to 2½ inches across, which are held above the water. Each flower lasts for only one day, but new ones appear all summer long. The thick green leaves, oval to heart-shaped, float on the surface of the water. Water poppy can also grow as a free-floating aquatic, dangling its roots in the water and not reaching the mud below.

Water snowflake (Nymphoides indica), with 4-inch-diameter leaves that look rather like a pygmy version of a water lily's leaves, is native to the tropics. All summer long, it has delicately fringed star-shaped white flowers up to 1 inch across. **Variegated water snowflake (N. indica 'Variegata')** has fringed yellow flowers and green leaves mottled or spotted with bronze or brown.

HARDY MARGINAL PLANTS FOR CONTAINERS

Numerous grasses, sedges *(Carex* spp.), rushes *(Juncus* spp.), and other grasslike plants, such as sweet flag *(Acorus calamus)*, variegated Japanese sweet flag *(A. gramineus* 'Variegatus'), flowering rush *(Butomus umbellatus)*, various horsetails *(Equisetum* spp.), various irises, and dwarf cattail *(Typha minima)*, are discussed in chapters 1 and 3. Their foliage can lend an attractive accent to container water gardens.

Vigorous, invasive plants like spike rush *(Eleocharis palustris)* can be kept within bounds in a container. Where these plants are used in combination, care must be taken to ensure adequate space for all the plants. One option is to use separate containers for plants with rampant habits. Arrange the containers attractively in a watertight tray. The setting will be most effective and the containers less distracting if the containers are similar in material and style.

Amphibious bistort (Polygonum amphibium) spreads with sufficient vigor to crowd out neighboring plants in a small pond. Where it is contained, its spikes of pink flowers in summer (July through September) are an attractive addition, complementing its floating leaves. It grows in 1 to 4 feet of water.

Plants grown for foliage have an extended period of interest. Consider plants such as astilbe, arrowhead, and pickerel rush, which are attractive both in and out of bloom, as possibilities. Others may have beautiful flowers but offer little other interest. Japanese primrose, for example, is most attractive when it is in bloom, but its coarse foliage, acceptable when combined with other plants in a naturalistic garden, takes up precious room in a small display area. Where space permits, it can be brought out for display and then either planted out into the garden or retired in its pot to a holding area when the flowering period is over. Obviously, plants with an extended period of bloom are more desirable than those that flower only briefly.

TENDER MARGINAL PLANTS FOR CONTAINERS

Water canna (Canna glauca) and the cultivars developed from the species thrive at the water's edge or can be submerged in standing water up to 6 inches deep. In fact, all cannas grow best in moist, humus-rich soil. *C. glauca* and selections made from it have glaucous bluish gray leaves that are over a foot long and relatively narrow (about 4 inches wide). The graceful plants are 4 feet tall. The species has attractive yellow flowers with thin, curved, narrow petals. Dr. Armstrong developed several cultivars at Longwood Gardens with *C. glauca* as one of the parent species. Among these are 'Ra', with yellow flowers; 'Endevor', with vivid red flowers; 'Taney', with bright apricot-orange flowers; and 'Erebus', with salmon-pink flowers. More refined than the leaves of the familiar cannas used as summer bedding annuals, the foliage of water cannas provides a bold and attractive contrast to the narrow linear leaves of sedges, rushes, grasses, cattails, and irises as well as to the lacier patterns of astilbe and ferns.

✎ GROWING TIPS. *At the New York Botanical Garden, water cannas are grown in attractive Malaysian pots, glazed ocher and umber in color with a raised relief of mustard-colored dragons, with a few inches of water above the soil. These are set out around the formal water lily pools in summer and brought into the conservatory with the onset of cool weather. They grow and flower all winter in the warmth and sunlight of the greenhouse. I also bring mine indoors to protect them from freezing, but they go into a holding pattern in the low light available, not flowering until they are moved back outdoors the following summer. Unlike other cannas, their tubers are not usually stored in dormant condition, but this should be possible if you can strike a balance between barely damp conditions and too much moisture, which results in rotting.*

Elephant's-ear *(Colocasia esculenta)* needs an elephant-size container and ample room for its coarse leaves. Other tall plants, such as papyrus, can provide a vertical accent in a narrow space, adding height without a wide-spreading growth pattern. Its tubers can be stored in a dormant condition over the winter.

✎ GROWING TIPS. *The tender bulbs of swamp lily (Crinum americanum) and spider lily, also called ismene (Hymenocallis occidentalis) and the tubers of calla lily (Zantedeschia aethiopica) need protection from freezing temperatures. If they are growing in containers, just bring them indoors for winter protection without disturbing their roots. (They are discussed elsewhere in the book; see the index for entries.)*

Papyrus or **Egyptian paper plant** *(Cyperus papyrus)* has tall, triangular dark green stems topped with numerous long, gracefully arching hairs. Clump forming, it can reach 4 to 5 feet tall. Papyrus grows in moist soil or in up to 4 inches of water. **Dwarf papyrus** *(C. haspan)* is a shorter, more compact plant growing 2 feet tall. **Umbrella plant** *(C. alternifolius* 'Gracilis')* is one of the most popular papyruses, with stems 2 to 2½ feet tall and a somewhat bushier, fuller appearance. It grows best in 2 to 4 inches of water.

Four-leaf water clover *(Marsilea drummondii),* from Australia, has light green cloverlike leaves. In shallow water, it grows erect to about 6 inches; in deeper water, the leaves float or even become happily submerged. **Cut-leaf water clover** *(M. quadrifolia)* has a more ornate leaf. It is hardy to Zone 5.

Water chestnut or **water caltrop** *(Trapa natans)* is actually a tender annual that functions as a perennial by freely self-sowing in warm water. It does this so successfully that it often crowds out native vegetation where it has become naturalized in North America. It has trailing stems with triangular green floating leaves that are mottled bronze-brown and turn red in autumn. In late summer, it has small, insignificant white flowers, followed by large black seeds, each having four sharp spines. **Chinese water chestnut** *(Eleocharis dulcis)* has tall, narrow, cylindrical leaves. In the muck at the bottom of a pond (or rice paddy), white-fleshed, nutlike edible corms with an ebony-black or brown skin form each year.

✎ EDIBLE PLANTS. *Although the large, spiny seeds of Trapa natans are edible, these are not the water chestnuts of Oriental cuisine, which are the corms of Eleocharis dulcis. The latter are referred to as Chinese water chestnuts to differentiate them. They are peeled and eaten raw, or used in stir-fry dishes. If your supermarket has fresh Chinese water chestnuts, plump and firm with no sign of shriveling or mold, you can plant and enjoy them in your container water garden in summer, then harvest and savor them in fall. Once dug, they store poorly; keep them in a container of water and peel just before using.*

FLOATING PLANTS FOR CONTAINERS

Some of these floating plants, such as duckweed, appear in ponds seemingly by magic. In reality, they are carried on the feet and feathers of waterfowl, which transport them from place to place. Shading the water, they moderate the growth of algae by reducing available sunlight. However, these floating plants, especially water fern and duckweed, tend to multiply profusely, spreading to cover the entire surface of the water. In a natural pond, they can be extremely difficult to control, but in containers or a small ornamental pool, the excess can be removed.

Water fern *(Azolla filiculoides)* is an emerald-green fern that forms a delicately textured ½-inch layer on the water's surface. In warm weather, it increases quickly, but it can disappear completely if not protected in winter. Its most intriguing aspect is that it turns a rich red, crimson, and brown in autumn. **Fairy moss *(A. caroliniana)*,** native to North and South America, is similar.

Water hyacinth *(Eichhornia crassipes)* (color photo, pages 129 and 131) is a hazard to water navigation in Florida and other southern states because it forms dense mats that clog boat propellers. The manatee is the only creature that seems to eat water hyacinth, and they are a partial solution to keeping the waterways clear. In an attempt to close the barn door, plants may not be sold across state lines, even to regions where this tender South American plant has no possibility of surviving the winter. Undeniably beautiful, it should be grown only in contained situations or in natural ponds located where cold winter weather is certain to kill it. Fat air-filled stems act as bladderlike water wings to provide buoyancy. Rosettes of cuplike leaves act as sails. The plants drift across the water, their dangling black roots, up to 3 feet long, providing shelter for fish eggs and fry. They increase by means of stolons, which form new rosettes at the ends, these easily break loose to set sail on their own. The 6-inch-high spikes of ten to thirty beautiful blue-violet flowers with gold and blue markings on the upper petals appear in summer. Water hyacinth needs high light intensity and is difficult to winter over indoors in an aquarium. When autumn comes, dispose of the plants in your compost heap.

Frog's-bit *(Hydrocharis morsus-ranae)* is a free-floating species with small (1 inch diameter) water lilylike leaves that grow in rosettes. In summer, it multiplies by means of short, horizontal stolons with new plants at the tips. In autumn, the stolons instead form large buds, which fall off and drop to the bottom of the pond, where they winter over in the mud. In spring, they float back up and begin to grow. Three-lobed white flowers with yellow centers appear in spring, male and female on separate plants. Frog's-bit tolerates partial shade. Its graceful appearance and origins in North Africa belie a robust constitution, as it is also native to Europe and western Siberia.

☙ GROWING TIPS. *You can get a head start on frog's-bit in the following manner. Scoop a few plants out of your outdoor water garden before they disappear for the winter. Put them in a jar of water with a little mud at the bottom, put a lid on it, and refrigerate. Earlier in spring than growth would begin outdoors, remove the lid and put the container on a sunny windowsill. To provide an early start on algae control as the water warms up, set the small leafy plants afloat in a pond as soon as the danger of hard frosts is past.*

Water fern can also be given a head start in this way. If you winter some plants over indoors and then use them to shade the surface, they limit the growth of algae, which otherwise begins before floating plants and submerged aquatics appear in spring.

Duckweed *(Lemna minor)* (color photo, page 129) is a major menace. Tiny green leaves form so thick a scum on the water's surface that people have been known to mistake it for solid land. It is eaten by waterfowl, goldfish and koi, but it out-proliferates their depredations, making new plantlets from old. Whether you purchase it or not, it will probably arrive in your garden as an accidental traveler on the roots or foliage of some other plant. Among the smallest of the world's flowering plants, duckweed has extremely inconspicuous flowers. In winter, the plants sink to the bottom, then float up again in spring.

Water lettuce *(Pistia stratiotes)* (color photo, pages 53 and 129) is a stoloniferous floating plant that forms 6-inch-diameter rosettes of velvety, fan-shaped pale jade-green leaves. Trailing feathery roots, dangling 6 inches down, provide shelter for fish eggs and fry.

OXYGENATING PLANTS FOR CONTAINERS

In the still, confined space of a container, submerged oxygenating plants are especially necessary for healthy fish; they also maintain the clarity of the water. For the fish, these plants add oxygen, more of which is present in moving than in still water and in cold than in warmer water. Neither of these conditions is generally present in a container water garden. As for water clarity, submerged aquatics and floating plants use the nutrients in the water. When there is insufficient plant growth, an overgrowth of algae and cloudy water usually result.

Waterweed or **Canadian pondweed** *[Elodea (Anacharis) canadensis]* is among the best oxygenating plants for pools; it is popular for aquarium use, too. The dense masses of lilylike foliage, grow in whorls of three on brittle stems. Pieces of stem easily break loose and float off to grow downstream. Goldfish eat the leaves, clumps shelter young fish, and all day long the leaves may be observed coated with fine bubbles of oxygen. This is a hardy, vigorous plant. In ponds, it may bloom, with small, three-petaled white flowers rising to the water's surface on threadlike stems. It is considered invasive in natural earth-bottom ponds, where the stems can grow to 5 feet long.

Parrot's-feather, featherfoil, or **water milfoil** *(Myriophyllum aquaticum)* has fine, feathery, bright green threadlike leaves on brittle stems that can grow long enough to form a carpet on the water's surface. In summer, it has tiny red and yellow flowers. Excellent for water purification and useful for spawning fish, it grows in 6 to 30 inches of water. In the evening as light becomes dim, the young leaves at the tops of the stems fold up. To replace any plants that might freeze outside, some cuttings should be wintered over indoors. To avoid unwanted dispersal, dispose of excess plants in your compost heap.

Arrowhead *(Sagittaria* **spp.)** has grasslike juvenile leaves that are well adapted to an underwater existence, especially in flowing water. With maturity or dropping water levels, freestanding arrowhead-shaped leaves appear. **Awl-leaf arrowhead** *(S. subulata)* from both North and South America has simple ribbonlike leaves only 6 inches tall, making it highly suitable for containers and aquariums. **Common arrowhead** *(S. latifolia)* is more suitable as a marginal, emergent aquatic.

Eel grass, tape grass, or **ribbon grass** *(Vallisneria americana)* is an important, common aquarium plant useful in outdoor water gardens. It has rosettes of translucent, pale green, ribbonlike leaves up to 3 feet long; it can grow in shallow water or in water up to 2 feet deep. It forms runners with new plants at the tips. Probably the most common species in aquarium sup ply stores is *V. spiralis,* named for the spiral stem that tethers the female flowers to the plant's base. The free-floating male flowers drift on the surface. After pollination, the stem contracts, pulling the fertilized flower under water, where the seeds ripen. This is a tender plant and must be wintered indoors in an aquarium.

SPECIALTY PLANTS FOR CONTAINERS

Some plants require more commitment than others. When an impatiens, coleus, or geranium dies at summer's end, it is a simple matter to replace it the next year. The decision whether or not to treat a tropical water lily as an annual often has larger budgetary implications, and you are also faced with providing suitable storage conditions. When you decide to grow rare and endangered plants, however, ethical considerations become as important as pragmatic decisions like these. Plants endangered in the wild need habitat protection for their continued survival. Removing any such plant for cursory enjoyment is wrong. At the same time, it is important to learn how to cultivate and propagate these plants. This is not a casual activity to be undertaken by a novice gardener. Orchids and insectivorous plants engender such excitement that it can be the cause of their death. If you decide to grow any of the native plants mentioned, especially endangered plants, be *sure* you obtain material from propagated stock, not wild collected plants, and then only if you can provide the plants with suitable growing conditions and the best care you can. (See also pages 117–126.)

Epipactis, among the easier orchids to cultivate, are less demanding than most of our native species. In fact, one European species, *E. helleborine,* has become widely naturalized in the eastern United States. **Marsh helleborine (E.** *palustris)* is an uncomplicated orchid to grow, something that has long been recognized. William Robinson, author of *The Wild Garden,* published in 1903, wrote, "The marsh *Epipactis palustris* is one of the easiest orchids to cultivate, growing well in an artificial bog or moist border." A creeping rhizome, just below the soil's surface, produces 12- to 18-inch-tall erect stems with prominently veined lanceolate leaves at regular intervals. In summer, ten to twenty reddish brown and pinkish white flowers open in succession, forming a loose, one-sided spray at the top of the stem. Marsh helleborine grows in partial to dense shade, requires bog conditions, and grows best in the company of bog grasses.

To grow marsh helleborine, plant it in a large plastic container, 16 to 24 inches across and 8 to 12 inches deep, to allow sufficient space for the plant community. Use a potting mix of one-quarter to one-third sedge peat, one-quarter composted fir bark, and the balance coarse silica quartz sand to provide a moisture-retentive mix, freely draining to prevent the soil from becoming too sour. Plant marsh helleborine in a natural manner, with its roots spread out horizontally. Plant low-growing, noninvasive bog or marsh grasses with it. Mulch any bare soil with composted fir bark.

After planting, supply moist conditions by keeping the container, which must have a drainage hole, in a watertight saucer. Add water as necessary to keep the soil continually moist but never soggy. Alternatively, use clean, weed-free live sphagnum moss over a sand substrate as a growing medium for this orchid. Take care to arrange the moss with its growing ends up. Get the moss established before you plant the orchid, placing its roots just under the surface of the moss. As living sphagnum must be kept constantly moist, it is important to keep water in the saucer at all times. Use rainwater or well water only. Chlorinated water or use of a water softener will kill or damage the sphagnum, and thus the orchid. Some growers use distilled water; aquarium or lily pool water are other alternatives. Once a week, water the sphagnum from above with distilled water heavily enough to flush out any mineral salts deposited in it. Let it drain. At the same time you water, clean and refill the saucer with fresh water. In winter, keep the plants at close to freezing temperatures (38°F), but do not allow them to freeze.

Like tropical orchids, *Sarracenia* **species** hybridize freely with each other, and the fertile hybrids may be crossed with each other or back to the species. It is an advantage to grow hybrids because these propagated plants have been selected for outstanding ornamental characteristics, such as color and markings of pitchers; production over a longer season; short, sturdy plants that stand up to normal wind and rain out-of-doors; evergreen rather than deciduous plants; and ease of cultivation. This work of hybridization, and the even more difficult task of selection, is in its initial stages. Fred Case in Michigan; T. Lawrence Mellichamp, Associate Professor of Biology and Director of the botanical gardens of the University of North Carolina at Charlotte; and Rob Gardner, curator of carnivorous plants at the North Carolina Botanical Garden in Chapel Hill, North Carolina, are at the same point, I imagine, as when Ahrends and Lemoine began their work with astilbe. Several pitcher plants have received formally published cultivar names:

'Moore's Melody' has a flamboyant wavy hood; 'Friar Tuck' is a diminutive cross of *S. minor* x *purpurea;* 'Carolina Cooler' is red and green; 'Dark Ladies' is a dark red dwarf form of *S. minor.*

Constant moisture is necessary, and plants will be harmed if they dry out for more than a few hours. Fertilization at the roots can kill them. Very dilute liquid fertilizer occasionally can be added to the liquid "soup" in the pitcher, but this is really not necessary, except for immature plants.

Pitcher plants can be grown in live sphagnum moss, as described for marsh helleborine, or in a substitute for the coastal plain soil of the Southeast. Measure by equal volume: one part fine peat (Canadian or German is preferred, as neither has any added fertilizer), one part small-grade perlite, and one part fine, washed silica quartz sand (sold in hardware stores as "play sand" or "sandbox sand"). Mix thoroughly and water until thoroughly wet. Allow the mixture to stand for one to two weeks. Plant pitcher plants individually in appropriate-size plastic pots, 3 to 8 inches depending on the size of the individual plant. For normal growth and best color, keep the pots standing in water, in full sun. Once a week, allow the pots to drain, then flush with distilled water. Freezing does not harm the plants; it does weaken the pots. A winter temperature of 40°F seems to give the plants the necessary chilling/resting period. Plants can be groomed and dead pitchers cut and removed at any time. Division and repotting can be done at any time during the growing season.

Chapter Eight

A Sampling of Water Gardens

A water garden can be quite simple and inexpensive; it can also be elaborate and costly. You may already have water in the form of a pond, stream, marshy woodland, or wet meadow, but if it is not naturally present, you can add water to your landscape. The challenge is to create a water garden that does not look artificial.

My first water garden was the essence of simplicity. I got a deep, single-bowl porcelain kitchen sink from a junkyard. Even though the surface was very worn, I washed it down (wearing rubber gloves and protective eye goggles) with muriatic acid. This cleaning process was to ensure that when I painted it with a couple of coats of black enamel, the paint would adhere firmly to the surface. A rubber stopper, sealed into place with aquarium silicone caulking, made it watertight.

At the edge of a shady bed planted with wildflowers, I dug a hole approximately the width and length of the sink and 8 inches deeper. I spread an 8-inch layer of coarse gravel on the bottom of the hole to serve as a sump, for when it rained and the water overflowed. When I set the former sink in the ground and masked its edges with some small ferns and low trailing ground cover plants, the effect was everything I had hoped for. The dark surface made the water seem much deeper and made the surface more reflective than a lighter color would have. I angled a small weathered branch partially into the water so that any small creature that fell in would have a path out.

After allowing the water to stand for twenty-four hours, then emptying it and repeating this procedure twice more, I felt that any noxious chemicals in the paint were leached out. I bought a few guppies for my pond from the local pet store. Their function was to eat mosquito larvae, which they did quite successfully. They were also very fecund, and when I went to dip them out in autumn (I was too tenderhearted to let them freeze), there were many more than the six I'd started with. With the knowledge that comes with experience, I'd now put in only males, or a couple of small goldfish. I loved my little water garden and, entranced, would stare into it imagining magic springs and forest pools.

Maintenance consisted of siphoning the water off each spring, removing the accumulated debris of autumn leaves, and wiping the basin clean before filling it with fresh water. At about tomato planting time, when the weather was mild and settled, I added the guppies. Because we were on a municipal system and had chlorinated water, I let the newly filled pool stand for a day before doing so.

Several years later, I felt I had outgrown that garden. I couldn't add new plants unless some were removed to make room. Our children were now in middle school and high school, and they were feeling crowded, too. My husband and I discussed what he wanted in a house and I wanted in a garden, and I began my search. Realistically, I wanted more space; I also wanted water, particularly a small brook, but that was not to be. Although the lowest corner of the garden is wet in a year of especially heavy spring rains, our yard cannot readily be characterized as a wetland. The only wetland plants that I have added are those adaptable to average soil conditions, such as false hellebore and royal fern. If I wanted a water garden, I would have to build it myself.

This time I wanted a pool big enough for water lilies, which also meant it would have to be situated in a sunny place. The front of the new property was the only possibility. It slopes from the street to a plateau where the house is situated, and that meant that the pool had to be sited at the toe of the slope. Water flows downhill to seek its own level; it is inconsistent to set a pool at the top of a slope without some rock outcrop or other impervious layer as justification for its placement.

When we had a man with a backhoe come to dig a hole for a new 1,000-gallon oil storage tank in the front lawn, I paid an extra $15 for him to scoop out a hole for my fishpool. My husband came home from work that evening and asked why we had an elephant trap in the front yard. When I murmured, "Fish pool," he pointed out that the soil was very sandy and did not look as though it would retain much water. Nonchalantly, I suggested that he could concrete it. He informed me that concreting the sides is not a simple matter and he was not interested in the process. So we had a hole in the front yard for a couple of years while I thought about things and saved some money.

After considering the different possibilities, I decided to use a preformed fiberglass pool. True, there would be no flexibility of shape as with a liner, but the fiberglass is more puncture resistant, and there are several shapes to choose from.

My first mistake was to order pool, fish, and water lilies simultaneously. The company assured me that the pool would be shipped first and they would wait to hear from me before delivering the fish and water lilies. You guessed it — the plants and fish arrived before the pool. A warning label on the bag of fish cautions the novice that oxygen has been added to the water and once the bags are unsealed, the fish can survive for only a couple of hours before the oxygen dissipates. I drove to the nearest discount store and bought two 30-gallon plastic trash pails. Blessing the fact that we were on a well and the water could be used as it came from the tap, I carefully decanted the fish into their temporary new home, set in a bathtub in case of leaks. The pool was delivered by motor freight a week later, on precisely the day the driveway was being resurfaced.

I began the installation by digging a shelf above the back rim area of the excavation. Here we set several large boulders, too heavy for me to move by myself. They function to keep soil from washing down the slope into the water. They are also aesthetically pleasing and help link the pool to the nearby rock garden. After the rocks were set, I climbed into the excavation and raked and leveled the bottom. I removed any pebble large enough to catch in the tines of the rake, and I excavated and cut out any roots from the adjacent cedar trees. I did not want anything lumpy putting pressure on the pool's bottom.

While bulky and awkward to handle, the pool was not heavy, and my husband and I could maneuver it easily. This was fortunate, as we must have had it in and out of the hole about twenty times. The critical thing with a pool is that it must be level. The water will be level whether its container is or not, so if the container is not level, the pool will always look tilted. When I thought the excavation was prepared, we set the pool in place and poured an inch or so of water in it. Not level, remove the pool, shift some sand, replace the pool. This step was tedious but not arduous.

When the pool was finally level to the satisfaction of my husband, the engineer, it was time to backfill the edges and tamp the soil so it could not shift. Then came the magic moment when the pool was filled for the first time. It looked awful! The raw dirt still showed at the edges; no plants masked the lip of the pool itself. It looked like a black wading pool sunk in the dirt. It needed the plants to settle it into the landscape.

The next day, I planted the water lilies in their brown dishpans — pink 'Rose Arey', yellow 'Chromatella', and white *Nymphaea odorata* 'Minor' — and mulched the containers with dark gravel. Then, after I slowly saturated the soil with the hose at a trickle, I carefully lowered them into place. I caught the goldfish, put them in a bucket, and gently tipped them into comparative freedom. Immediately, things looked better.

I had previously purchased a couple of low trailing shrubs, so *Juniperus procumbens nana* and a ground cover cotoneaster were right there, ready to be planted. They were small (2-gallon size), and the temptation was to plant them so they would overhang the pool right away. Realizing that I needed to allow room for them to grow, however, I set them sufficiently far away from the edge, even though it made the planting look skimpy. For the first couple of years, I used trailing herbaceous plants, both perennial and annual, to disguise the bare spots.

That summer (and every summer since), the pool mesmerized me. I caught some bullfrog tadpoles at a nearby pond, not realizing the adults would come and take up residence on their own. Dragonflies skimmed the surface, and water boatmen skated like demented whirligigs. Then autumn came.

The pool is 9.3 feet long by 8 feet wide by 17 inches deep. When we first installed it, there was no electricity to the pool and thus no way of using a stock tank heater to keep a small area of surface free of ice. (Besides, my husband pointed out that because we were heating our house with wood to conserve energy, it was contradictory to use electricity to keep a bunch of fish comfortable. If I could find a stove to burn under water, he'd split wood for the fish, too.) I thought the fish could make it. That was a very cold winter, and the ice froze 14 inches thick. I know, because I frequently went out and used an awl-like tool and a small maul to make a hole in the ice to provide for a carbon dioxide/oxygen exchange. I could not just whale away at the ice: water is a noncompressible medium, and shock waves traveling through it harm the fish.

The fish died. It was not the cold. Perhaps one fish died, and then the process of decay, sealed under the ice, consumed the oxygen needed by the remaining fish. Or maybe it was the debris at the bottom, again using up even the scanty amount of oxygen needed by the sluggish fish in winter. In the years since that experience, come October I drain the pool partway down, catch the fish, and move them indoors to a 55-gallon aquarium for the winter. We enjoy watching them perform their aquatic ballet. In spring, I move them outdoors again.

There have been surprises. Like the autumn following the summer when heavy growth of underwater plants hid infant goldfish. That year, I brought in seven adults and fifty-two babies. Most springs, there will be one or two adults that by maneuvers evaded the net the autumn before and have come through the winter unscathed. Obviously, one or two fish can survive where greater numbers cannot.

The "shoreline" plants have grown, and the juniper is about the same dimensions as the pool. The hardy water lilies grow so well that every three or four years, they require separating. The fish (I've been selecting for calico and pure white ones) add to the enchantment. All in all, this is one of the most satisfactory parts of my garden. Children and adults alike home in on it. Birds come down to get a drink; a frog sits solemnly on a lily pad; big and little dragonflies dart about. Even in winter, when snow softens the landscape and I look at the boulders, juniper, and ice, it continues to provide pleasure.

There is more to the story of my water garden: one year my husband and children gave me a waterfall for my birthday. We buried the wires and kept it safe with a ground fault interrupter. The pump sits in the bottom of the pool, and at the flick of a switch, water comes trickling over the rocks a foot or so above the pool, gurgling as it moves to the lower level. When I installed the fountain, I spent delightful hours standing in the pool arranging and rearranging those rocks, fish nibbling at my legs.

There are many other water gardens with stories worth telling. Some gardens, like mine, are created. Others resulted from the enhancement of natural sites. They are suburban, urban, rural. What they have in common is the satisfaction they provide for all who see them, owner and visitor alike.

Shady Stream with Marshy Borders

Dick Redfield and his brother Herb are both retired now, able to devote even more time to gardening than before. Theirs is a garden in the rural community of Scotland, Connecticut. They began planting the water garden, which consists of a stream winding through the low area of the garden with marshy borders, in 1975. The factor that most influenced them to do so was the natural terrain, which in Dick's words "almost demanded it." At its peak in spring, from mid-April until early July, the garden requires little maintenance. Some summer and autumn weeding and trimming are all that is necessary. Only very occasionally is there a problem, and primarily it consists of flooding in periods of very heavy rain. The aspect of their garden that seems to attract the most comment from visitors is the integration of exotic plants such as Japanese primrose (*Primula japonica*) and Welch poppy (*Meconopsis cambrica*) with the existing native flora. Native wildflowers include marsh marigold (*Caltha palustris*), skunk cabbage (*Symplocarpus foetidus*), cardinal flower (*Lobelia cardinalis*), blue lobelia (*L. siphilitica*), and many ferns. Most of the native plants already grew on the site naturally and were encouraged to thrive and spread. Others were raised from seed or were gifts from friends. Many of the plants naturally self-sow. The only one that has been extensively propagated is the exotic Japanese primrose. It is commercially available from seed-raised plants. By now the Redfields' plants are doing so well that they supply seeds each year to a wholesale nursery.

When the garden is in bloom from mid-May to mid-June, it provides a major display and is a favorite with visitors. When I asked Dick which plant was a particular favorite, he promptly replied, "All of them. If a favorite must be chosen, perhaps it would be *Primula japonica.*"

About the only problem they have in their garden overall is deer, which in the past few years have become serious pests. Otherwise, they share the water garden with fish, frogs, salamanders, and dragonflies. The garden provides a place to wander or sit and enjoy the natural beauty and serenity, a place for the two men to share with their friends and visitors from distant places who share their love of nature.

An Artificial Waterfall

When Midge Riggs and her husband moved to suburban Hastings-on-Hudson, New York, in 1986, their third of an acre contained not only a house but also a waterfall. Hoisted by a ½-horse-power electric pump, the cataract tumbles over mossy rocks down a steep natural cliff to a pool at its base. Adjacent to the pool is a deck just off the house. The pool was excavated by a bulldozer, and then lined with concrete poured on-site.

Midge says that maintenance of the pool consists of cleaning out debris such as fallen leaves. The only problems are worms, which seem to be fatally attracted, crawl in, and die, and mosquitoes. She cannot add fish to the pool because they would be sucked up by the pump. And when it is hot, the dogs climb into the pool to cool off. Midge confesses that she does not run the pump constantly — in general, only when there are visitors, as it is the waterfall that attracts the most comment from visitors.

The garden sustains its display not by deliberate propagation or purchase of additional plants, but through the self-seeding of plantings at the top of the waterfall, replacing trailing clumps of *Campanula poscharskyana* and arabis. Midge introduced ferns by wedging pieces of soft tufa mix into the cracks so the plants could take hold. (Tufa is a porous deposit of calcium carbonate, or a manmade, porous, rocklike substance consisting of peat and cement.) Frogs and dragonflies arrived on their own and are now part of the ambience. For Midge, the waterfall and pool garden provide peace, a place outside her hectic daily routine as a genetics counselor, a place where she "can just sit and relax for a long time and listen to the water."

A Pond and a Bog and Another Bog

Morris West and Nick Klise have complex careers — Morris as a microbiologist and Nick as a designer. Their rural 10-acre property in Brouge, Pennsylvania, currently has approximately 4 acres of garden. Their wish to grow bog and water plants led to the construction of a pond. The stream on their property made an appropriate site for such a water garden. A backhoe was used to excavate the pond area, and it was lined with several layers of 3-mil polyethylene (membrane liners were not readily available when the pond was constructed in 1982). Maintenance is simple, including the usual removal of leaves, debris,

THE WEST-KLISE PLANTS

POND
Dwarf water lily cultivar	*Nymphaea pygmaea*
Arrowhead	*Sagittaria latifolia*
Water poppy	*Hydrocleys nymphoides*
Bamboo sedge	*Dulichium arundinaceum*

BOGS
Acorus	*Acorus gramineus* 'Ogon'
Acorus	*A. gramineus* 'Variegatus'
Marsh marigold	*Caltha palustris*
Bottle gentian	*Gentiana andrewsii*
Swamp pink	*Helonias bullata*
Japanese iris	*Iris ensata*
Iris	*I. graminea*
Siberian iris	*I. sibirica*
Cardinal flower	*Lobelia cardinalis*
Great blue lobelia	*L. siphilitica*
Monkey flower	*Mimulus guttatus*
Golden-club	*Orontium aquaticum*
Japanese primrose	*Primula japonica*
Meadow beauty	*Rhexia virginica*
Globeflower	*Trollius laxus*
Pitcher plant	*Sarracenia purpurea*
Nodding ladies'-tresses	*Spiranthes cernua*
Bog rosemary	*Andromeda polifolia*
Andromeda	*A. polifolia* var. *glaucophylla*

Visitors are fascinated with the naturalistic appearance of the pond, insisting that it must have originated from natural sources. The success of the pond led to the creation of a bog in 1985. That flourished, so they built a second bog in 1989. One bog is their own creation; the other involved the use of a backhoe to dig a hole into which a concrete casket liner was placed to retain the water.

Some of the plants were already present on-site; others were gifts from friends or raised from seed. Purchased plants came from Siskiyou Rare Plant Nursery in Medford, Oregon; We-Du Nursery in Marion, North Carolina; and Wicklein Aquatic Gardens in Baltimore, Maryland.

Morris and Nick propagate many of their plants. Bottle gentian, both species of lobelia, primroses, *Rhexia virginica*, pitcher plant, and *Trollius laxus* are propagated by seed. *Mimulus guttatus* is propagated through cuttings, and both species of *Acorus*, swamp pink, all the irises, water lilies, *Trollius laxus*, and arrowhead are propagated by division.

They introduced fish and tadpoles, while salamanders and dragonflies found the water gardens on their own. Occasionally snakes eat a frog; snakes, raccoons, and feral cats are probably also responsible for the disappearance of fish.

Like all the gardens on their property, the pond and bogs are attractive garden features that provide the unique habitats necessary for nurturing plants that need or prefer water, constant moisture, and/or acid soil. For skilled gardeners, such challenges exist in order to be met.

and excess vegetation, especially with such invasive plants as the two species of *Acorus,* both lobelias, Japanese primrose (*Primula japonica*), and water poppy (*Hydrocleys nymphoides*). There is sufficient water loss that the pond may require replenishment as often as twice a week in high summer. This may be due to evaporation as much as leakage.

Fresh Kills Reclamation

Not too many of us can say that we "garden" on 2,400 acres. Bill Young, landscape architect and project manager for the Fresh Kills Landfill on Staten Island, began working on this project in 1987. Creeks already present on the site influenced the shape of the landfill, which includes estuarine tidal creeks, freshwater ponds, palustrine wetlands, and ephemeral (seasonal) wetlands. The ponds look great in early summer, says Bill, because more wildlife is using them at that time. And he likes the creeks when they are under the influence of the moon tide.

Several wet sites were already in existence when Bill arrived at the landfill. Under his guidance, and with the help of other people who contributed to this project, four or five wetland sites were created. Others who were involved include: Andropogon Associates of Philadelphia, which helped on numerous projects (not necessarily related to water); Sven Hoeger of Creative Habitat of White Plains, New York, who designed the first two tidal wetlands; and Richard Lynch of the Staten Island Native Plant Center, who helped on the first native reclamations. Serendipitously, one pond was even created by accident, when a culvert that was installed for a road they were building allowed tidal water in but not back out.

Always, the projects were done with additional help, some in-house and some involving outside professionals. For example, a contractor graded and planted the "dunes" site, which has two ponds. Those ponds are on a modified landfill cap of compacted glacial till and a spillway of riprap. Bill admits that it could probably use some maintenance, but there is no funding or personnel. Nothing was ever deliberately planted in the two ponds. Nature brought in cattail, rushes, sedges, and phragmites. A major problem comes from the phragmites, as both ponds are shallow and nearly dry up at times. A meadow was seeded around the ponds, using switchgrass plugs, little bluestem, black-eyed Susan, and asters. The two tidal wetland plantings were done with prairie cordgrass (*Spartina alterniflora*).

The plugs were obtained from Dale Hendricks of North Creek Nursery in Pennsylvania; the spartina was contract-grown by Creative Habitat; and the seed mix came from Stock Seed Farms in Murdock, Nebraska. "We cannot afford to get too fussy about any plants," Bill says. "We're doing a large-scale reclamation. They [the plants] have got to hold their own, or they do not belong."

Bill was not really sure that the Fresh Kills project fit within the scope of *Waterscaping*. He said that, as it relates to wetlands, the project seemed to engender "mostly chagrin from the engineers who detest ponds on landfill caps. Mostly delight from others, especially when the ducks are there." For himself, he says, "I get a feeling of wonderment that these wet areas exist on a landfill. They support a surprising diversity of wildlife. The resiliency of nature manifested at Fresh Kills inspires me."

Small Pond, Waterfall, and Tiny Bog

I have not bothered to figure out how many times Ken Druse's Brooklyn, New York, garden would fit into Fresh Kills. A typical 20-foot by 50-foot city lot might seem minuscule—unless you have Ken's imagination. A garden author and photographer, he crams more plants than I would ever have believed possible into the fenced confines of the garden hidden behind his Brooklyn brownstone.

He began his water garden in the spring of 1987, assisted by some friends. One friend, for instance, helped lay the electrical line; another watched from an upper floor of the house next door, offering advice on positioning and placement; still a third helped smooth the flexible PVC (polyvinyl chloride) liner into place from inside the empty pool — definitely a two-person job, says Ken. He did use some concrete, poured on-site, to hold the rock edge for the pool and the rocks for the waterfall, as well as to form a concrete basin for the waterfall reservoir.

About the only regular maintenance necessary is cleaning the filter. Originally, the pond was perfectly balanced with plants and fish. But then the eight koi began to grow. So the filter was added. In the third year, a second filter had to be added to handle the ever-growing load. This was a biological, rather than a mechanical, filter. The pump needed replacement in the fifth year. Periodically, water needs to be added, to replace evaporative losses and also because surrounding plants sometimes send roots into the water and start to drain the pool.

One year Ken thought there was a leak in the pool's liner, as the water was going down by several gallons each day. Finally he realized the problem was caused by the watercress he had tossed into the top of the waterfall, started from a bunch bought at the greengrocer. The watercress actually sucked water up through the roots and out through the leaves, in a natural process of transpiration. And he had a problem with duckweed (*Lemna* spp.), which arrives as some innocent-looking green pinheads that seem inevitably included with a shipment of plants from any water garden nursery and then grow to develop a solid blanket that looks sturdy enough to walk on.

Some of the original plants are still there. Others have departed. In some instances, this has occurred through the browsing habits of the koi. They eat nearly all plants with floating leaves, such as water lilies and water clover (*Marsilea mutica*), and will also pull them out of their pots. Ken can grow only those plants that can tolerate having the rims of their pots above the water line, such as umbrella plant (*Cyperus alternifolius*) and pickerel rush (*Pontederia cordata*). Narrow-leaved cattail and zebra rush add elegant linear foliage.

An incredibly wide variety of plants which enjoy moist soil are grown next to the pool, especially in an area which is wick-fed with water from the pool: *Acorus gramineus* 'Variegatus'; marsh marigold (*Caltha palustris*), buttonbush (*Cephalanthus occidentalis*), variegated sweetgrass (*Glyceria aquatica* 'Variegata'), yellow flag (*Iris pseudacorus*), cardinal flower (*Lobelia cardinalis*), *Rodgersia tabularis*, and more. Two tender plants enhance the display: elephant ear (*Colocasia esculenta*) and calla lily (*Zantedeschia aethiopica*).

In Ken's words, "Nothing brings life to the garden like a water feature. Besides the light that is reflected from the water, there is the sound of the waterfall — especially welcome in an urban setting. The fish are a constant amusement and bring joy. During the growing seasons, most of my garden is obscured by plant growth. In winter, the pond is in full view from the windows of my house, and the fish are fantastic to see. When my little Eden is covered with snow, the koi are spectacular."

A Nature Center's Water Garden

The Nature Center in New Canaan, Connecticut, is well-known for its commitment as an environmental education facility. With programs directed at both children and adults, this is very much an organization focused on teaching the general public about their natural surroundings. There is a two-story solar-heated greenhouse and classroom space developed with modern technology. Deciduous forest, meadow, and several wetlands are part of the property, which includes a red maple swamp, a cattail marsh, and two large constructed earth-bottom ponds, with trails and boardwalks allowing ready access.

It seems appropriate to the Center's environmental concern and focus on nature study that the staff created the Naturalists' Garden adjacent to the main building. The garden contains two water features — an 8-foot-by-24-foot figure-eight still pond constructed in the spring of 1991 and a 4-foot-by-10-foot four-part waterfall pond built in August of that year. These water features are an important part of the design, intended to provide a living and breeding habitat for a variety of plants and animals and to highlight the visual beauty and musical sounds of the water.

The water gardens have different attractive features from April through October. In spring, breeding amphibians — frogs and salamanders — are night visitors. In summer, the diversity of wetland plants in flower and eye-catching insects like dragonflies are the best features. And in autumn, the pond surfaces capture the colors of nearby foliage.

The pond designs are the work of Lisa Beebe, New Canaan Nature Center greenhouse manager, and a landscape designer. The details of the pond and waterfall construction were worked out by Richard Haley, assistant director of the Nature Center. Peter Falcione of The Norwalk Aquarium in Norwalk, Connecticut, provided professional advice on materials and construction. These are created ponds, sitting above the local water table. The actual construction work — digging, lining excavations with a cushioning protective layer of used carpet liner and carpet remnants, and lining the two ponds with 30-mil PVC liners manufactured by the Tetra Company — was done by staff and volunteers.

The aquatic and emergent plants are grown mainly in pots. Among these are American lotus *(Nelumbo lutea);* water lily *(Nymphaea virginalis),* which was chosen for its beautiful flowers, as was pickerel rush *(Pontederia cordata);* arrowhead *(Sagittaria cordata);* blue flag iris *(Iris versicolor);* and miniature cattail *(Typha minima).* Floating plants include water hyacinth *(Eichhornia crassipes)* and water lettuce *(Pistia stratiotes).* The ponds contain cabomba *(Cabomba caroliniana)* as a submerged oxygenating plant. Planted in the moist soil adjacent to the ponds is yellow flag iris *(Iris pseudacorus).* Some plants were relocated from elsewhere on the property; others were purchased from Waterford Gardens in Saddle River, New Jersey.

Maintenance is minimal — some manual removal of algae in late spring and occasionally replenishment of evaporative losses in hot, dry weather. There is also a problem with the edging rocks, as some are unstable and easily knocked into the pools by children. To correct this, the edges will be redug and the stones reseated. Both Lisa Beebe and Richard Haley agree that children are most attracted to the frogs and turtles. Adults are captivated by the waterfall, commenting on its soothing quality and the serenity it lends to the garden as a whole.

As is appropriate for a nature center, the fish of choice is the native bluegill, some of which were introduced from other local ponds. Painted turtles also were brought in, but they have disappeared. It is uncertain whether they left on their own or were taken. Bullfrogs, green frogs, gray tree frogs, spring peepers, and American toads all moved in on their own, and several now breed in the ponds. Dragonflies, damselflies, water striders, and other invertebrates moved in on their own, too, and were also introduced when some bottom muck from another pond was brought in. Recently a great blue heron has eaten a few of the frogs, but, say the naturalists, that is what they are supposed to do.

The ponds function as a live exhibit for some of the nature center's classes. Children spend time watching all the animals that live in and around the water. Adults come to the garden to paint or sketch, picnic, or just sit. Though only a few years old, the ponds are highly successful on many levels, providing both habitat for small wildlife and pleasure for visitors of all ages.

An Elaborate Pool and Waterfall

Water gardens can be simple — designed, built, and planted by the homeowner. They can also be more luxurious, with the final result the effort of professionals. Just such a garden is that of Beth and Bruce Becker of Ridgefield, Connecticut. A serious gardener, Beth wanted to enhance their 1-acre lot with moving water, the only thing she felt lacking on their scenic property overlooking a lake and their suburban town. The first water garden was built in 1988, the effort of a landscape architect who suggested a stream with a series of waterfalls around the perimeter of the property. No plans were actually drawn up, and the concept was conveyed orally to the mason contractor who did the work. It was unsuccessful.

When Glen Gate Company of Wilton, Connecticut, was subsequently consulted, Joe Scott, Jr., president and conceptual designer, realized that they could not salvage any of the previous work. The structure, as designed, would not survive winter weather. It was also out of scale and competed with the existing natural features, including the view.

Together with Mark Hoffman, the firm's landscape designer, Joe Scott drew up a new design for the structural, mechanical, and stonework design. After approval by the Beckers, construction was begun. They then built the reinforced concrete structure and the plumbing system. Under Joe's supervision, a crew consisting of a mason, his helper, a crane operator, a backhoe operator, and one trained laborer took several weeks to do the stonework. The introduced rocks were laid in strata to match the preexisting ledge and give a totally natural look. The primary waterfall stone is a single flat slab discovered by Glen Gate in an old Connecticut stone wall and set aside for just such a special use. It is 18 feet long and 18 inches thick, and it weighs 14 tons. The masons, using Carborundum blades on a power saw, cut a sluiceway in it, as there was no natural channel to function as such. Rocks were used within the pond itself; to allow for maintenance (for example, to clean the pond and for the fun of getting close to feed the fish), to create a sense of rock tumbled down off the ledge, and to interrupt an otherwise too-perfect shoreline.

The pool itself was built of reinforced Gunite (shotcrete), given a finish coat of dark gray marble plaster. Small, flat rocks were placed on the floor to enhance the natural look. A manifold was created with PVC valves to offer twenty different options for controlling the water flows to various points of the water feature and its falls. These vary from small rivulets trickling over the stones all the way up to a thunderous cataract.

Maintenance is simple. A fine fibrous mulch is used on the planting beds to help hold back siltation into the water. This reduces but does not eliminate early spring cleanup of winter debris and erosion into the system. In summer, hand-pruning and hand-trimming also reduce the debris and litter that would otherwise fall into the water. The recirculating system needs to be protected against winter freeze-up, but the pool remains full of water year-round. (Once they tried to keep the waterfalls running into December. A sudden snowstorm and power loss caused a frantic winterization of the system.) The ribbon grass that they planted is invasive and needs to be controlled; slugs (which thrive in moist conditions) seem to have no preferences — they go after all the herbaceous plants. And unless particular care is taken to aim the lawnmower's discharge chute in the other direction, grass clippings get into the water. Raccoons were a problem, but an area on the side of the cliff was developed into a feeding station. The raccoons seem happy with that and stay away from the water garden.

The waterscape is in full view to anyone entering or exiting the front door. The waterfall and its primary stone attract the most comment from visitors, but the design is definitely a garden, with foliage, texture, and color accents used to blend it into the landscape. Stonecrop *(Sedum ellacombianum)* and *Sedum* 'Lemon Drop' fill crevices and niches, softening the edge, while grasses at the water's edge provide a shoreline effect, shifting and swaying in the breeze in contrast to the static rocks and conifers. Astilbe, especially the cultivar 'Peach Blossom', with soft pink plumes of flowers in summer, Siberian iris, and ferns add to the wetland appearance. Using a Japanese design technique, a weeping Norway spruce was planted, mimicking the visual effect of cascading water. Azaleas are used to conceal portions of the water feature, creating a feeling of discovery, as viewers cannot see the design in its entirety from any single point, any one angle.

Hemlocks and laurels were planted, receding back into the natural surroundings to integrate the design into the landscape. Less-than-perfect laurels were deliberately chosen to match the existing ones and avoid a landscaped appearance. A grassy slope comes down to the water's edge, both allowing access and mimicking the natural process: water at the lowest part of the land.

The garden awakens in April, as bulbs begin to bloom. At season's end, as leaves drop in October, the ruggedness of the outcrop is heightened. In winter, conifers — bird's nest spruce, weeping hemlock, weeping Norway spruce, and evergreen Kurume azalea — provide a foliage backbone, accenting the garden paths and replicating the cascading water and rugged rocks. Running myrtle *(Vinca minor)* becomes more evident in winter, as its tidy foliage forms an evergreen carpet of ground cover.

This is a complex project, which interrupts its surroundings as little as possible to fold the water garden back into the landscape. Its natural look successfully adds a water feature to the property while avoiding any sense of artificiality.

Vernal Pool

Probably the most frustrating and difficult water garden situations are those where water is present only some of the time. This is the case with Sydney Eddison's Newtown, Connecticut, vernal pool. From November through June, the site is naturally wet. Then decreasing moisture shrinks the brook and dries the pool completely. Sydney does not have enough water to supplement rainfall and so is required by dictates of nature to cope with the situation in a natural manner. Yet for all the difficulties it presents, no part of her garden means as much to her as the 170 x 60 foot woodland garden and its trickle of a stream.

Development of this garden began with the stream near the border of her semirural property on the last day of April in 1979, when she built a little wall along the trickle that goes into the old pond behind the barn. (That pond is itself a construction — scooped out by previous owners who were deceived by spring freshets into thinking a swimming hole was possible; instead, it dries to a summer mud wallow.) All the while, Sydney kept thinking of the fun she and her younger brother Hugh used to have as children, playing in the brook on their parents' property in Woodbury. Nostalgia — and the fun of playing in water — was the impetus for this waterscape.

In a site as exacting as this, plants must be chosen in part by trial and error. For instance, plants at the edge of the pond are often submerged for considerable periods during cold weather, for standing water in winter is a major problem with this site. Linc Foster, noted plantsman and rock gardener, thought that Japanese iris (*Iris ensata*) would tolerate these conditions and gave her some seedlings to try. They could not take it and died.

When I walk around the garden with Sydney in spring and see the diversity of plants in vigorous growth, I understand how a determined, knowledgeable gardener can meet and surmount such a challenge. At the pond's edge are marsh marigold (*Caltha palustris*), cardinal flower (*Lobelia cardinalis*), great blue lobelia (*L. siphilitica*), *Ligularia dentata, Rodgersia sambucifolia,* and *R. tabularis,* Japanese primrose (*Primula japonica*), and other candelabra primroses such as *P. beesiana, P. bulleyana,* and *P. pulverulenta.* The primroses must be those that flower by mid-May, as after that it is too shady for good bloom. *P. florindae,* which flowers later than Japanese primrose, just languishes in the shade. Shrubs that tolerate wet feet — summer-sweet (*Clethra alnifolia*), black alder (*Ilex verticillata*), and swamp azalea (*Rhododendron viscosum*) — thrive on the pond's edge.

In the adjacent woodland garden — moist but not inundated in spring — grow cinnamon fern (*Osmunda cinnamonea*), interrupted fern (*O. claytonia*), and royal fern (*O. regalis*), ostrich fern (*Matteuccia struthiopteris*), shield fern (*Dryopteris* spp.), and several others. Jack-in-the-pulpit (*Arisaema*), goatsbeard (*Aruncus dioicus*), foxglove (*Digitalis purpurea*), bottle gentian (*Gentiana clausa*), Siberian iris (*Iris sibirica*), Virginia bluebells (*Mertensia virginica*), violets (*Viola* spp.), and more create a wonderful tapestry of spring flowers and summer foliage.

Many birds visit the woodland garden in spring, in part because the Eddison property is adjacent to 800 acres of state forest and a nearby lake. The candelabra primroses attract hummingbirds. In early spring, the pond is home to hundreds of vociferous green frogs. As the pond recedes, they depart and mosquitoes arrive. There are snakes and an occasional spotted turtle. Deer are kept at bay with an electric fence.

Maintenance is minimal and consists of mowing or string-trimming the foliage around the empty pond in late autumn so that the weed stalks do not rise above the water in spring. Fallen leaves naturally mulch the plants, with occasional help from Sydney. A thorough weeding once a year is the goal, intended to keep perennial weeds under control. Annual jewelweed is deemed rather harmless, providing additional shade for the primroses. The paths are edged with small logs, and these need periodic replacement as they rot out. And unless the self-sown infant Japanese primroses are mulched with evergreen boughs in winter, there are significant losses. The small rosettes have very shallow roots, which are pulled from the earth when the waterlogged soil rises up as it freezes.

Older plants withstand winters more successfully. Some especially vigorous plants, like celandine poppy *(Stylophorum diphyllum)*, are a problem, self-sowing into the smaller, choicer primroses and overwhelming them. The same can be said for the spreading tendencies of goldenseal *Hydrastis canadensis;* it is welcome as a ground cover but must be kept in control. An excess of dying bulb foliage (snowdrops in this instance) is not good for other plants. Even tough, sturdy creeping phlox *(Phlox stolonifera)* dies out in patches where the deliquescent bulb foliage smothers it.

Those plants that do well are the basis for the next step. A skilled gardener and author, Sydney explains, "I have by no means sorted out the warring factions. Nor, alas, do I have the energy to tear things up and start again. No part of the garden means as much to me as the woodland garden and its trickle of a stream. I suppose it is a combination of childhood memories and a feeling that my roots go deep into uncultivated Connecticut. If I could no longer keep up this part of the garden, it would be all right. It was a secret before I found it. The possibilities were always there, but they might not have been discovered by someone else. It's mine, but by its very nature, on loan. A wild garden puts your tenure in perspective."

A Postscript

As we have seen, waterscapes come in a diversity of styles and sizes. Simple or elaborate, sunny or shady, permanent or seasonal, each offers a unique challenge and a special opportunity to be playful and at the same time create magic in the garden.

Chapter Nine

PLANTING AND CARING FOR WATER GARDENS

*N*o garden of any kind is finished when it is installed. For that matter, gardens are never installed precisely as designed. There are always what might be termed field adjustments, necessary accommodations to preexisting conditions that were not anticipated on paper.

Certainly one major factor that influences a garden is time — plants grow, plants die, tastes change, and new plants are added to replace others that are no longer as desirable as they once were. In one sense, this is still design, as it affects the appearance of the garden, yet we tend to call this work maintenance, regarding it as an entirely different aspect. Although it may not be as concentrated an effort as the original layout and installation, the two processes are really part of the same whole. Without the design, there would be no garden to maintain; without maintenance, there would be no garden to admire.

Caring for Plants in Wet Soil

There are a few special considerations when dealing with plants for wet meadows, marshes, and swamps. Wetland soils are fragile, subject to compaction. If the area is extensive enough that a path is necessary, a boardwalk or viewing platform might be a good idea. As well as protecting the soil, it will allow you to walk through your garden and enjoy it without getting your feet wet.

A garden in wet places differs from one with "average" moisture in that most of the time you do not dig over the entire bed before planting. Such digging is destructive to wetland soils. Furthermore, where you are introducing plants to enhance an existing plant community, this is unnecessary.

In general, planting techniques are the same, but the presence of water adds some constraints. Extreme caution is necessary when herbicides or insecticides are used in, or even near, wetlands. This may even be a regulated activity. Fertilizers can also be a problem, leading to eutrophication — the accelerated aging of ponds. Fertilizers can become ground-water contaminants. (This happened on Long Island, where agricultural production, particularly of potatoes, allowed fertilizers and other chemicals to seep through the sandy soil and left water unfit to drink.) Restrict, or even better, eliminate your use of fertilizers, insecticides, and herbicides in or near wetlands. If such constraints appear extreme or intrusive, just consider, would you want toxic chemicals to enter the water supply that comes into your home?

Emergent and Wet Meadow Plants

Plant containerized emergent plants such as cattail, arrowhead, sweet flag and irises in an artificial pool using the same method as described for water lilies (pages 167–168). Pot in either open-sided containers, plastic buckets, or plastic flowerpots or in sturdy nursery containers. Adjust the size of the container to the vigor of the plant: dainty dwarf Japanese cattail *(Typha minima)* does not need the depth that the larger cattails require. Use a heavy loam, top with gravel, and water before lowering the container into shallow water. Plant only one kind of plant in each container.

During the growing season, trim any unsightly yellowing foliage and remove spent flowers, the same as you would for perennials in the herbaceous border. Some marginal aquatic plants spread very quickly beyond their allotted space. When they are confined in a container, their reduced vigor results in poor growth, and the plants produce few flowers. In early spring, remove overgrown plants from their containers and divide them. Plants can be split, or a chunk can be carved off. Repot only as much as you need and dispose of the rest.

Preparing Nursery Stock for Wet Sites

Don Knezick of Pinelands Nursery in New Jersey is a wholesale supplier of trees, shrubs, and herbaceous wetland plants. He maintains his stock ready to plant into a mitigation site or for stream bank stabilization. Some plants are maintained under heavy irrigation; others are grown in holding beds edged with railroad ties and lined with black plastic. The potted plants are kept constantly saturated with water standing in these temporary shallow pools. This is not the usual case for adaptable facultative wetland plants that can be grown in a herbaceous border as well as in wet sites. Plants like yellow flag iris, for instance, are not usually available prepared for truly wet conditions.

More typically, nurseries offer plants grown under "normal" conditions. These plants, used to growing with average moisture conditions, develop root rot if suddenly immersed in water. They need a period of adjustment, much as you would harden off tender plants in the spring to acclimate them to outdoor conditions. In this instance, you want to adapt the plant roots to saturated soil.

Set the container in a sturdy plastic saucer. One that is 24 inches in diameter and 3 inches deep will hold six or seven pots of various sizes. Water the plants thoroughly. In a day or two or three, depending on the weather, water the pots again before the soil dries out. In another day or two, add an inch of water to the saucer. Before it can evaporate, add more. In this manner, the plants gradually adjust to saturated soil. Now they are ready to be potted in their planting containers and set in the pool or planted in a wet soil location.

OTHER TECHNIQUES

Hardy marginal aquatic plants can also be planted directly into the mucky soil along a pond shore, in a marsh, or near a stream. Wear rubber boots and, if it is early in the season, rubber gloves as well. Cold, wet hands become numb and make it difficult to handle the plants. Use smaller plants, remembering that many of these, such as arrowhead, cattail, mint, and rushes, spread quickly by means of stoloniferous roots. Scrape a hole with a trowel or narrow-bladed shovel and set the plants in place. Use your feet to push the soil over the roots.

One interesting technique where erosion may be a problem makes use of coconut fiber. This method is used by Pinelands Nursery and by Sven Hoeger of Creative Habitat Corporation in White Plains, New York. The coconut fiber is available as long rolls, called Biologs or Fiber-Schines. They are about 12 inches in diameter and up to 20 feet in length. The rolls are staked into place at the bottom of a bank, partway into the water. Any soil coming down the bank becomes trapped in the sturdy fibers, while water, cleansed of silt, percolates through. Actively growing herbaceous facultative wetland plants, usually in 2-inch-diameter peat pots, are plugged into the Fiber-Schine. If planted in spring, the plants root into the bank within two weeks. They fill in and provide good cover within three months.

The coconut fiber is also available as a blanket. This has tremendous potential. The mats are laid into a holding bed made from railroad ties. Lined with plastic to create temporary pools, the mat can be kept constantly wet with an inch or two of standing water. Seedlings or plugs are

inserted into the fiber. Within a period of several weeks to three months, depending on the season, the plant carpet is ready for installation. It is loosely rolled up, put in a plastic bag to keep it wet, delivered to the site, unrolled, and pinned into place. Within a single growing season, a disturbed site has a new cover.

PROPAGATING EMERGENT AND WET MEADOW PLANTS

Many of these herbaceous plants are easy to propagate from seed: blue flag and yellow flag iris, pickerel rush, cattail, swamp milkweed, and various sedges. Duck potato also is easy from seed, as it produces a small almond-size tuber in one year. Some are easier to propagate by division: sweet flag, marsh marigold, soft rush, bogbean, arrow arum. Most home gardeners propagate tender marginal plants by division, which is how they usually increase their water lilies. Cultivars of iris, or named forms of marsh marigold, must be propagated by division to produce plants that are identical to those with which one began. Some plants that grow readily from seed can also be increased by division, including arrowhead and pickerel rush.

PLANTING AND MAINTAINING TREES AND SHRUBS

Think how messy it must be driving down a highway with a wet truckload of 4-foot-tall catalpa, silver maple, black gum, and sweet gum; 3-foot swamp white oak; and some smaller Atlantic white cedar, winterberry, and swamp azalea, draining and dripping as you go. (To get some of the excess water drained off, let them sit on a pallet for an hour or two, if possible.) Even pin oak, available at many nurseries, will take the transition to a wet site more smoothly if it has been preadapted to wet soil. Although you might wish for ease of planting without needing to adapt the woody plants first, it is necessary.

Plant adapted trees within a day or two, if possible; otherwise you must provide alternative means of keeping the root balls wet. Trees and shrubs adapted to saturated conditions begin to show signs of stress in as little as three days, especially under sunny, breezy conditions.

Trees and shrubs do better if moved as balled-and-burlapped specimens or container-grown plants. Certain trees, especially birch, maple, magnolia, and holly, do best if planted early in spring, before they begin to leaf out.

When you prepare the site, remember that in nature, the landscape, even in a wetland, is not absolutely flat — only the surface of a pond or lake is level. Think of a winterberry swamp in the Northeast, with sedge tussocks supporting the growth of deciduous hollies and herbaceous plants such as cinnamon and interrupted ferns. Just as there are these swales and hollows in a marsh or swamp, you can create similar depressions in the garden, with corresponding high spots. Trees and shrubs planted on such berms will get better drainage. They can have the constant moisture the site provides by reaching their roots down to it rather than sitting in a puddle.

There are alternative methods for planting shrubs as erosion control, but timing is critical. Certain shrubs root very easily from branches. Anyone who ever picked or bought a bunch of daffodils and some pussy willows in spring understands: the pussy willows root and send out leaves almost before the daffodils are ready for disposal. Sandbar willows behave similarly, an adaptation that allows them to survive the shifting sand and gravel rearranged by the river.

Pinelands Nursery has a 5-acre cutting block just to propagate these quick-rooting species. In 1989, stock plants of pussy willow, black willow, and silky dogwood, useful for this technique, were planted. After they were established, the main stems were cut back to within 1 or 2 feet of the soil in early spring. The plant's response is to produce long whiplike shoots. This technique, called *stooling*, is traditionally used to produce long, pliable willow withes for basketry. In early March, before the buds begin to open, long, straight lengths of this juvenile wood are cut and tied into bundles, called *fascines*. Within twenty-four hours, they are planted on eroded banks in the following manner: A shallow trench is dug parallel to the watercourse. A bundle is laid in the trench, and some soil is kicked over the shoots. If the bank is badly scarred and space permits, another row or two are installed uphill in the same manner. This is not intended as window dressing, for aesthetics. The primary goal is to stabilize a site. It also has high wildlife value, providing good nesting cover for birds, shelter for small mammals, and browse for deer; in addition, shaded watercourses are more attractive to fish.

Brush layering on steeper sites is accomplished by laying the bundles at right angles to the watercourse. A layer of riprap forms the base. Some soil is scattered over the stones, and brush bundles are placed over it, with their butts uphill and their tips toward the water. Another layer of soil is laid down, then more brush bundles, staggered to avoid placing them directly over the plants on the row below. The final layer of soil is covered with a straw mulch to slow erosion.

Still a third technique uses the whips as living stakes, installed individually with a vertical orientation. It goes more quickly with several people; even children can help, making this a suitable school or scout project. First make a planting tool from a metal bar or pipe, with a short horizontal handle fastened at one end. Weld a spike to the other end and, about 12 to 18 inches away, a short plate at right angles to the shaft. Drop the spike to the ground, step on the foot bar while you push down on the handle. Wiggle it back and forth to make an opening, then go on to the next spot. Someone follows behind, dropping a cutting into the hole — butt down, shoot up. A third person shoves some dirt in the hole. Respectable numbers can be planted in a very short time with this technique, especially if you trade off positions to avoid fatigue from boredom.

There are two drawbacks to this project. One is the limited availability of the long, whiplike juvenile growth necessary if the cuttings are to root quickly. The other is the speed necessary to handle the material. It is important that planting follow cutting within twenty-four hours. If some delay comes up, you can gain one, or possibly two, days (if it is still cool and early in the season) by mulching with straw and wetting it down.

IMPROVING THE WATER-HOLDING CAPACITY OF SOIL: POLYMERS

Traditionally, gardeners are told to add organic matter (including peat moss) as a soil amendment to improve the water-holding capacity of their soil. This is adequate for more conventional herbaceous plants that need that mystical sounding "moist but well-drained" condition that gardening books advise, but it is not enough for many wetland species. Help exists if you want to grow plants like wet meadow and marsh plants, which may be used in water-retentive sites created with an impervious liner. These are happiest with constantly moist conditions but not necessarily standing water. Assistance also comes in the form of special polymers.

Soil-treatment polymers are particles of superabsorbent polyacrylamide polymers. One of these is sold under the brandname Terra-Sorb. It is important that the product you use is a *polyacrylamide,* which is designed to absorb and release water repeatedly. (Some products on the market are *polyacrylates;* these are used in disposable baby diapers and only absorb liquids.) The sugarlike crystals of polyacrylamide absorb many times their weight in water, with precise amounts depending on the salt content of the water.

The manufacturer recommends 1 pound of Terra-Sorb per 300 square feet of surface for each 2-inch depth of soil, or 150 pounds per acre. Don't use too much, or it will come bubbling out of the ground like frog spit as it expands.

To use, thoroughly mix the dry crystals with the soil. One ounce of crystals will soak up 1 gallon of water; 1 pound of crystals will absorb 25 to 40 gallons of water, expanding from their sugarlike dry state into clear, translucent ¼- to ⅜-inch gel particles. Drench the soil thoroughly, wait an hour, and soak it again.

Where Terra-Sorb is used in a small area, such as when planting individual trees and shrubs, mix half the dry crystals you estimate you need throughout the planting hole and use the remaining half to amend the backfill. Suggested rates are 6 ounces for 3-inch-caliper balled-and-burlapped trees and 1 pound for 6-inch-caliper specimens. It takes woody plants at least a couple of weeks to attach their roots to the gel particles, so you will have to water during that period. After that, watering will be required less frequently. The manufacturers claim that the particles last for four or five years, simply because this is a relatively new product and tests for longer periods do not exist; probably it has a longer effective period. It is a plastic and thus does not biodegrade.

Terra-Sorb is sold in small 3-ounce packets, as well as in 4- and 10-pound jugs and 55-pound containers. The granules are available in three different sizes: up to 1.0 mm, for use as a soil amendment for small container-grown plants and as a bare-root treatment (small plants are dipped into a slurry of expanded gel particles before planting); 1.0 to 1.5 mm as a soil amendment in potting mixes; and 1.0 to 3.0 mm as a soil amendment in large containers and when transplanting trees and shrubs.

I have used it as an amendment in half whiskey barrels, adding 6 ounces of the coarsest grade mixed with the soil for a 24-inch-diameter container. For bulk soil preparation, the suggested application rate is 2 pounds per cubic yard of mix. Smaller containers for individual plants would have their soil amended with 1/3 ounce for a 1-gallon pot, 1/2 ounce for a 2-gallon pot, and 1-ounce for a 5-gallon pail.

For individual containers, even half barrels, it is easier to mix the polyacrylamide crystals with the soil if they are expanded first. Dump the required amount in a large pail and add water.

Wait an hour, see if more water is needed; add it and again wait an hour. The gel particles should make a loose slurry, neither tightly packed nor with free water over the surface. Blend with barely moist potting mix. Use about 15 percent gel to 85 percent potting mix, or one part gel to six parts potting mix. Fine soil particles will coat the individual gel pieces, separating them from each other, like flouring blueberries before adding them to muffin batter. After filling the containers with the amended mix, set your plant and water.

Remember, this material does not eliminate watering. The polymers retain water that would normally drain from the soil, eliminating fluctuations in moisture level.

Planting and Maintaining Aquatics

In general, it is advisable to plant and transplant aquatic and emergent plants in spring and early summer. This allows the plants to become established and develop strong roots to support new leaf growth before they begin to flower. Variation in actual planting dates depends first on geographic location; for example, water lilies for a pool in Florida can be planted earlier than those for a pool in Maine. It also depends on whether the particular plant is hardy or tender. Hardy water lilies can be planted earlier than tropical water lilies — in late April or early May in Connecticut and in mid- to late May in Denver. Tropical water lilies are set out when the water temperature reaches, and maintains, 70°F. Hardy emergents like yellow flag iris can remain out all winter, their pot sitting in the pool. In cold-winter areas, tender water canna may be moved outdoors only when the weather is mild and settled.

Using a Container to Set Plants in Your Pond or Pool

In lined constructed pools, water lilies are planted in containers placed at the appropriate depth. One advantage of this technique is that the level of the container can be adjusted with the season: propped up on blocks or bricks to bring it near the surface when growth is just beginning in spring, lowered so that 6 to 12 inches of water covers the container, and lowered again to the bottom of the pool for winter protection. (If you have used a flexible membrane, pad them at the point of contact to be certain you don't damage it with bricks or blocks.) The depth of water over the container in summer is dependent on the variety of water lily. Some dwarf varieties require less; other vigorous cultivars and species need more. In general, the most vigorous water lilies are planted either in the large display pools of public parks and gardens or directly in the soil of a large earth-bottom pond. Remember, too, that water filters sunlight, and if your pool is in a partially shaded site, submerged plants should have less water over the container.

Planting in containers has other advantages. It is easier to remove the plants to propagate them. And in the case of vigorous, spreading, invasive plants, growing them in containers controls their spread.

Nurseries specializing in aquatic plants sell containers designed for planting water lilies and other aquatic plants. These look like small plastic laundry baskets or milk crates with lattice sides. Line these containers with natural burlap before planting, to keep the potting mix from spilling through the coarse openings. Instead of the containers manufactured for the purpose, I have used plastic dishpans from a discount store. Their drawback is that after a couple of years, the water lilies have made so much root growth that the roots appear over the top of the containers and wave in the water, indicating that it is time to lift and divide the plants. I have heard that pressed-pulp containers work well, but I wonder what happens when you try to lift the container out of the pool in a few years to separate an overgrown plant. Soil and water are heavy, and I can easily envision the container breaking from my grasp and falling back into the pool, dumping mud into the water.

Whatever type container you use, choose a brown or black one. It will be less noticeable.

In this small manufactured pool, container-grown aquatics can be raised and lowered seasonally to provide appropriate conditions. They can also be easily removed for propagation.

Turquoise or any other light color is glaringly obvious.

For most hardy water lilies, a container 15 inches in diameter and about 9 inches deep, providing a little over 1 cubic foot of root-growing space, is the minimum suitable size. The more vigorous tropical water lilies need a larger container — one 19 inches in diameter provides a little over 1½ cubic feet of space. Larger containers produce more vigorous growth, greater spread of foliage over the surface, and a longer interval between division.

Do not use soil from a natural pond bottom in containers. It is likely to have seeds or root pieces of vigorous native weeds, or even eggs of insects harmful to your pool fish. Avoid manure, compost, or other similar organic matter, which can foul the water in the pool. I use Michigan sedge peat, a heavy, fine-textured black muck peat. If this is unavailable, sterilized topsoil will do. Mix a handful of 5-10-5 fertilizer with the soil in the lower half of the container. Fill the container with soil to within 1 inch of the top.

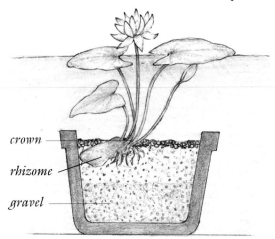

crown

rhizome

gravel

The thick rhizome of a hardy water lily should be placed slanted at a 45° angle against the side of the container, with the growing point barely below the water surface.

PLANTING HARDY WATER LILIES

Plant hardy water lilies (which have been kept wet in a bucket of water or wrapped in wet newspaper) with the end with the thick rhizome (it looks sort of like a bearded iris tuber, but thicker and rougher) against the side of the container and the growing point toward the center. If there is any mature, uncurled foliage, remove it. The rhizome should be slanted at a 45° angle, with the growing point barely below the surface and the end of the rhizome set more deeply in the soil.

Gently saturate the soil, driving out air bubbles and helping it settle around the roots. Top the soil with an inch of coarse sand or fine gravel, ½ inch in diameter, to keep fish from disturbing the soil and muddying the water. I find light yellow sand and gravel conspicuous and so prefer to use a darker stone, such as crushed traprock or bluestone. The container is now ready to set in the pool. It will be heavy and awkward to handle, and often two people are required to manage this task more easily.

PLANTING TROPICAL WATER LILIES AND LOTUSES

Tropical water lilies have a more rounded bulblike tuber, which is placed in the center of the container. Often there will be a white line on the tuber showing you how deeply the bulbous tuber should be planted. If you cannot see it, just cover the roots with soil, leaving the crown exposed. The leaves of these plants are very sensitive and should be covered with wet newspaper or burlap while you are preparing the containers prior to planting.

Lotuses are treated a little differently. After filling the container as described for water lilies, make a depression in the center of the soil for the tuber. The thickest portion of the tuber should be covered with about 2 inches of soil, and the growing tip should be about ½ inch above the soil. Mulch with gravel, keeping the tip clear by using a thinner layer in that area.

Lotuses should be planted in a depression in the soil, with the thickest portion of the tuber covered with about 2" of soil and the growing tip about ½" above the soil.

PLANTING DIRECTLY IN SOIL

Planting directly in the soil of an earth-bottom pond or pool is easy. One rather fanciful method suggests rolling the hardy water lily's tuber in a piece of sod, grass side out. Leave the growing crown peeking out the edge. Tie the sod in place, not too tightly, and fasten a rock to the underside. Drop the bundle into water of the appropriate depth. The rock should pull the bottom of the bundle to an inferior (lower) position. The tuber will then root into and through the sod, establishing itself in the mucky soil at the bottom of the pond.

Another method, suggested by Sara Stein in her book *Noah's Garden,* is based on the same principle. Cut an ample square of natural burlap — the kind made from jute rather than plastic, and brown rather than green (which indicates treatment with rot-retarding chemicals). Put a few quarts of potting soil in the center of the burlap and set the tuber on top. Bring up two diagonally opposite corners and tie them together, allowing the burlap to bunch loosely over the contents. Repeat with the other two corners. Gently drop the bundle into the water and allow it to sink to the bottom. The water lily's leaves can emerge through the four openings between the knots and edges of the burlap. In time, the burlap will rot away, but by then the water lily will have rooted into the bottom of the pond.

SUMMER MAINTENANCE

Summer maintenance is fun. Once a month or so, I put on a pair of shorts and, barefoot, step into the pool. I take a small, shallow dishpan or tray with me and let it float on the surface of the water. As I trim off dead flowers and yellowing leaves, I toss them in the container for collection. I usually clip one or two flowers in good condition to use as cut flowers indoors. Water lilies stay open for four days. Although they close at night,

One method of planting hardy water lilies directly into the soil entails placing the tuber on top of potting soil on a piece of burlap. Loosely tie corners over the contents, and drop bundle into water.

I enjoy seeing their flowers close-up and inhaling their sweet fragrance.

Water lilies do quite well without supplemental fertilization, but feeding them does encourage more flowers. Fertilize once a month during the active growing season. You can buy tablets, called Lilytabs, made specially for this purpose. Just push a couple deep into the soil on opposite sides of the pot. Work fast, as the tablets start to dissolve if you hold them under water for more than a few seconds. Or you can use 5–10–5 fertilizer. Wrap about a tablespoon of fertilizer in an unfolded single-ply white paper napkin, then plunge it into the soil. Prepare these bundles in advance and have them in a floating container at your side. With one hand, make the hole by pushing a couple of fingers into the soil. Leaving that arm under water as a guide, briskly plunge the fertilizer packet into the opening.

Fertilize aquatics once a month during the growing season by plunging fertilizer into the soil. Use a fertilizer tablet sold for water plants or a tablespoon of fertilizer tied in a paper napkin.

Autumn Maintenance

In late autumn when growth is halted, trim off all growth close to the surface of the container. This removal reduces oxygen depletion caused by decaying foliage in winter. Hardy water lilies can remain in pools that do not freeze solid, if you lower their containers to the bottom. Tropical water lilies are often discarded; alternatively, they can be stored as described in chapter 6. If you find walnut-size tubers attached to the original tuber, these are generally easier to keep through the winter. Night-blooming tropical water lilies often have these small tubers above and below the old tuber; day-blooming varieties usually produce them only at the base.

Algae

Algae growth is a natural occurrence in pools. It is a sign that the balance has been disturbed. Triggered by fresh water that is higher in nutrients than the old water and by sunny conditions before the water lily leaves shade the surface, algae begin to grow in my pool every year when I clean it in spring. Plant submerged plants as part of the system to adjust the balance. Floating-leaved plants, by reducing the available sunlight, also are useful. In natural ponds, filamentous algae can cause tremendous problems, forming large slimy green mats. Your pool also will have algae. Don't expect it to be as crystal clear as a swimming pool. That is unnatural, and the fish will be unhappy. If your hand, plunged 6 or 8 inches down, is palely visible, it's fine. A bubbler will reduce algae growth, but it also will mean that you cannot grow water lilies, which require still water.

Dividing and Propagating Water Lilies

In three to five years, depending on the vigor of the plant, growing conditions, and the size of the container, it will be necessary to divide and replant hardy water lilies. This should be done in early spring, about the time you would plant new water lilies. Hoist the container out of the water and remove the plant. Hose it off to remove the muddy soil, giving you a clear look at the tubers. Using a sharp knife, cut away and discard all the old tubers and fibrous roots, keeping only the strongest young shoots with 4 to 6 inches of tuber attached. Scrub the container free of algae and replant the tuber in fresh soil. You will have more water lilies than you need, so either introduce a friend to the joys of water gardening or discard the tubers. An overplanted pool with crowded water lilies concealing the surface and thrusting their leaves out of the water is not attractive.

Another means of propagation is useful with many tropical water lilies. These viviparous plants produce miniature plantlets where the leaf joins the petiole. Notice a cluster of tiny leaves and, underneath the mature leaf, a small tuber and roots. Carefully detach the plantlets from the leaf. If several plantlets are clustered together, separate them and pot them individually in a shallow clay pot filled with rich soil. Set the pots in shallow water. They are often easier to manage in a separate basin, as the 3- to 4-inch pots readily tip over in a large pond. The plantlets grow into full-size replicas of the original plant, often with increased resistance to moderately cold weather — more so than tropical water lilies propagated by division of tubers or from seed.

Planting and Maintaining Submerged Plants

Submerged plants like elodea can be planted spring or summer. They are especially susceptible to sun and wind and are quickly damaged if they are exposed to these conditions even briefly while you are preparing to plant them. Keep them temporarily in a bucket of water or in a plastic bag with a sheet of wet newspaper over it to prevent overheating.

Some elodeas are easy to propagate from cuttings. In fact, you may find that what you have purchased is a clump of rootless cuttings, bundled with a lead weight crimped around the lower end. Just plant the whole thing in a 1-quart pot and mulch with gravel. Make sure that the lead weight is buried in the soil; otherwise it can damage the stems. If you remove the weight, the rootless stems will have a tendency to float out of their pot and drift about the pool. The foliage should look bright and fresh; the presence of long white roots along the stem is an indication they have been sitting around for a while.

Submerged plants help keep the water clear, using up nutrients that would otherwise encourage the growth of algae. They are appreciated by goldfish, among others, which lay their eggs on the leaves; the leaves also shelter the small fry that would otherwise be eaten by larger fish. Goldfish and koi eat submerged plants. On the other hand, certain insect pests and snails lay their eggs on submerged plants. If you suspect this might be the case, briefly soak the plants in a mild solution of potassium permanganate before planting, using just enough of the crystals to turn the water pale pink.

Free-floating plants are simply tossed out at the appropriate time. I have noticed that water hyacinth has a tendency to get sunburned when it makes the transition from an aquarium or pet store to my pool, but it swiftly recovers.

MAIL-ORDER SOURCES

Before ordering or purchasing plants, be sure to confirm with the nursery that the material is propagated, not wild collected.

AQUATIC AND MOISTURE-LOVING PLANTS AND POOL SUPPLIES

Creative Habitat Corporation
253 Old Tarrytown Road
White Plains, NY 10603
(914) 948-4389
Supplies, consulting, services for stream bank and shoreline stabilization; wetland construction, restoration, and reclamation

Gilberg Perennial Farms
2906 Ossenfort Road
Glencoe, MO 63038
(314) 458-2033
No mail order; water lilies, aquatic plants, and aquatic supplies, plants for terrariums; liners; pumps

Lilypons Water Gardens
P.O. Box 10
Buckeystown, MD 21717
(800) 723-7667
    or
P.O. Box 188
Brookshire, TX 77423
(800) 765-5459
    or
P.O. Box 1130
Thermal, CA 92274
(800) 365-5459

Little Giant Pump Company
3810 N. Tulsa Street
Oklahoma City, OK 73112
(405) 947-2511
Submersible pumps and related equipment

Maryland Aquatic Nurseries, Inc.
3427 N. Furnace Road
Jarrettsville, MD 21084
(410) 557-7615
Retail and wholesale; catalog $2.00; will ship to Canada

Matterhorn Nursery, Inc.
227 Summit Park Road
Spring Valley, NY 10977
(914) 354-5986
Water lilies, aquatic plants, and aquatic supplies

Resource Conservation
    Technology Inc.
2633 N. Calvert Street
Baltimore, MD 21218
(410) 366-1146

Revere Plastics, Inc.
16 Industrial Avenue
Little Ferry, NJ 07643
(201) 641-0777

Slocum Water Gardens
1101 Cypress Gardens Blvd.
Winter Haven, FL 33884-1932
Catalog $3.00
(813) 293-7151

Tetra Pond
Tetra Sales (U.S.A.)
201 Tabor Road
Morris Plains, NJ 07950

Tilley's Nursery/
    The Water Works
111 E. Fairmount Street
Coopersburg, PA 18036
(215) 282-4784
Catalog $3.00

William Tricker Inc.
7125 Tanglewood Drive
Independence, OH 44131
(216) 524-3491
Catalog $3.00; will ship to Canada

Van Ness Water Gardens
2460 N. Euclid Avenue
Upland, CA 91784
(909) 982-2425
fax (909) 949-7217
Catalog $4.00

Waterford Gardens
74 E. Allendale Road
Saddle River, NJ 07458
(201) 327-0721
Catalog $5.00

Wicklein's Water Gardens
1820 Cromwell Bridge Road
Baltimore, MD 21234
(410) 823-1335
Catalog; will ship to Canada

OTHER PLANTS

Kurt Bluemel, Inc.
2740 Greene Lane
Baldwin, MD 21013-9523
(410) 557-7229
Retail and wholesale; ornamental grasses, sedges, rushes, bamboos, ferns, aquatic plants

Country Wetlands Nursery &
Consulting Ltd.
S75 W20755 Field Drive
Muskego, WI 53150
(414) 679-1268
fax (414) 697-1279
*Many sedges; native wetland
plants for wet meadows, sedge
meadows, and bogs; two native
water lilies; catalog $3.00*

De Vroomen Bulb Co., Inc.
P.O. Box 189
Russell, IL 60075
(708) 395-9911
*Wholesale only; hardy water lilies
by color; hardy marginal, bog,
floating, and submerged plants; a
few tropical water plants*

Fancy Fronds
1911 Fourth Avenue West
Seattle, WA 98119
(206) 284-5332
*Ferns; catalog $1.00; will ship to
Canada*

Forest Farm
990 Tetherow Road
Williams, OR 97544-9599
(503) 846-7269
*Extensive list of trees and shrubs,
including many hard-to-find
species, most as smaller plants to
grow on before planting in the
garden, some available in 1- and
5-gallon sizes. Catalog $3.00; will
ship to Canada*

Hungry Plants
1216 Cooper Drive
Raleigh, NC 27607
(919) 851-8699
*Insectivourous plants produced by
tissue culture; catalog $1.00; will
ship to Canada*

Lee's Botanical Garden
390 Davis Street
LaBelle, FL 33925
*Insectivorous plants (Sarracenia,
Drosera, and Dionea)*

Limerock Ornamental Grasses
RD 1, Box 111C
Port Matilda, PA 16870
(814) 692-2272
*Retail and wholesale; grasses,
sedges, rushes, a few ferns; catalog
$2.50; will ship to Canada for
wholesale only*

Niche Gardens
1111 Dawson Road
Chapel Hill, NC 27516
(919) 967-0078
*Southeastern native plants, some
for waterscapes; a few bog plants;
Sarracenia; catalog $3.00; will
ship to Canada*

North Creek Nurseries, Inc.
RR 2, Box 33
Landenburg, PA 19350
(610) 255-0100
fax (610) 255-4762
*Wholesale only; plants for
naturalistic landscaping,
including many starter plants for
wet meadows, particularly native*

Orgel's Orchids
18950 S.E. 136th Street SW
Miami, FL 33196
(305) 233-7168
*Hybrid Sarracenia, Drosera, and
Pinguicula; will ship to Canada*

Plant Delights Nursery
9241 Sauls Road
Raleigh, NC 27603
(919) 772-4794
*Seven species of Saracenia,
Dionaea, and some wet soil
natives; catalog $2.00*

Peter Pauls Nursery
4665 Chapin Road
Canandaigua, NY 14424-8713
(716) 394-7397
*Dionaea, Sarracenia, Drosera,
Pinguicula, and live Sphagnum;
supplies; seeds of insectivorous
plants*

Pinelands Nursery
323 Island Road
Columbus, NJ 08022
(609) 291-9486
*Wholesale; woody and herbaceous
plants for wetland mitigation and
stream bank stabilization; bio-
engineering erosion-control
products*

Prairie Nursery
P.O. Box 306
Westfield, WI 53964
(608) 296-3679
*Excellent source for young plants
and seeds of prairie, woodland,
and wetland plants; catalog $3.00
for 2-year subscription*

Siskiyou Rare Plant Nursery
2825 Cummings Road
Medford, OR 97501
(503) 772-6846
*Catalog $2.00 refundable with
order; will ship to Canada;
specialize in poolside plants*

Wildlife Nurseries
P.O. Box 2724
Oshkosh, WI 54903-2724
(414) 231-3780
*Wild rice, native water lilies and
lotuses, aquatic, wetland and seed
plants for wildlife food*

Triple Brook Farm
37 Middle Road
Southampton, MA 01073
(413) 527-4626 (evenings)
*Northeastern native plants;
aquatics; will ship to Canada*

We-Du Nursery
Route 5, Box 724
Marion, NC 28752
(704) 738-8300
*Catalog $2.00; specialize in
wildflower bulbs*

Woodlanders, Inc.
1128 Colleton Avenue
Aiken, SC 29801
(803) 648-7522
*Catalog $2.00; Specialize in
native plants; rare and hard-to-
find*

SUGGESTED READING

Allison, James. *Water in the Garden*. Boston: Bulfinch Press, 1991.

Ammann, Alan P. *Method for the Evaluation of Inland Wetlands in Connecticut*. DEP Bulletin No. 9. Hartford: Natural Resources Center of the Department of Environment Protection, October 1986.

Angel, Heather, and Pat Wolseley. *The Water Naturalist*. New York: Facts On File, 1982.

Armitage, Allan M. *Herbaceous Perennial Plants*. Athens, GA: Varsity Press, 1989.

Benyus, Janine M. *The Field Guide to Wildlife Habitats of the Western United States*. New York: Simon & Schuster, 1989.

Boon, Bill, and Harlen Groe. *Nature's Heartland: Native Plant Communities of the Great Plains*. Ames: Iowa State University Press, 1990.

Brooklyn Botanic Garden. *Water Gardening*. 41 (Spring 1985).

Brown, Lauren. *Grasses: An Identification Guide*. Boston: Houghton Mifflin, 1979.

Bruce, Hal. *How to Grow Wildflowers and Wild Shrubs and Trees in Your Own Garden*. New York: Alfred A. Knopf, 1976.

Coon, Nelson. *Using Wayside Plants*. New York: Hearthside Press, 1969.

Correll, Donovan Stewart. *Native Orchids of North America North of Mexico*. Stanford, CA: Stanford University Press, 1978.

Dalton, Patricia A., and Alejandro Novelo R. "Aquatic and Wetland Plants of the Arnold Arboretum." *Arnoldia* 43 (Spring 1983)

Densmore, Frances. *How Indians Use Wild Plants for Food, Medicine & Crafts*. New York: Dover Publications, 1974.

Finlayson, Max, and Michael Moser. *Wetlands*. New York: Facts On File, 1991.

Flint, Harrison L. *Landscape Plants for Eastern North America*. New York: John Wiley & Sons, 1983.

Greenlee, John. *The Encyclopedia of Ornamental Grasses*. Emmaus, PA: Rodale Press, 1992.

Grounds, Roger. *Ornamental Grasses*. New York: Van Nostrand Reinhold, 1979.

Hansen, Richard, and Friedrich Stahl. *Perennials and Their Garden Habitats*, 4th ed. Portland, OR: Timber Press, 1993.

Johnson, Charles W. *Bogs of the Northeast*. Hanover, NH: University Press of New England, 1985.

Jones, Samuel B. Jr., and Leonard E. Foote. *Native Shrubs and Woody Vines of the Southeast*. Portland, OR: Timber Press, 1989.

Jones, Samuel B. Jr., and Leonard E. Foote. *Gardening with Native Wildflowers*. Portland, OR: Timber Press, 1990.

Kavasch, Barrie. *Native Harvests: Recipes and Botanicals of the American Indian*. New York: Random House, 1979.

Knap, Alyson Hart. *Wild Harvest: An Outdoorsman's Guide to Edible Wild Plants in North America*. New York: Arco Publishing Company, 1975.

Luer, Carlyle A. *The Native Orchids of the United States and Canada Excluding Florida*. New York: New York Botanical Garden, 1975.

Magee, Dennis W. *Freshwater Wetlands: A Guide to Common Indicator Plants of the Northeast*. Amherst: University of Massachusetts Press, 1981.

Marshall, Nina T. *The Gardener's Guide to Plant Conservation*. Washington, DC: World Wildlife fund, 1993.

Mitsch, William J., and James G. Gosselink. *Wetlands*. New York: Van Nostrand Reinhold, 1986.

Niering, William A. *The Audubon Society Nature Guides: Wetlands*. New York: Alfred A. Knopf, 1985.

Niering, William A., and Richard H. Goodwin. *Inland Wetland Plants of Connecticut*. Connecticut Arboretum Bulletin No. 19. New London, May 1973.

Oakes, A.J. *Ornamental Grasses and Grasslike Plants*. New York: Van Nostrand Reinhold, 1990.

Paul, Anthony, and Yvonne Rees. *The Water Garden*. London: Frances Lincoln Limited, 1986.

Perry, Frances. *The Water Garden*. New York: Van Nostrand Reinhold, 1981.

Rae-Smith, William. *A Guide to Water Gardening*. London: Bracken Books, 1989.

Stein, Sara. *Noah's Garden: Restoring the Ecology of Our Own Back Yards*. New York: Houghton Mifflin, 1993.

Swindells, Philip, and David Mason. *The Complete Book of the Water Garden*. Woodstock, NY: Overlook Press, 1990.

Taylor, Sally L., Glenn D. Dreyer, and William A. Niering. *Native Shrubs for Landscaping*. Connecticut Arboretum Bulletin No. 30. New London, September 1987.

Thomas, Bill. *The Swamp*. New York: W.W. Norton, 1976.

Thomas, Graham Stuart. *Perennial Garden Plants*. London: J.M. Dent & Sons, 1982.

Tomikel, John. *Edible Wild Plants of Eastern United States and Canada*. California, PA: Allegheny Press, 1976.

Weller, Milton W. *Freshwater Marshes: Ecology and Wildlife Management*. Minneapolis: University of Minnesota Press, 1987.

Wells, B.W. *The Natural Gardens of North Carolina*. Chapel Hill: University of North Carolina Press, 1979.

GLOSSARY

Algae. Aquatic nonvascular plants, pond scum, and seaweeds

Aquatic. Growing or living in water

Bog. Wetland in northern Europe and North America with a high water table and little significant flow of water in or out of the area; consisting of peat deposits and supporting the growth of acid-loving plants, especially *Sphagnum*

Bottomland. Periodically flooded lowland adjacent to rivers and streams, often forested

Coastal plain. Region of sandy, peaty soil supporting sparse growth of longleaf pine; historically subject to periodic fires; from Virginia south through the Carolinas; natural habitat of many specialized plants, such as Venus's-flytrap *(Dionaea muscipula)*, pitcher plants *(Sarracenia* spp.), and numerous orchids

Ecotone. Transitional zone between two adjacent plant communities, such as meadow and forest

Emergent plants. Sedges, rushes, cattails, and other such herbaceous plants that are rooted in soil and protrude above the water's surface

Ericaceous. Relating to plants in the family Ericaceae (heathers), including erica (heathers), calluna (heath), rhododendron, and other lime-hating plants that require acid soils with a pH of 6.5 or lower.

Eutrophication. Nutrient enrichment of a pond, usually referring to nitrogen and phosphorus, resulting in oxygen deficiency

Facultative plant. Plant sometimes found growing in wetlands (34 to 66 percent of the time) but also found in nonwetland sites [examples: Jerusalem artichoke *(Helianthus tuberosus)* and poison ivy *(Toxicodendron radicans)*]

Facultative upland plant. Plant naturally found growing in nonwetland sites and seldom in wetlands (only 1 to 33 percent of the time) [examples: goatsbeard *(Aruncus dioicus)* and quaking aspen *(Populus tremuloides)*]

Facultative wetland plant. Plant naturally found growing in wetlands 67 to 99 percent of the time but occasionally found in nonwetland sites [examples: cinnamon fern *(Osmunda cinnamomea)* and river birch *(Betula nigra)*]

Floating-leaved plants. Water lilies and other such plants that are rooted in soil and have their leaves floating on the water's surface

Floodplain. Level land adjacent to a river periodically covered by floodwaters

Free-floating plants. Duckweed *(Lemna* spp.) and other such plants that float on the water's surface and are not rooted in soil

Geogenous. Referring to a bog formed from surface water and/or groundwater sources; having picked up dissolved minerals as the water passes through bedrock and soil, these bogs are higher in nutrients than ombrogenous bogs

Hibernaculum. Winter-resting bud formed when leaves and roots die back, as in sundews *(Drosera* spp.)

Hydrophytes. Plants adapted to wet conditions, growing in either water or soil too waterlogged for most plants to survive

Hydrosere. All the stages in natural plant succession from shallow lake through marsh to swamp to terrestrial climax forest; the serial progression of wetland plant communities and soils

Lacustrine. Of, relating to, or growing in a lake

Lake. An open-water wetland deeper than 8 feet and larger than 20 acres situated in a topographic depression or dammed river channel (as an oxbow) without trees, shrubs, or emergent plants

Marsh. Wetland continually or frequently inundated and characterized by emergent herbaceous plants

Obligate wetland plant. Plant always found growing in wetlands under natural conditions (may persist in nonwetlands that have been drained or if planted there) [examples: white water lily *(Nymphaea odorata)* (nonpersistent) and common monkey flower *(Mimulus guttatus)*]

Ombrogenous, ombrotrophic. Referring to a bog that collects water from rain or snow (through precipitation) as opposed to groundwater or surface water runoff (very low in nutrients, as the water contains no dissolved minerals that would have accumulated if it had passed through or over soil)

Oxbow, oxbow lake. Portion of a former riverbed when the bend is cut off from the main stream (named for the U-shaped frame that supports the yoke and forms a collar around an ox's neck)

Palustrine. Referring to wetlands with water less than 6 feet deep and dominated by trees, shrubs, and persistent emergent plants; of, relating to, or growing in marshes

Peat. Incompletely decayed dead plant material that has accumulated in low-oxygen conditions

Phyllode, phyllodium. Leaflike structure from widened petioles, formed in autumn or winter by some pitcher plants *(Sarracenia* spp.)

Pocosin. Upland evergreen shrub swamp of the coastal plain of the southeastern United States

Pond. Smaller and shallower than a lake — 1 to 8 feet deep and generally less than 8 acres

Pothole. Shallow marshlike pond that may dry up in times of low rainfall; found in the prairie states, especially Minnesota, North Dakota, and South Dakota, and adjacent regions of Canada

Riparian zone. Land adjacent to a river, stream, or other body of water that is at least periodically affected by flooding

Riverine. Referring to a wetland habitat contained within a channel; situated beside a river; of, relating to, or growing in or on the banks of a river

Siltation. The filling of a wetland by waterborne sediment

Slough. Shallow swamp or marsh with sluggish, slowly flowing water

Submerged plant. Plant that is rooted in soil and grows below the water's surface [example: elodea *(Elodea canadensis)*]

Swamp. Wetland dominated by woody plants, trees, or shrubs

Tussock. Thick clump of sedge forming a small hummock in a marsh, swamp, or bog

Upland plant. Plant naturally found in wetlands less than 1 percent of the time [example: whorled milkwort *(Polygala verticillata)*]

Vascular. Referring to a channel for conveying fluid; in plants, the system of xylem and phloem for transporting sap

Vernal pool. Seasonally wet pool, most frequently wet in winter and spring and dry in summer

Viviparous. In plants, a situation where plantlets are produced on the leaves or stems of the parent plant

Wetland. Distinguished by the presence of water that may be permanent, intermittent, or temporary; often has soils that differ from nearby uplands; supporting the growth of hydrophytes

Wet meadow. Grassland with waterlogged soil near the surface and open, standing water absent for most of the year, woody plants few or entirely absent.

INDEX

Numerals in italics indicate illustrations.